Understanding the Somalia Conflagration

UNDERSTANDING THE SOMALIA CONFLAGRATION

Identity, Political Islam and Peacebuilding

Afyare Abdi Elmi

First published 2010 by Pluto Press
345 Archway Road, London N6 5AA and
175 Fifth Avenue, New York, NY 10010

www.plutobooks.com

Pambazuka Press
51 Cornmarket Street
Oxford
OX1 3HA
www.pambazukapress.org

Distributed in the United States of America exclusively by
Palgrave Macmillan, a division of St. Martin's Press LLC,
175 Fifth Avenue, New York, NY 10010

Distributed in Africa exclusively by Pambazuka Press

British Library Cataloguing in Publication Data
A catalogue record for this book is available from the British Library

ISBN   978 0 7453 2975 8   Hardback
ISBN   978 0 7453 2974 1   Paperback (Pluto Press)
ISBN   978 1 906387 76 1   Paperback (Pambazuka Press)

Library of Congress Cataloging in Publication Data applied for

This book is printed on paper suitable for recycling and made from fully managed
and sustained forest sources. Logging, pulping and manufacturing processes are
expected to conform to the environmental standards of the country of origin.

10   9   8   7   6   5   4   3   2   1

Designed and produced for Pluto Press by
Chase Publishing Services Ltd, 33 Livonia Road, Sidmouth, EX10 9JB, England
Typeset from disk by Stanford DTP Services, Northampton, England
Printed and bound in the European Union by
CPI Antony Rowe, Chippenham and Eastbourne

This book is dedicated to the hundreds of thousands of Somalis who perished during Somalia's brutal civil war and the subsequent Ethiopian occupation. I also dedicate this book to the aspirations of the millions of Somalis who are striving and struggling to establish a peaceful and prosperous Somalia.

Markay dani meeday tidhi
Maxaan talo meel ka deyey,
Markay dani maaha tidhi
Weyddiiyey qof meel ka deyey,
Markay dani maaha tidhi
Ku laabtay halkaan ka deyey,
Markay dani maaha tidhi
Ka sii deyey meel la-deyey.

When a need arose,
I searched for a solution
When that solution did not work
I asked someone who also tried to resolve
    the problem
When that solution did not work [again]
I looked again in the same place I searched
    before for the solution
When that solution did not work for me
I searched again in a place that has already
    been looked [by someone else] *for a solution.**

Mohamed I. Warsame (Hadrawi), 'Dabahuwan'

---

* These are the first lines of 'Dabahuwan' (Covered from the bottom), which
Hadrawi composed in 1995. In the poem, Hadrawi asserts that those who are
trying to resolve the Somali problems are searching for solutions in the wrong
places. In this first stanza, he argues that the imported foreign mechanisms that
are used cannot address the Somali problem at all.

Contents

Acknowledgements

Completing a book project requires the efforts of more than one person. My case was no exception, and I benefited from many people while researching and writing this publication. I would like to thank Dr W. Andy Knight and Dr Terrance Carson, who supervised my PhD thesis. Without their guidance, help and understanding, I would not have produced this book. I am also grateful to the members of my dissertation committee, Dr Ali A. Abdi, Dr Yasmeen Abu-Laban and Dr Tom Keating, for their support and encouragement.

Many of my friends were able to discuss the project and provide feedback over the past three years. Special thanks go to Said Mohamud Mohamed (Said Suugaan) and Dr Abdullahi Ahmed Barise. I spent many hours debating with Said on the findings and contentious points. Said also read most of the chapters and critiqued my arguments and assertions. Moreover, I thank Said for allowing me to use his library, as he has a large collection of books, reports and electronic resources on Somalia and East Africa. Similarly, Dr Barise's comments helped me clarify my arguments. In addition, I am grateful to Katie Lehman, who read the manuscript several times to edit and format the book. The discussions that I had with Abdulrahman Aynte, Ali Weheliye, Mohamed Duale, Abdirashid Khalif, Hassan Mahadalla, Mohamud Khalif, Awalle Abdi, Mohamed Elmi, Abdullahi Sheikh Aden, Zainab Hassan, Sahal Abdulle, Hussein Santur, Yusuf Hassan and Ladan Affi helped me clarify arguments, and I would like to thank them for their support and invaluable advice.

Many more people helped me to complete this book. Among them are those whom I interviewed, Somalis and non-Somali individuals. During my two field research trips to Somalia, Kenya, Djibouti, Eritrea, Qatar and United Arab Emirates, I met and discussed the issues in this book with many Somalis. Their information, analysis and thoughts enriched and strengthened this study, and I would like to thank all of them.

Moreover, since I joined the University of Alberta, I benefited from the institutional resources of the university. As a student, I completed courses that directly and indirectly contributed to this publication. I am grateful to my teachers: Dr W. Andy Knight,

Dr Terrance Carson, Dr Tom Keating, Dr Fred Judson, Dr Jenine Brodie, Dr George Richardson, Dr Malinda Smith, Dr Dianne Conrad and Dr David Smith. While at the University of Alberta, I taught several courses including Theories of International Relations, Introduction to Political Science, and Conflict and Peacebuilding. More than 150 students took this last course and critiqued some of my views. I am grateful to all of them. I also taught similar courses at the Qatar University's International Affairs Department, where students' discussion and critique was useful to me – I thank them as well.

I am also grateful to Dr Lois Harder, Coordinator of the Graduate Program of the Department of Political Science at the University of Alberta, for her understanding, advice and support. The administration staff of the Political Science and Secondary Education departments have always addressed my questions and have made my stay at the university enjoyable. I thank Tara Mish, Marilyn Calvert, Cindy Anderson, Donna Coombs-Montrose, Dawne Cook, Donna Lauritsen, Kateryna Nowytzkyj, Vanessa Ianson and Nancy Evans.

Most important of all, I would like to thank my wife, Sahro Ali Ebar, and my children, Mohamed, Maryama, Faizo and Abdulrahman, who not only understood the long hours I spent away from home but always supported me. Without their understanding, commitment and sustained support, this project would not have come to fruition.

With respect to funding, I am grateful to the International Development Research Centre in Ottawa, as it provided a grant that helped me to carry out this research. Information on the Centre is available at www.idrc.ca. I also appreciate the grants and scholarships I received from the University of Alberta in order to complete this research project.

Preface

Somalis as well as the international community have tried many times to resolve the conflict that persists in Somalia. More than 20 conferences have been held in an attempt to reconcile the Somali groups. Obviously, none has produced the intended results of ending the civil war and establishing a functioning state. Despite the conflict persisting for so long, studies that relate to Somali reconciliation and peacebuilding are sparse and those that investigate Islamist perspectives are non-existent.

I have two aims in writing this book. First, that so little has been published about the reasons behind the failure of all Somali peacemaking efforts proves that there is a huge need for research on this topic. The book explains the complex factors of identity, religion ('political Islam') and foreign interventions that perpetuate the Somali conflict. Second, the book does not just analyse the *problems* of Somalia. Instead, it offers solutions in the areas of governance, education and conflict resolution.

Few would question the need for a critical investigation of the Somali conflict, as the issue is both important and timely. But the question is, why me? First of all, I am Somali. The politics of my background shaped my interest in peace in this country. The civil war has and does affect me directly. I fled from my home country after experiencing the harsh realities that Somalia's political situation created. Like many other Somalis, I lost several relatives and family members because of the civil war. Moreover, some members of my family now live in different parts of the world: Canada, the United States, Norway and Kenya. Therefore, my interest in studying peace is multi-layered: domestic and international, theoretical and practical, personal and scholarly.

I want to understand sources of conflict and how they can be addressed. News of wars and pictures of civilian victims of violence have always aroused my emotions. I always believed that if leaders used their minds and controlled their greed, many conflicts could have been averted. Whenever I have an opportunity to study or write, I choose issues that relate to peace. For instance, while at the University of Alberta, I wrote my PhD dissertation on the Somali conflict. I also wrote my MA thesis from the University of Toronto on 'Promoting a Culture of Peace in Canada', and I investigated the 'Barriers to Peace in Somalia' for my second MA from Brock University. I have taken several courses and read many publications on peace, conflict and conflict resolution, with the intention of contributing to the theoretical and practical issues of peacebuilding in general literature and in the particular case of Somalia. This book builds on my previous works.

Moreover, one of the fundamental assumptions I hold is that research and researcher cannot be separated fully. I believe that locating oneself within research is necessary. Several identities and experiences informed my worldviews, basic assumptions and values as I began to study the Somali conflict. As I was born in Somalia, my intellectual journey started with the Somali culture and Islamic religion. Somali is my mother tongue. In particular, the poems of Somalia's legendary poet and composer, Mohamed Ibrahim Warsame, nicknamed 'Hadrawi' (translated as 'the master or father of speech'), have had a significant impact on how I conceived of politics and change in Somalia. Hadrawi composed many critical poems against Somalia's military dictatorship. Hadrawi's powerful poems and songs, such as 'Deyn maayo heesaha' (I will not stop singing; 1973), 'Dibadyaal' (The excluded; 1981), 'Gudgude' (Heavy rain; 1989), 'Sirta nolosha' (Secrets of life; 1984) and 'Dabahuwan' (Covered from the bottom; 1994) influenced my understanding of the complex nature of the Somali conflict and how the Somali culture can help in resolving the hostilities.

Second, as a typical urban Somali child, I joined Koran and Islamic studies school at age five. This experience equipped me with a worldview that is based on Islam. I learned basic Arabic language, the memorization and interpretation of the Koran and basic Islamic jurisprudence. Like Hadrawi, the story of Sheikh Mohamed Moallim Hassan, as narrated by his students, has had a significant impact on me. Sheikh Mohamed is considered to be the father of Somalia's Islamic awakening. The rise of this Islamic awakening coincided with the rise of socialism in Somalia in the 1970s. The Somali government promoted scientific socialism in schools and media. Ironically, many Islamists were teaching in these schools that promoted socialist ideas.

Hadrawi, the poet, and Sheikh Mohamed, the Islamic scholar, had something in common. They were both courageous in that they faced the military dictatorship, unarmed. They said what they thought was in the current interest of the people, without fear or favour. But the regime could not tolerate such behaviour and both men were imprisoned. Released after five years, Hadrawi defected to Somali rebel groups in Ethiopia. Sheikh Mohamed never left Somalia and was imprisoned there several times, serving twelve years in total and suffering physical attack.

What appealed to me about the actions and principles of these two individuals is that they were not opposing the system for self-serving reasons; their life attests to this fact as they continued preaching what they believed in and they never participated in the factional politics after the Somali state collapsed in 1991. During the revolutionary era, they regarded the system as insensitive to the needs and aspirations of the people. Both men were principled and persistent in their beliefs and actions. In fact, Hadrawi, in one of his poems, argues that persistence and good actions are the two major 'secrets of life'. For Hadrawi, he walked the walk as, to this day, he is consistent in opposing injustice wherever it appears. Sheikh Mohamed Moallim Hassan passed away in 2000; tens of thousands came to his funeral in Mogadishu, including myself. I later realized that the power of the message of these two individuals lay in the Somali culture and language and the Islamic faith. These two indigenous sources of knowledge have shaped my worldview and these individuals appealed to values that were already present in me. Parallel with these two indigenous sources of education was Somalia's secular socialist education system. The military government promoted socialism and required students to study revolution and related subjects. As a student, I also attended these schools.

As the country disintegrated, I tried to make sense of the conflict that destroyed my country. So I decided to read as much as I could before I joined formal higher education institutions in Canada in the 1990s. Through friends I was introduced to many publications by the International Institute of Islamic Thought. I read books and articles on Islamic epistemology, Western paradigms, and differences in the area of ontology and methodology. Long before I joined Ryerson University, I read works by Taha Jabir Alwani, Abdul Hamid A. Abu Sulayman, Ismael Faruqi, Ali Mazrui, Mohammed Ayoob and many other subaltern authors. Abdul Hamid A. Abu Sulayman's book, *Crises in the Muslim Mind* (1993), fascinated me as it critiqued both Muslims who uncritically adopted Western models and those who followed blindly the Muslims of another era (Salaf-Saleh), arguing that these imitations would not address the problems of today's colonized Muslims. I also rejected the idea of imposing (as the Europeans did during the colonial era and as they now do in peacebuilding activities) one civilization's way of living on others by force.

Although both Somali culture and Islam have contributed to the way I see the world, I am also Western-educated. I attended some of the major Western universities to complete my higher education. My academic background in political science and education convinced me that one single paradigm cannot help us fully understand and appreciate the complexity of the conflict in Somalia. Therefore, I employ both social constructivism and post-colonialism paradigms when analysing the events in Somalia. The ontological and episte-mological assumptions of constructivism are useful for making sense of the unique social realities of the Somali people. In particular, the idea that social realities are rooted in specific structures that can be changed is important for this book. Second, the constructivist framework is a helpful tool for accounting for the formation of identity in a given context. Scholars such as Alexander Wendt and Emanuel Adler note that the constructivist paradigm is sensitive to the ways in which identities and interests inform each other.[1] In this way the constructivist paradigm is appropriate in trying to understand this unique problem, accommodating the local conceptions of learning within the Somali culture and within Islam in Somalia.

While elements of the social constructivist paradigm are useful in making sense of the conflict in Somalia, post-colonialism is the main paradigm that may help untangle the complex problems and issues that form the basis of the conflict. Although there is significant diversity within this school of thought, most post-colonialist scholars share three major assumptions. First, there is an agreement on the need to revisit the colonial past and its effects on colonized peoples. Second, most post-colonialist scholars believe that it is imperative to look at issues and events from the perspective of the marginalized groups.[2] Finally, proponents of the post-colonialist framework reject the universalization of specific values, particularly those of colonial groups. The argument here is that theories and interpret-ations are value-laden. They are linked to the place and the time that these theories emerged.[3] Obviously, the above assumptions of this school of thought are related to the meanings and representations associated with different cultures. Edward Said, one of the founders of the post-colonial school, argued that a negative representation of indigenous communities resulted from the interaction of European and Southern peoples.[4]

Said also argued that the negative representation of the 'other', particularly Islam, Arabs and Muslims, is not neutral or innocent. He contended that there are interests behind representing Islam, Muslims and Arabs in the way they are being represented in the West. In one of his interviews, he said: 'It is an unfortunate reality and perhaps that is why we have this gigantic military.'[5] Said argued that even those who claim to be experts on the Arab and Muslim world present these communities as 'oil-producers' at best and 'terrorists' at worst. He criticized the way the West represents the other, arguing that the difference between human beings is based on history and experience rather than genetics or biology or culture/civilization. He blamed Western scholars and media for misrepresentation, both knowingly and unknowingly. I agree with Said that the biased and self-serving misrepresentations of the other contribute to a marginalization of the billions of people in the Third World.[6] I also share in his conclusion that the current unbalanced system is a byproduct of the West's long and brutal colonialism and imperialism.

Social constructivist and post-colonialist frameworks are also useful in understanding the links between the concepts of conflict, violence, identity, peace and peacebuilding, education and peace education, and citizenship. Conflict is inherent in human relations, and thus it is inevitable. It can occur in multiple ways including when there is the mere presence of identity difference. Violence and non-violence are also two possible ways of reacting to the conflict. I argue that violence is a means (either reaction or instrument) that people use to resolve conflicts. In addition, I acknowledge that identity has had a role in the Somali conflict. On the other hand, reviewing concepts of peace and peacebuilding, education and peace education, and citizenship is useful in shedding light on human beings' constructive approaches to handling conflict non-violently. As such, when states collapse or chronic civil wars tear societies apart, different governance and peacebuilding mechanisms are suggested. Keeping the meaning of these concepts in mind, I investigate how members of many Somali groups (including Islamists, nationalist intellectuals, members of the business community and average Somalis) view efforts to build durable peace and a functioning state in Somalia.

A great respect has to be accorded to the context being studied; the values and issues and interests of the people involved must be taken into account. With respect to the theories and concepts of conflict resolution and peacebuilding, it is clear that peacebuilders heavily depend on a particular European worldview. I hope that the current calls for inclusion of other ways of seeing the world will be heeded. The indigenous values involved in the case of Somalia have their own conflict-resolution mechanisms that resonate with Somalis. I come to this research with the assumption that employing the tools that the culture and Islamic faith offer for building peace in Somalia cannot be ignored. I, as researcher, will be one of the subaltern voices pushing for inclusion. This is the perspective I come with when analysing the Somali conflict.

Note on Methods

I have collected documents, peace accords, education textbooks and policy guidelines that relate to Somali conflict and peace from institutions I visited in Somalia, Kenya, Djibouti, Eritrea, United Arab Emirates and Qatar. I interviewed Islamists, business leaders, many average citizens, nationalist intellectuals, and officials from the leading education umbrella group, Formal Private Educational Network in Somalia (FPENS), which has regulated Somalia's education system since the Somali state failed. FPENS has 46 member-organizations throughout Somalia. The textbooks that the member-schools use are often printed by UNESCO, UNICEF and the Islamic Development Bank. In addition to textbooks, I also collected copies of the five major peace accords that have been signed by Somali factions since 1991. (Even though there were 17 peace conferences, only five of these have produced peace accords or transitional charters.) Besides analysing peace accords and textbooks, I also gathered data through interviews. I interviewed Somalis and non-Somalis who have been involved in one way or another in addressing the Somali conflict.

1
Introduction: Conflict and Peace in Somalia

Wax la heybiyaba dowladnimo waa, la soo helaye
Nin walbaa haruub buu toshoo, hoorso leeyahay
Hayeeshee sidii loo hantuu, hadal ka joogaaye

Although it has been a long struggle for a long time,
nationhood [freedom] has finally been attained.
And, every person is trying to benefit from the spoils of
independence.
However, there is a question of whether [Somalis] can
maintain the acquired nationhood [freedom].

Ali Hussein, Somali nationalist poet[1]

Somalia is a small state in the Horn of Africa. While the country is extremely poor by any world standards, the Somali people, who are largely homogeneous, have a long history and rich language. Although a significant number of Somalis are farmers, most are considered to be nomads. With the onset of unorganized mass urbanization, however, many Somalis, farmers and nomads alike, have lost their basic livestock resources in the countryside. Somali people continue to be resilient in the face of economic poverty and civil wars that have been so much a part of their history. Many authors classify Somalis as an independent and proud people who maintain a living from sparse resources.

Before the Western colonization of Somalia in the late 1800s, the Somali culture and Islam were the primary sources of knowledge for most Somalis. Despite some claims that Somalis have Arab roots, I am of the view that Somalis are Muslisms and Africans. Geographic proximity, culture and religion unite Somalis with Arabs and the Arab world.

Terrorism, piracy and humanitarian catastrophe have been associated with this poor nation and Somalia is now increasingly in the news and the subject of political discussion. The purpose of this book is to explain the specific nature and character of the conflict in Somalia and to discuss ways and means to resolve it.

THE SOMALI CONFLICT: WHY WE SHOULD CARE

From the beginning of the Somali civil war in 1978 to the present, hundreds of thousands of Somalis have lost their lives either directly or indirectly due to the conflict. Millions have been displaced internally and externally, thus making the majority of the Somalis aid-dependent. Interestingly, while many other countries that experienced civil war within this time frame have recovered, Somalia's conflict has persisted despite all attempts to build peace and restore a functioning state.

As evidenced in the number of domestic and external actors involved, Somalia's conflict and peacebuilding is everyone's business – a Somali proverb says that when someone is sick, many people would decide for that person (*Qof buka boqol baa u talisa*). In fact many actors consider that building peace in Somalia is an important goal globally, regionally, and locally. The rise of extremism in Somalia and the country's status as a 'collapsed state' within the context of the US-led 'war on terror' raises concerns for the United States. Washington openly argues that since Somalia is 'ungoverned space', it has therefore become a recruitment site for terrorists. The United States is particularly concerned with the presence of Al-Shabab Al-Mujahideen, one of the Islamist groups in Somalia. As such, when the Somali warlords that Washington supported were defeated in June 2006, the United States collaborated with Ethiopia (Somalia's hostile neighbour) to destroy the Union of Islamic Courts (UIC). As Jendayi Frazer, former Assistant Secretary of State for African Affairs repeatedly said, the United States considers Somalia a priority.

In addition, the United Nations seeks a solution to the conflict since it is the custodian of international peace and has invested heavily in several peacebuilding efforts in Somalia. From October 2006 to February 2007 the UN passed three different Security Council Resolutions: 1724, 1725 and 1744. In passing Resolution 1744 on 20 February 2007, the Security Council unanimously agreed to send African forces to Somalia for six months. Both the African Union and the East African regional organization Intergovernmental Authority on Development (IGAD) are heavily involved with the Somali conflict and peacebuilding efforts. In addition, the Arab League, under the Sudan leadership, has also shown strong interest in ending the Somali conflict. It has hosted several peace conferences in Khartoum and pressed the Somali government and the Union of Islamic Courts to settle their differences peacefully.

It is the Somali people who have paid the heaviest price for the civil war. After the deaths of hundreds of thousands and the displacement of millions, war-weary Somalis wish for peace and want to see their own government reflect the citizens' needs. Thus, both the well-being of Somalis and the international community are at stake in efforts to attain a sustainable peace in Somalia.

In this introductory chapter, I will outline my major arguments concerning the Somali conflict. I will discuss the interrelated components of statelessness and peacebuilding, with specific emphasis on the rising problem of piracy. Then I will examine the impact of statelessness on the Somali conflict and the general themes that relate to conflict resolution and peacebuilding. Specifically, I will look at the potential for radical groups to use Somalia as a safe haven where they could launch attacks against Western interests. Last, I briefly discuss the role of education and peace education in ending the civil war.

MAJOR ARGUMENTS

This book advances many arguments. As the verse at the start of this book suggests, the international community's approach to building peace in Somalia is confused. Thus far, peacebuilding efforts have been based on organizing peace conferences outside the country. In addition, such efforts have brought little in terms of implementation: Often before the outcomes of a peace conference have been implemented, the next one is being organized. This book asserts that in the twenty peace conferences that have taken place nothing of substance has been done to construct the Somali state. And it is this statelessness, I argue, that is the source of the country's conflict. If peace is to be built, the coercive capacity of the state has to be reestablished. This shifts the agenda of the Somalia debate from that of organizing peace conferences to building the capacity of the state, particularly by establishing inclusive, professional and well-disciplined security forces.

Moreover, I argue that, like other wars in Africa, the causes of the Somali conflict and the actors that are present in this context are complex and multiple. While competition for power and resources are the main engine of hostility, colonial legacy, unhelpful political culture, and a ready availability of weapons are also fuelling the fight. In terms of actors, many clans, a number of Islamist groups, tribal entrepreneurs using different slogans, hostile neighbouring states, and a confused international community are pulling the country in different directions.

In examining clan identity and its implications for peacebuilding, I argue that such ties are strong within the Somali people and that any attempt to design political institutions will have to deal with issues of representation. It is this representation issue, I contend, that is one of the most difficult problems facing the nation. As such, the book proposes that any effective way of dealing with this issue will require both short- and long-term mechanisms. The two main Somali identities, clan and Islamic identities, will have to be represented within the political system. The book further contends that, for the short term, a temporary formula that represents all clans will be necessary. Perhaps the current '4.5 formula' can be replaced with one that divides the power to five or six clans. The presence of Islamists, who largely disapprove of the usage of clan identity in politics, complicates the matter. Some of the Islamist movements call for clan-blind policies. The book proposes a bicameral system where one of the houses represents clans while the other uses some form of geographical or population-based constituencies.

As argued in Chapter 4, the international community has to accept the reality that, as in other Muslim countries, political Islam is a force that is to be reckoned with on the ground in Somalia. Both moderate and radical groups are present in the country. The book contends that most of Somalia's Islamists have a national agenda and can be accommodated within the peacebuilding process. Further, I assert that conditions (at times created by external forces) will determine whether moderates or radicals are empowered. For instance, during the first six months of the Union of Islamic Courts, the prevailing conditions favoured moderate Islamists and thus they were more powerful. But the Ethiopian occupation reversed this and created conditions that empowered extremists. The irony here is that Ethiopia, and to lesser extent Kenya, share the goals of preventing the emergence of a Somali state with the same radical groups that they are determined to fight. Both of these countries have worked against building the Somali state for their own geopolitical reasons.

Finally, the book concludes with the argument that Somalia's peacebuilding does not have to wait until the conflict ends. The international community and Somalis must begin to invest in education, governance and economic development. I consider progress in these areas to be an important part of the long-term approach to the conflict. Moreover, one of the main obstacles to peace has been the lack of resources. Previous peace processes failed because donors were not forthcoming with cash; Somalia does not have the revenue sources to pay for peace. In short, the resources needed to build peace in Somalia are billions of dollars – yet no country is willing to foot this bill. As such, the book argues that, like the case of East Timor, the issue of Somalia's resources has to be on the table when negotiating for peace. As James Fearon and David Laitin note, this will require the United Nations to be fully involved to ensure that Somalia is not taken for a ride.[2] The international community and super powers also benefit from building peace in Somalia and therefore, I argue, have an interest in providing financial assistance.

By advancing the above arguments, the book aims to contribute to the policy and academic debates in conflict and peacebuilding in general and to the debates in peacebuilding in Africa. I explore how Somalis of various persuasion (Islamists, business leaders, nationalist intellectuals, average citizens) understand the challenges of and responses to building durable peace and a functioning state in Somalia. The book proposes a fresh way of understanding and interpreting events in Somalia and suggests context-appropriate political structures. This is significant because of the growing concerns among major powers and the international community regarding the persistence of the Somali conflict and the ever-increasing suffering of the Somali people. In addition, I hope that my proposals find application in other collapsed states such as Afghanistan, Liberia and Sierra Leone, as well as in other African states struggling with similar problems. This book will help peacebuilders and policymakers better understand the nature of the problems behind such conflicts and help them to design suitable remedial strategies and institutions.

STATELESSNESS, PIRACY AND PEACEBUILDING

Legitimate or not, one relevant question is, why should anyone but the Somalis care about Somalia? The Great Powers of the day only care what happens to small countries and poor peoples when they feel that their own 'interests' are threatened. Statelessness, civil wars, anarchic conditions or lack of democracy become a concern to the Great Powers when their national interests come into play. There are numerous examples to illustrate this. For instance, in Uganda in the 1970s under Idi Amin and in Rwanda in 1994, no Western powers intervened to stop the bloodbaths, as they saw no reason to do so. Although such complacency is changing, historically, the case in Somalia has witnessed a similar hesitancy on the part of the international community to intervene. In 1990, the international community, led by the United States, abandoned Somalia when the state collapsed. Soon after, the US launched Operation Restore Hope, which saved many people from starvation. But when the forces of Somali warlord General Aideed killed 18 American soldiers, the West withdrew and adopted a 'wait and see' attitude.

At present Somalia is strategically important to Western interests, at least as such interest is defined by the United States. There are three interconnected factors of concern to the US. First, with the collapse of the old secular regime in Somalia, religion in the form of Islam has and will play a major political role in the building of a state in Somalia. This is further complicated by the presence of many different organized Islamist forces (both radical and moderate). Because the United States has had a foreign policy based on denying power to Islamist groups, if it is to have any involvement in the securing of Somalia, its policies toward a new Islamic state there will need to be addressed. Second, even if the United States were to disengage from an Islamic state in Somalia, threats to shipping from piracy would still necessitate Western intervention. Third, because of the energy needs of the United States, Africa as a whole is one of the latest arenas for the setting up of military enclaves by the US, which has a direct oil interest along the western borders of the continent.[3]

In the view of Washington, statelessness and civil war in Somalia provide the conditions for 'Bin Ladens' to set up shop and plan attacks on Western interests around the world. Moreover, in an environment of stateless anarchy, entrepreneurial Somalis find an opportunity to make money from seizing ships that pass the Somali coast. This is piracy, by any definition. But to Somalis, illegal fishing and toxic-waste dumping in their waters by Western companies also represent a type of piracy.

All of this leads to the need for the establishment of durable peace and the creation of a functioning state in Somalia. Of course, the question is peace for whom, and through what methods. This book is concerned with the connections between the important issues that stem from statelessness of Somalia as they affect both Somalis and the world community, and the solutions that can be entertained in order to resolve this conflict. Indeed, one of the major reasons for writing this book is to propose solutions that work for both domestic and external players.

THE SOMALI CONFLICT

A State Collapse and its Implications

Using a sophisticated methodology and twelve social, economic and political indicators, *Foreign Policy* magazine and The Fund for Peace annually publish what they call the 'Failed States Index'. As of 2008, according to the index, Somalia is on the top of the list of failing and failed states. Robert Rotberg conducted similar research on states that are not performing well, determining state performance on the ability (or inability) of a country to provide public goods – the most important public good being security. Using data from the Human Development Index (HDI), Transparency International and the World Freedom Report, Rotberg identifies four categories of states: functioning states, failing states, failed states, and collapsed states. He defines collapsed states as the 'extreme version of a failed state'.[4] For Rotberg, Somalia is the best example of a fully collapsed state.

Failed states, Rotberg argues, pose a significant threat to the international community. He writes, 'the existence of these kinds of countries, and the instability that they harbor, not only threatens the lives and livelihoods of their own peoples but endangers world peace'.[5] Other proponents of this view argue that non-state actors could exploit a collapsed state environment, as has been the case in Afghanistan.[6] One assumption that guides US policy toward Somalia is that because Somalia is a poor Muslim country within which the state has collapsed,[7] non-state actors, such as terrorist organizations, could similarly exploit this condition and use the country as a base to attack Western interests.

Although the context has changed now, Ken Menkhaus and Ted Dagne previously questioned this assumption.[8] Menkhaus argues that the same forces that hinder humanitarian agencies also haunt terrorists. He writes, 'the case of Somalia suggests that we may have been partially mistaken in our assumption about the relationship between terrorism and collapsed states'.[9] Taking the debate further, he notes that 'terrorist networks in a region such as East Africa would have a strong and logical preference to work out of Nairobi, Dar es Salaam, or even in the Ugandan capital of Kampala, rather than in Somalia'.[10] Scholars come to this conclusion because, according to them, terrorists cannot find targets in a failed state environment since the presence of Westerners in such an environment is limited. Moreover, these scholars argue that since Somalia disintegrated, local authorities are too weak and fragmented to provide shelter. In contrast, because of corruption, fragile states can offer better alternatives to terrorist organizations – an argument, as stated above, to which US policy is still geared.

Regardless of the theoretical possibilities, in early 2002 the Western media speculated about a possible US attack on Somalia.[11] In an effort to save Somalia from bombardment, its greatest writer, Nurudin Farah, argued in the *New York Times* that it was highly doubtful whether Al-Qaeda could operate in Somalia because the conditions that statelessness created would not allow foreign organizations to survive. Farah argued, 'the West should not be fooled by the misinformation doled out by both the Ethiopian regime and its allies in Somalia and by the untrustworthy men now leading Somalia's murderous factions. They can be expected to point censorious fingers at their rivals, describing them as associates of Al-Qaeda.'[12] Although many experts have agreed with Farah, the United States's view of Somalia has remained hostile and focused on terrorism.

Menkhaus, however, agrees with Herbst and Rotberg that the problems of collapsed states could easily go beyond their borders.[13] He points out that there are other apparent security problems that could arise from a collapsed state environment. For Menkhaus, such environments can produce humanitarian disasters, refugees, and sometimes communicable diseases that impact both local populations and the international community. As examples, Menkhaus identifies Rift Valley and drug-resistant tuberculosis as two diseases that have appeared in Somalia, which could easily move across borders to infect citizens of other countries. Additionally, the Somali media has reported that there were disease outbreaks[14] following the 2004 tsunami disaster, because Somalia's coast was used by European companies as a toxic waste dump site.[15] Nobody knows the future impact of this on the people of the region.

Obviously, it is dangerous to generalize too broadly from the cases of Afghanistan and Somalia, and each case should be understood according to its own specificities and historical, geopolitical and social contexts. The Somali context is changing on a daily basis. The US and many Westerners believe that the Al-Shabab movement is linked to Al-Qaeda. But, it is not yet clear whether this link is ideological or organizational. Al-Shabab spokesmen have stated openly that they were not members of the Al-Qaeda network, but it is known that they share the same views, enemies and objectives with Bin Laden's movement. Whether a link exists or not, many Somalis reject Al-Shabab's actions and their interpretations of Islam. That said, there are other clear dangers for the Somali people, such as health problems and humanitarian crises that fall to the wayside or are compounded upon.

Despite the views of Somalis and experts, the US government has enacted policy based on its information and its understanding of the dangers that are associated with the collapsed state environment in Somalia. After 9/11, the US closed down Al-Barakaat, Somalia's largest bank and telecommunications company, as well as its subsidiaries. Former US Treasury Secretary Paul O'Neill went as far as to say, 'Al-Barakaat companies are the money movers, the quartermasters of terror.'[16] Some media accounts suggested that Bin Laden was receiving at least $25 million a year from the commissions that Al-Barakaat made.[17] Al-Barakaat managers denied the charge and invited the US government to check its books. UN officials in Somalia also questioned the US decision to close Al-Barakaat and suggested the move may affect many ordinary Somalis.[18] These calls for caution did not alter the Bush administration's decision on closure. However, in 2004 the National Commission on Terrorist Attacks Upon the United States released its 9/11 Commission Report, and stated that its investigation did not find evidence linking Al-Barakaat to Al-Qaeda. Despite the fact that the Commission concluded that there was no credible terrorist evidence against Al-Barakaat, the company was not de-listed as a terrorist organization. In addition to Al-Barakaat, the US added Al-Ittihad al-Islami and the Al-Shabab Islamic movement to its 'terrorist list'. In 2006 the US helped depose the Union of Islamic Courts from power.

Piracy in Somalia: Global Problem and Local Response

After the Cold War, many commentators hastily claimed that Somalia's strategic importance ended with the collapse of the former Soviet Union. But, the recent upsurge of piracy on the high seas reminds us that Somalia remains very important for the globalized world economy. As piracy off the coast of Somalia became an increasingly persistent problem over the last decade, it came to affect the lives of millions of people throughout the world. The Gulf of Aden, the 'hunting ground', is strategically too important for the world community to lose to the pirates.

According to the International Maritime Bureau, in 2008, Somali pirates attacked 111 ships (a record number) and captured 42 of them.[19] Some 92 of these attacks took place in the Gulf of Aden. This problem peaked when a Saudi Arabian supertanker, the *Sirius Star*, was hijacked on 18 November 2008.

Explaining the broader context in a recent article in *Foreign Affairs*, Robert Kaplan argued that the Indian Ocean will be the world's centre-stage and whoever controls it will dominate the world for years to come. According to Kaplan, 70 per cent of the world's petroleum-related products transit the Indian Ocean.[20] Most products shipped from China, Japan and India are transported through this route.

Somali pirates have collected ransom money estimated at between $80 million and $150 million. Moreover, because of the piracy, ship owners now pay ten times more insurance than they used to in the past.[21] The reason is that underwiters consider pirates as terrorists and do not cover terrorism risks in the policies they offer to the owners.[22] With respect to the human cost, besides hundreds of hostages that are being held by pirates, pirates' activities have a negative effect on millions of Somalis. Ships carrying food aid and commercial products to Somalia have been hijacked. As a result, domestic food prices there have sky-rocketed.

Piracy off the coast of Somalia has been the direct result of the increased illegal fishing and toxic-waste dumping in Somali waters. Somali pirates have spoken of the abuses committed against local Somali fishermen by foreign vessels fishing illegally in the area.[23] According to the UN Food and Agriculture Organization, more than 700 foreign vessels have been fishing illegally in Somali waters since 2005.[24] As so little has been done to rectify these issues, many Somalis now regard the intentions of the international community as suspect. Interestingly, the Somali writer Mohamud Khalif, asked the French Navy Commander based in East Africa if French forces or others securing the Indian Ocean would protect Somali waters from 'other pirates' – that is, illegal fishermen and the dumpers of toxic waste. The commander responded by saying that his forces did not have the mandate to do that.[25]

Efthimios Mitropoulos, secretary-general of the International Maritime Organization, appealed to the UN Security Council to help address the problem of piracy. As a result, the Security Council passed Resolutions 1816, 1848 and 1851. These resolutions call on the international community to act in order to end the piracy off the Somalia coast. As a result, the European Union, NATO, the Combined Maritime Force and 16 individual countries sent 24 warships to guard the coast – but to no avail. Pirate attacks increased after the United States Navy freed Captain Philips from Somali pirates by killing three and capturing one.

It is becoming increasingly clear that these half-baked solutions suggest the world community's poor understanding of the magnitude of the problem. The security of the Somalis and the safety of the goods on the high seas are linked. Thus, instead of calling more of the same old and failed policies, the international community must adopt a comprehensive approach that addresses the root causes of the problem of piracy: illegal fishing, toxic-waste dumping, and most importantly, human insecurity. Building durable peace and a functioning state in Somalia should be the common sense approach.

CHALLENGES TO ENDING THE SOMALI CIVIL WAR

Generally, civil wars end either through a military victory or through a negotiated settlement. If one faction, for instance Yoweri Museveni's National Resistance Army in Uganda or Meles Zenawi's Tigrayan People's Liberation Front in Ethiopia, emerges as a winner by defeating the rest militarily, then that group imposes its will on others. But when no faction wins, all groups involved in the conflict may opt for a negotiated settlement, as has been the case in Mozambique, Burundi and South Africa.[26]

As was clear from the outset of the civil unrest in the 1990s, none of the Somali factions could win the war by defeating other groups militarily. Therefore, to end the conflict a negotiated settlement became the only option available to all factions involved. Subsequently, between 1991 and 2004, 17 reconciliation conferences were held for the opposing Somali groups. Several countries, such as Djibouti, Kenya, Yemen, Ethiopia, Libya and Egypt, hosted these conferences. For the most part only warlords were invited to attend, although at times the host country would allow civil society and traditional leaders to participate. For instance, five of the many peace processes were major conferences in which the international community provided substantial support. These were the Djibouti conference in 1992, the Addis Ababa conference in 1993, the Cairo conference in 1997, the Arta conference in 2000, and the two-year-long Nairobi conference held from 2002 to 2004. After each of the five conferences, a peace accord was signed or a transitional government was established in Somalia. Unfortunately, none of the conferences produced a legitimate, functioning government capable of creating a viable state in Somalia.

The Somali civil war cannot end through military victory since there is no one faction that can defeat clans, factions, Islamist groups and self-governing regions. On the other hand, the many peace processes that were held for Somalis did not end the conflict. Does this then mean that there is no solution? To the contrary, the thrust of this book's argument is that peace in Somalia is not only desirable but also possible, albeit with many challenges.

Peace, Peacebuilding and Statebuilding in Somalia

In general, this book does not conceive peace as the absence of violence or absence of threat of violence. Instead, peace is understood as the presence of skills and processes for dealing with conflicts non-violently.[27] While 'negative peace' (the absence of violence or war) is necessary, it is not a sufficient condition for achieving sustainable peace. With respect to peacebuilding, former United Nations Secretary General Boutros-Ghali defines it as a process that helps establish durable peace by 'addressing the root causes and effects of conflict through reconciliation and institution building'.[28] Scholars approach peacebuilding in different ways. For instance, Barbara F. Walter argues that building peace requires the presence of a credible third party. For her, when third parties assure protection for different groups, these groups are willing to sign and implement peace accords.[29] George Downs and Stephen John Stedman contend that disarmament of combatants and demilitarization of politics would lead to peace.[30] Fen Osler Hampson, on the other hand, argues that peace will prevail only when the situation on the ground is ripe for resolution, the international community provides timely assistance, and the quality of the peace accord reflects the needs of the groups.[31] Moreover, Thomas Keating and Andrew Knight in their review of the concept of peacebuilding identify six themes: conceptualizing peacebuilding; broadening the time and scope of peacebuilding; promoting a local culture of peace; evaluating the role of international actors; looking at the relations between civil and military aspects of peacebuilding; and addressing issues of justice.[32]

However, as Roland Paris argues, the international community's peacebuilding efforts are not ideologically neutral; for the international community, governance and other peacebuilding efforts have to produce, eventually, a liberal democracy and a free market.[33] In other words, whether a peacebuilding effort is successful will be judged on the extent to which it produces a market economy and liberal democracy. For Somalia, the facts on the ground present a different reality. Popular and well-organized Islamist movements challenge the Western-driven peacebuilding efforts.

Peace Education and Citizenship Education

Education, and in particular peace education, is considered as one such institution through which the root causes of conflict might be addressed. As Kathy Bickmore asserts, all kinds of learning in different contexts (formal and informal) and from a variety of sources (culture, language, schools and environment) are considered as education.[34] I believe such a broad conception is necessary for this book, as Somalia has been a collapsed state for the last two decades and most of its formal education institutions have been destroyed. If, as Michael Wessels argues, peace education is a necessary 'condition for and a cornerstone' of building peace, then, according to Wessels, 'families, communities, ethnic groups, and nations must be socialized in ways that promote non-violent conflict resolution, sustainability, and social justice' in all possible forums, including formal, informal and non-formal education.[35]

Gavriel Salomon classifies types of peace education according to a particular context of conflict: peace education in regions of intractable conflicts (such as Rwanda and Israel-Palestine), peace education in regions of interethnic tension (Belgium and United States), and peace education in regions of experienced tranquillity (Canada). He argues that those who design peace education programmes must have a conceptual clarity of the type of conflict being addressed and the appropriate peace education programmes for a given context.[36]

Keeping these in mind, how is peace education conceived? Where does peace education, and ultimately, peace, begin to deal with the Somali conflict? What determines and constitutes the curricula of peace? What values should peace education programmes teach? This book utilizes Susan Fountain's definition of peace education as 'the process of promoting knowledge, skills, attitudes and values needed to bring about behavior change that will enable children, youth and adults to prevent conflict and violence, both overt and structural; to resolve conflict peacefully; and to create the conditions conducive to peace, whether at an intra-personal, interpersonal, inter-group, national or international level'.[37] This definition emphasizes behaviour change and targets both children and adults. Finally, Fountain's understanding of peace education, like Salomon's, addresses different types of conflicts at all levels. The book will also discuss some of the peace education programmes that have been used in the Somalia context and the values they promoted.

ORGANIZATION OF THE BOOK

This book explores the main challenges of and responses to the Somali conflict. Chapter 2 examines the sources of the conflict and provides historical context. Chapter 3 looks at clan identity and its implications for peacebuilding in Somalia. It addresses the following questions: How does clan identity work in the Somali context? Why is it important? What is the role of clan identity in the Somali civil war? How does it affect the efforts towards building durable peace and functioning state institutions? How can it be addressed? Chapter 4 analyses the history and role of Islam in Somalia, and the concept and future implications of Islamic awakening or 'Islamism'. The chapter looks at the challenges that Islamist forces and the values they stand for pose to Western efforts to build a liberal peace in Somalia. Also examined are the origin and role of Islamic courts in creating a more secure environment in this troubled country.

Chapter 5 examines US policy toward Somalia. It argues that US policy deals with the symptoms, but does not address the statelessness problem that US administrations use to justify America's limited and negative involvement in Somalia. Chapter 6 then examines the impact of regional players. In particular, it analyses the roles that Ethiopia, Kenya and Djibouti have played in the initiation and perpetuation of Somali conflict, arguing that Somalia's hostile neighbours have exploited the miseries of the Somali people for self-serving purposes. Chapter 7 looks at the role that education can play in building peace, and assesses options available to the international community for assisting Somalia. It further analyses Somali children's access to education, peace education, and peacebuilding education. Chapter 8 then discusses the role of the international community and the mismatch between the Western ideology that drives peacebuilding efforts and the indigenous institutions – Islam and Somali culture – in the country. It also examines several options for building sustainable peace in Somalia: trusteeship, transitional administration, and supporting a home-grown solution. Chapter 9 sums up the main points of the book and provides recommendations.

CONCLUSION

In light of growing concerns among major powers and the international community regarding the persistence of the Somali conflict and the ever-increasing suffering of the Somali people, this book examines the challenges of and responses to building peace in Somalia. It advances our understanding of the challenges of peacebuilding by identifying primary obstacles and the policies that have attempted to address those obstacles. The book analyses failed peacemaking attempts of the past in an effort to help peacebuilders and policymakers better understand the nature of the problem and help them design appropriate strategies, thus contributing to theories of conflict resolution and peacebuilding. Such accounts give insight to knowledge-building at the theoretical level as well as provide practical policy advice in regard to peacebuilding and the role education might play in the peace efforts in Somalia. Such knowledge also gives insight to addressing African states struggling with similar problems as well as to efforts to build stability in other collapsed states, such as Afghanistan, Liberia and Sierra Leone.

2
Understanding the Sources of Somali Conflict

Xumaan ka guur, xumaan u guur
Xaggee bannaan, xeraan galnee

Moving from bad to worse
Where can we go, we are in prison

Farah Gamuute, Somali writer and poet

In the early 1990s when the Soviet Union disintegrated many people expected that peace in a unipolar world would prevail. Instead, many intra-state wars broke out in different parts of the globe. Different factions, identity groups and regions challenged existing states' monopoly over violence. As a result, a number of states collapsed and many others to this day remain precipitously on the verge of failing. Somalia, Sierra Leone, Liberia, the former Yugoslavia, Congo and Cambodia are examples of states that have totally collapsed. Many African countries such as Ethiopia, Sudan and Zimbabwe are under extreme pressure from domestic and external forces. Many scholars and some important political actors often characterize these conflicts as identity-based civil wars.[1] This chapter discusses the causes of the Somali conflict. As I argued elsewhere,[2] the main causes of the Somali conflict are competition for resources and/or power, the colonial legacy, and repression by the military regime. Politicized clan identity, availability of weapons, and the presence of large numbers of unemployed youth are considered as contributing causes. The chapter further outlines the peace processes held and it discusses some of the main factors that led to the failure of these efforts.

SOMALIA: BRIEF BACKGROUND

Early European writers called Somalis a mixed race of Arab and African origins but more reasonable accounts suggest that Somalis are related to other ethnic groups in the Horn of Africa. In other

16

words, Somalis, as an ethnic group, are African in race and Muslim in faith. Moreover, Somalis are largely homogeneous people. Within the Somali ethnic group, there are many clans and sub-clans that are based on patrilineal kinship.[3] Prior to European colonial arrival, Somalis did not have a central state in the sense of a Western, Weberian bureaucratic state. However, they used home-grown conflict resolution mechanisms of *Heer* (traditional law) and Islam for resolving disputes among individuals and groups. Socioeconomically, Somalis have depended on livestock and farming and many are pastoral-nomads.[4]

Colonial countries partitioned Somalia into five parts. Great Britain took two parts while France, Italy and Ethiopia divided the remaining three among themselves. In response to the partition and the colonization that followed, Somalis fought back. Sayid Mohamed Abdulle Hassan led a long struggle against Great Britain while several groups resisted France, Italy and Ethiopia in other parts of Somalia. Besides Sayid Mohamed Abdulle Hassan's protracted struggle between 1899 and 1921, the most significant organization was the Somali Youth League (SYL) which was established in 1943. Following Italy's defeat in the Second World War, the League of Nations put Southern Somalia into trusteeship for ten years. Northern and Southern Somalia gained independence on 26 June 1960 and 1 July 1960 respectively, and they united under one state. Somalia's first state was determined to unite all the regions under 'Greater Somalia'.

For the first nine years after its independence (1960–69), Somalia was a democratic state. Although the SYL was the dominant political party, there were as many as sixty political parties in the 1969 election.[5] But, Cold War politics and the winds of change in Africa affected Somalia. The military coup on 21 October 1969 turned Somalia into a socialist state. Although Siyad Barre's military regime built many schools and roads, it has repressed the Somali people for over twenty years. As a result of the military regime's repressive tactics, several clan-based armed groups organized rebellions. Among these were the Somali Salvation Democratic Front (SSDF), the Somali National Movement (SNM), the Somali Patriotic Movement (SPM), Somali Democratic Movement (SDM) and the United Somali Congress (USC).

In 1978 military officers from the Majeerteen clan attempted to overthrow the regime.[6] In response the Siyad Barre government used the national army and police to punish civilian members of the Majeerteen clan and the military was involved in the killing of civilians, mass abuses, and the destruction of areas inhabited by the clan. The current civil war started with these events. As more clans began to challenge the state, so the regime became more abusive. In 1981 politicians of the Isaaq clan established an opposition movement (the Somali National Movement) in London. Again the Siyad Barre regime began to punish innocent civilians, murdering many people when the SNM attacked the cities of Hargeysa and Bur'o in 1988. Human rights organizations reported that more than 50,000 people were killed in these conflicts.[7]

After Siyad Barre was overthrown in 1991, most of the country's institutions, as well as law and order, were destroyed. Anarchy spread in the country. While successful in overthrowing the regime, opposition factions failed to fill the power vacuum because no faction (including the United Somali Congress that expelled Siyad Barre from Mogadishu) had the power to dominate the other groups militarily. They also failed to reach a negotiated settlement. As a result, the factions kept fighting against each other for different motives. Most of the major factions have been fighting for domination, while smaller ones have been fighting for survival.[8]

COMPETITION FOR RESOURCES AND POWER

Outside urban centres, different clans contest over resources such as water, livestock and grazing land. In the past Somali nomads have fought over the ownership of camels because of their utility for survival in Somalia's harsh environment. In this context, clan identity is useful because to obtain and keep a large number of camels one needs to rely on the support of one's clansmen. As Abdalla Omar Mansur notes, after urbanization, the type of assets seen as important changed.[9] State-power, weapons, jobs and foreign aid became important resources for which clans and other groups competed. To access these, again one had to rely on the relationships that clan identity provided. In relying on clan identity, clan lines were strengthened.

Indeed, during the first round of the civil war, between 1988 and 1992, militias were organized along major clan lines and major cities changed hands.[10] In fact, it was at that time common to hear from the media, and Somalis, that faction X had captured a particular city or was occupying an important location within the capital. Militias from Hawiye clans expelled other Somali clans from Mogadishu and other towns in central and southern regions.

Militia groups that belonged to the Darod clan also controlled the Lower Jubba and Puntland regions while Digil and Mirifle took charge of the Bay and Bakool regions. Soon this changed, and the sub-clans of the major clans began to compete for the control of major cities. In Mogadishu, Habar-Gidir and Abgal militias fought for four months and destroyed what was left of the city. Habar-Gidir also fought against the Murusade and Hawadle clans. Similarly, the Absame and Harti clans of the Darod clan clashed a number of times for control of Lower Jubba, particularly the city of Kismayo. The Marihan and Harti sub-clans have also fought over the same issue. These examples were repeated in Baidoa as the Digil and Mirifle clans fought over control of the city. Even the breakaway region of Somaliland was not spared from this intra-clan warfare – the Isaaq clans (Garhajis and Habar Awal) fought a bitter civil war in north 'Somaliland'.

COLONIAL LEGACY AND MILITARY REPRESSION

At the macro level the colonial legacy has also played a significant role in the Somali conflict. In 1884, the colonial powers divided the Somali peninsula into five different regions. Great Britain took the northwest regions and Northeast Frontier District (NFD). France colonized Djibouti and Italy controlled southern Somalia. During the 'scramble for Africa', Ethiopia was given the western portion of Somalia for its cooperation with the colonial powers. After colonization, Great Britain handed over several regions of the Somali territories to Ethiopia and Kenya. Indeed, it was because of this division that Somalis started to mobilize for independence and fight against colonial forces. Moreover, after Somalia became independent in 1960 it spent most of its resources regaining the lost regions.[11] The current collapse of the Somali state is rooted in the 1977 war between Somalia and Ethiopia over the 'Ogaden' region. Due to direct military intervention from the Soviet Union and Cuba, Somalia lost the war.

With respect to repression, injustices that stemmed from the use and abuse of power during the period of the Somali state (1960–91) produced many of the grievances that Somalis have against each other. Both civilian and military governments were essentially controlled by the elites of respective clans who held the levers of state power. Somalis call the first civilian government, as democratic as it was, 'the corrupt government' (Dowladdii Musuqmaasuqa). Qasim, a famous Somali poet, eloquently characterized how Somalia's civilian government failed to meet the expectations of Somalis. He said, 'Isma doorin gaalkaan diriyo, daarta kii galaye'[12] (there is no difference between the infidel I expelled [from the country] and the one that occupies the building [the government parliament]). Although not widespread, there were cases in which the government used the Somali police against clans who held grievances against the regime.[13]

It is true that civilian leaders in the period between 1960 and 1969 embezzled state resources, mishandled judicial cases and scholarships, or else used nepotism when hiring and firing government employees, acting in part from the fact that Somalia's military regime committed heinous crimes against civilian populations. The military leaders used brute force against opposition groups and the general public. The first incident came when military officers attempted to overthrow the government in 1978 (after the 1977 war). The coup failed, and Siyad Barre's regime killed many innocent Somalis who belonged to the Majeerteen clan in the Mudug and Bari regions. From the regime's perspective, those people were guilty by association or because they shared an identity, at times a distant one, with the officers allegedly responsible for carrying out the coup. Hadrawi, Somalia's greatest poet, protested this barbaric act and wrote his poem 'Heelliyo' (Female monkey), in which he criticized the military regime's practices.[14] A similar event, albeit bigger in terms of magnitude and human suffering, occurred in northwest Somalia in 1988. After a long war Siyad Barre signed a deal with Ethiopia's dictator in which they agreed to stop supporting the respective opposition groups of both regimes. This agreement forced Mengistu Haile Mariam of Ethiopia to stop supporting Somali opposition groups, including the Somali National Movement (SNM). As a result, the SNM moved into Somalia, captured Bur'o city and then attacked Hargeysa, the second capital of Somalia. The Siyad Barre regime retaliated, killing thousands of people with military airplanes and tanks. Several human rights groups condemned this act and in fact, even the United States, which earlier supported the Barre regime, stopped providing military assistance to the Somali government [15]

Clan pride and the culture of taking revenge against any member of the perpetrator's clan (i.e., collective punishment) are not only causes of traditional clan wars but the cause of the recent civil war. For some theorists, pride or prestige is considered a type of resource, albeit not a quantifiable one.[16] There are numerous examples that show how clan pride motivated conflicts. For example, when the Abgal and Habar-Gidir sub-clans of Hawiye fought in Mogadishu, it was clear (at least from the perspective of the Abgal) that clan pride was a pertinent factor. Members of the Abgal clans considered Mogadishu as their own city and believed that the Habar-Gidir clan came all the way from the central regions of the country. Similarly, when Habar-Gidir's militia captured the Hiran, Lower Shabelle and Bay regions, clans that traditionally populated those areas internalized the defeat as an injury to clan pride.[17] Clan pride causes conflicts between clans when a member of a clan kills another person. The clan of the victim often takes such an act as an injury to its pride and takes revenge. Besides competition for resources and/or power, there are many examples where a war began between two clans because of a perceived injury to clan pride and the collective punishment that followed it. In the 1940s clan wars among the Habar Yonis, 'Ogaden' and Dhulbahante clans began, and according to Guba poems, it was because of perceived injury to clan pride.

THE PEACE CONFERENCES: WHY DID THEY FAIL?

There were five major conferences that the international community supported (see Table 1). However, at least twelve additional conferences were held, all outside of Somalia and all of which also failed. Djibouti sponsored the first peace conference in August 1991. It also hosted two rounds of conferences in May and June 2008 for the Transitional Federal Government (TFG) and the Alliance for the Re-liberation of Somalia. Kenya hosted a conference for the Somali groups in April 1994 and October 1996. Moreover, in 2001 Kenya hosted two more conferences, in Nairobi and Nakuru. Some Somali groups met in Cairo in November 1993. Yemen held talks for the Somali groups in April 1997. This conference was useful as it destroyed the green line in Mogadishu between the United Somali Congress (USC) groups. Moreover, Yemen mediated the two factions of the TFG in 2005. Ethiopia organized two conferences: Sodere in 1996 and Awase in 2001. Sudan hosted three rounds of conferences between the TFG and the Union of Islamic Courts.

Several factors contributed to the failure of the first two peace conferences in Djibouti and Addis Ababa. Some of the faction leaders that participated in the conferences thought they could win the war through military victory and therefore were not interested in negotiated settlement. For instance, the six groups that met in Djibouti signed a peace accord, but General Mohamed Farah Aideed rejected the deal even though his representatives signed the agreement. He believed the agreement did not reflect the realities on the ground. Right after the accord, war broke out between the factions of General Aideed and Ali Mahdi over power-related issues.

Table 1 Major Peace Conferences for Somali Factions

Location	Date	Sponsored	Participants	Outcome	Status
Djibouti conference, Djibouti	08/1991	Djibouti	Six factions	Accord	Failed
Addis Ababa conference, Ethiopia	03/1993	UN	15 factions	Peace accord	Failed
Cairo conference, Egypt	12/1997	Egypt	28 factions	Peace accord	Failed
Arta conference, Djibouti	05–08, 2000	Djibouti	More than 3,000 civil society members	Charter	Failed
Mbagathi conference, Kenya	10/2002 10/2004	IGAD	Three main factions (SRRC, Group 8 and TNG) and many individuals	Charter	Failed

Although thousands of people were killed during the Mogadishu fighting between the USC groups and other inter-clan wars, none of the groups emerged as a winner. The international community and the regional actors called for another conference in Ethiopia. The 15 factions that participated in this conference produced a detailed peace agreement. The creation of a Transitional National Council was agreed which had to be elected from Somalia's 18 regions. Each of the regions would choose three members, of which one would be a woman. Again, the question over who would select these members resulted in a dispute between General Mohamed Farah Aideed and the leadership of the United Nations. General Aideed believed that since he controlled many regions his faction would nominate while the UN wanted to respect the local people's wishes. Again, General Aideed's forces fought against the US-led United Nations forces, thus leading to another failure.

While the first two conferences were unsuccessful due to the lack of will on the part of Somali faction leaders, the Cairo and the Arta conferences failed due to foreign meddling too. When Somalis signed the Cairo Peace Accord, Ethiopia convinced Colonel Abdullahi Yusuf and General Aden Abdullahi Nur (Gabyow) to quit the conference. These leaders left Cairo and rejected the outcome. Moreover, Hussein Aideed, Ali Mahdi and others were also not interested in implementing the agreement. Hussein Aideed refused to leave Baidoa which his forces controlled. In addition, Ali Mahdi and Hussein Aideed failed to pacify Mogadishu. Many Somalis believe they had neither the will nor the capacity to do so.

THE MBAGATHI CONFERENCE AND TRANSITIONAL FEDERAL GOVERNMENT

Since the Mbagathi conference lasted for two years and the transitional government that resulted officially ruled the country for the longest time, in depth analyses are warranted. The peace conference held for the Somali factions and warlords in Kenya concluded on 10 October 2004, with the formation of a transitional government. The Intergovernmental Authority on Development (IGAD), a regional organization of East African countries, sponsored the conference, which was hosted by the Kenyan government. During this period, as IGAD claims, the Somali factions enacted a transitional charter and selected a 275-member legislature. The selected parliament then elected Abdullahi Yusuf Ahmed as president.

According to Stedman, badly designed and poorly implemented peace agreements can lead to a renewed civil war, not to peace. Stedman cites the examples of Rwanda and Angola where, according to him, more people died after a peace agreement was signed than during the conflict.[18] At the outset, there were serious problems with the process that produced Somalia's Transitional Federal Government. Ethiopia dominated the peace process. In particular, it rewarded the warlords that supported its policies by appointing them as members of the parliament and cabinet, and it punished those who were not on its side: civil society, nationalist intellectuals, and Islamists. Since representation problems have always been the most difficult challenge, Ethiopia and Kenya, with the help of IGAD, arbitrarily selected most of the 275 members of the parliament. They also alienated factions and countries that were important for any successful peace agreement in Somalia.

Ethiopia and Kenya had their own reasons for manipulating the peace conference. They had concerns with the notion of a greater Somalia since they both control Somali regions. So in this venture, they wanted to install a regime that was opposed to the idea of a greater Somalia. Besides, Ethiopia is a large, landlocked country, and it is interested in gaining access to a sea corridor. The current Addis Ababa regime, therefore, wants to create several mini-states that are hostile to each other and have good relations with Ethiopia.

It prefers to deal with different clans that populate the areas in which it has an interest rather than dealing with a strong united Somali state.[19]

Ethiopia and Kenya imposed this transitional government on the Somali people, and for the first time in history they had a charter, a parliament and a government of their design in Somalia. Without a national debate or referendum, Ethiopia and Kenya, while using their proxy warlords, also forced an undefined and obscure form of federalism on Somalia. Interestingly, the argument here was that the state is not federal but the government is federal – the Transitional Federal Government of the Somali Republic. This logic was strange because the confusion it created is still with the new Government of National Unity.

The conditions that often necessitate federation are not present in Somalia. In addition, Somalia lacks the capacity to run several layers of governments: local, regional and federal. There are also practical problems, as currently there are no agreed-upon regions or states in Somalia. Depending on the popular opinion of different clans, some (federalist northerners) want two regions while others (Puntland and Rahanweyn Resistance Army) call for four or five regions. But there are also those, such as some members of the Darod clan, who want the federation to be based on the 18 regions that Siyad Barre left. On the other hand, some members of the Hawiye clan call for the eight regions that existed before Siyad Barre came to power. None of the above criteria are based on an objective system or the economic reality of the country; each clan wants to maximize its share. Adopting such an undefined form of federalism is likely to lead to more conflicts, not solutions. More important, as has been noted previously, the Somali people did not have an opportunity to participate in the process that was used when adopting federalism.

Although the Somali peace process in Kenya had been ongoing for two years, unfortunately it did not have time to address justice-related issues. The question of how Somalis should deal with their past never made it to the table because the warlords did not want to face up to their crimes. Avoiding this important justice issue will not help solve it. Blanket amnesty, punishment and lustration (i.e., limiting the political rights of the warlords) are all possible ways of addressing the issue; but the justice issue has to be addressed in the first place.

In addition to these structural issues, the transitional government faced external and domestic challenges. Externally, although Ethiopia and Kenya were on board, some countries in the region such as Eritrea and Egypt were not happy with the outcome of the conference in Kenya. As media reports suggest, Egypt received Abdullahi Yusuf coldly when he visited Cairo in November 2004 to attend the funeral of Yasir Arafat, indicating that Egypt was not interested in working with his government. Arab countries and Somalia's two neighbouring countries, Ethiopia and Kenya, have always been rivals. Arab countries share a culture and religion with the Somali people. Ethiopia and Kenya, on the other hand, share geographical boundaries with Somalia and consider it an historic enemy. Kenya and Ethiopia also have political, economic and military ties against Somalia.[20] Moreover, Ethiopia undermined Egypt's efforts to end the Somali conflict in 1997 at the Cairo conference.

Many Western countries have not clearly stated how they would deal with the new regime after it was established – although this changed in 2006 when the Union of Islamic Courts emerged. The US and Great Britain cautiously welcomed the development, but their recognition and support were conditional on how the new government functioned in the country – in fact, Washington ignored the government and decided to work with the Mogadishu warlords in undermining the government. These countries' past policies toward Somalia did not change. When former president Abdikassim Salad Hassan and his prime minister, Dr Ali Khalif Galaidh, asked for assistance in 2000, the US and other Western countries told the Transitional National Government they would receive assistance when their government was fully functional in the country. Had the Western political and economic support come right after the conclusion of the conference, the survival chances of the Transitional Federal Government of President Abdullahi Yusuf would have been much better.

Internally, the TFG faced many challenges. After its inception the government broke down into two factions in 2005. The president and the prime minister were on one side, and the speaker and several Mogadishu warlords were on the other. The president of Yemen mediated the two groups in 2005. The parliamentary speaker and the president agreed to end their hostility and hold a parliamentary meeting in Baidoa.[21] But again, the transitional government broke down into two groups. The parliamentary speaker and forty other members fled the country after Ethiopian invasion forces crossed the Somali border. The president and the prime minister and most of the members of parliament went to Baidoa where they chose another speaker. The difference between these two groups is largely based on the presence of Ethiopian troops. Interestingly, there was another rift between the president Abdullahi Yusuf and the new prime minister, Nur Hassan Hussein, which escalated and resulted in the resignation of the president.

Since Somalis did not own the process that produced the new charter, many Somalis were cautious in dealing with the transitional government. Neither the Somali people nor their representatives have elected the members of parliament; most members obtained their parliamentary seats with the help of the countries managing the peace conference. Many Somali grassroots groups such as civil society organizations, independent media, human rights organizations and religious institutions were not happy with the outcome of the conference. Many chose not to cooperate with the regime while many more actively resisted both the Ethiopian occupation and the installation of the transitional government it controlled.

Abdullahi Yusuf, president of the Transitional Federal Government in Somalia, brought heavy political baggage with him. His style of leadership, his attitude toward those who differ with him and his loyalty to Ethiopia did not sit well with many important sectors of Somali society whose support was necessary for the success of his regime. These groups considered him Ethiopia's determined spoiler. In addition, the timing and the way Abdullahi Yusuf handled his first major policy decisions – calling for peacemaking troops that included those of Ethiopia and Kenya – was also controversial. These actions fuelled mistrust among rival clans because some interpreted the moves as hostile. As different Somali media outlets have reported, the price of weapons in Mogadishu has dramatically increased since he became president; a sign of war, not peace.

In addition, Abdullahi Yusuf has had poor relations with most of Somalia's intellectuals and religious leaders. Yet the support of these groups was necessary for any government to function in Somalia. In the past, he alienated intellectuals and antagonized the religious community, calling them 'terrorists' in order to win sympathy from the Ethiopian government and Bush administration. Moreover, inviting Ethiopian troops, although the US was also involved in this project, was a serious blunder on the part of the government. In fact, the transitional government did not recover from this move.

CONCLUSION

In short, the causes of the Somali conflict are multiple. I have argued here that the main causes are competition for power and resources, colonial legacy and state repression. Moreover, I discussed the roles of clan identity and the clan pride that comes with it. Regarding the reasons that led to failure of the efforts to end the Somali conflict, a combination of factors including lack of will and capacity on the part of Somalis and foreign meddling are behind the collapse of the five major peace conferences.

3
Clan Identity and Implications for Peacebuilding in Somalia

Abtirsiimo waa dacar jinnoo, waan danqanayaaye
Dalkii nimanka tagayow fariin, dowga qabadsiiya
Dadka kale ha joogee warkaa, Cali dareensiiya

Kinship is like evil aloes, and it is hurting me
Those men, who are leaving for home, convey a message
Besides others, make sure Ali gets this news

Mohomed Omar Dage, 'Damane'[1]

Identity, in general, can be defined as a 'self-locating device in an uncertain social world'.[2] Amartya Sen, in his recent book on identity and violence, argues that identity is a 'double-edged sword' and that individuals can have multiple identities.[3] Sen rejects the argument that places one specific identity over other identities and he also rejects any ensuing claims that individuals helplessly act on one overarching identity. Sen contends that, albeit constraining, individuals have agency over the importance they attach to a specific identity. Although Sen warns against the idea that a singular identity overrides human agency, many scholars repeatedly put clan identity at the centre of the Somali conflict.[4]

The Somali state collapsed in 1991. As a result of the ensuing civil war, hundreds of thousands of people lost their lives and millions were forced to leave their homes. Many scholars, analysts and writers, Somalis and non-Somalis, argued that clan identity and clanism were responsible for Somalia's ills. They claimed that clan identity and the culture attached to it could not be reconciled with the institutions necessary for building a viable state.[5] This chapter explains how clan identity works within the Somali context and why it is important and relevant for the conflict and peacebuilding. It examines the functions of clan identity and how clan identity affects peacebuilding efforts. The chapter further analyses various responses to dealing with the challenges that come with clan identity, in particular by looking at four strategies: partitioning the country among competing clans, ignoring and/or suppressing clan identity, power-sharing, and identity reconstruction.

THE NATURE OF CLAN IDENTITY

Most Somalis are homogeneous in terms of religion, culture and language. While there are Arabs, Baravans and Bantu groups who are also Somalis, the overwhelming majority of the population, particularly those that have been fighting, have minimal differences. Most of the fighting from 1978 onwards has occurred among the Somali clans, in particular, along clan lines, although unarmed clans such as Baravans, Jareer, Madhibaan and Yibir are also affected.[6] Besides religious Islamic identity and national Somali identity, clan identity is very strong among the Somali people and has played a significant role in the conflict. Indeed, a glaring fact is that most militia groups are organized along clan lines.

There are five major clans in Somalia: Darod, Dir, Digil and Mirifle, Hawiye, and Isaaq. There is also a coalition of smaller clans. The Isaaq clan, which is the dominant clan in 'Somaliland', is sometimes considered a sub-clan of Dir. But some scholars, such as I.M. Lewis and Said Sheikh Samatar, separate the Isaaq from the Dir clan. Members of the Isaaq clans strongly identify themselves as the Isaaq clan. In fact, Lewis sees six major clans: Darod, Dir, Digil, Mirifle, Hawiye, and Isaaq.[7] In August 2000 the Somalis who attended the Arta peace conference agreed to put the Isaaq clan under the Dir clan. Many members from the Isaaq clan considered the delegates' decision as an act of aggression against them. One elderly man said to me, 'The southerners failed to annihilate us even when they used war planes against us, now they are trying to deny us our own identity.'[8] The Isaaq clan is traditionally considered a major clan by scholars. Moreover, given that identity in general is a basic need of and therefore of primary importance to individuals and groups, I consider the Isaaq clan to be one of Somalia's major clans on its own accord. Of course, there are many other Somalis who do not belong to these five or six major clans, but, like other Somali groups outside the main clans, they are not key players in the conflict.

Clan identity in Somalia is based on patrilineal descent. Starting with the first name of male members of family, Somalis count their names as far back as twenty or more generations. For example, if the name of an individual is Ali Mohamed Hassan, Ali is the first name, Mohamed is his father's first name, and Hassan is his grandfather's first name. Depending on its size and resources, a major clan can consist of many sub-clans and sub-sub-clans. The following example may illustrate this better. The Darod clan families consist of five sub-clans: Yusuf (Awrtable), Lel-Kase, Harti, Absame, and Sade – the latter three are the major sub-clans within Darod. The Harti is further divided into four clans: Majeerteen, Warsangeli, Dhulbahante, and Dashishe. These four clans are not necessarily equal in terms of the number of their members, land they occupy, and resources they mount. The major sub-clan among the Harti is the Majeerteen, and it in turn has many sub-sub-clans. Similarly, the other three major sub-clans of the Dir, the Hawiye, and the Isaaq, are structured the same way. The Digil and Mirifle are also not much different from other clans.[9] As Lewis writes, 'Everyone knows [his or her] genealogy up to the eponym of his clan-family.'[10] Moreover, Lewis uses clan family (*qabiil*), clan (*qolo*), primary lineage (*jilib*) and Dia-paying group (*reer* or *tol*) in descending order. Dia-paying is the smallest kin group which shares blood-wealth; this means that when a member of a given Dia-paying group kills someone, the perpetrator's group is expected to give a blood-wealth of one hundred camels – although specific requirements can vary in different regions. Lewis recognizes the fluid nature of the clan identity system, saying that 'a man is a member of lineage only in opposition to another'.[11]

While clan identity is based on the idea of common ancestral kinship, there are numerous cases where the perceived kinship is not based on blood or a common founding father. In almost all of Somalia's major clans one finds sub-clans that may not be related by blood – some anthropologists call such a relationship 'fictive kinship'.[12] Mohamed Abdi Mohamed 'Gandi', a well-known Somali anthropologist, presented a case in which a clan identity was socially constructed in the Bakool region. According to Gandi, a number of smaller communities who did not share one common ancestor came together and named their newly found clan *Isma-Dhaxasho*, a name which translates as 'the members of the clan will not inherit each other as those who are related by blood do'. Gandi also pointed out that both the Hawadle and Gal-Je'el, two major sub-clans of Hawiye, cannot be traced to the same ancestor of the other Hawiye clans. It is believed that the Digil and Mirifle have a significant number of people who migrated from other regions and adopted the identity of the respective sub-clans they joined.[13]

As Lewis notes, a daughter keeps her father's name as her surname but her children take her husband's genealogy or what

Somalis call *abtirsiimo*.[14] Generally, Somali clans inter-marry and the marriages establish a special kind of relationship between individuals and groups. It is common to come across clans that are named after mothers: Bah Majeerteen, Bah-Hawadle, Bah Hawiye, Bah Ogaden, and so on. Lewis writes: 'in practice, every point of lineage segmentation – every ancestor in the genealogies – is at least potentially an axis of political division and unity'.[15]

Traditionally, different clans may fight over resources such as water, grazing or livestock. Such conflicts happen both at macro (clan family) levels and at micro (Dia-paying group) levels. For instance, as evidenced by poems and oral history, in the north, Dhulbahante (Darod clan family) and Habar Je'lo (Isaaq) or Habar Yonis (Isaaq clan family) and Ogaden (Darod clan family) fought.[16] In addition, on several occasions there were conflicts between Majeerteen and Habar-Gidir in the central regions of Somalia. Most of the time, these conflicts were settled by using the Somali traditional legal system (*Heer*).

Ahmed Sheikh Ali Ahmed (Burale) has written a book on Somalia's *Heer*, *Xeerkii Soomaalidii Hore* (Legal System for the Somali People), in which he defines *Heer* as fundamental decisions that are adopted for regulation of the affairs and relationships of society.[17] Ahmed argues that even though the Somali *Heer* was not written as a constitution, it was practised as a convention, and most elders are still familiar with the different articles of the *Heer*. Elders and religious scholars once played the role of legislators, Ahmed claims. Ahmed classifies the *Heer* by the type of people who use it. For example, he states that there are laws for farmers, laws for nomads, laws for merchants and laws for hunters. Most significant among Ahmed's classification are laws that deal with murder or injury (*dhiig*) and laws that deal with unacceptable criminal behaviour (*dhaqan*) – this consisted of marriage-related issues and property (*xilo iyo xoolo*). Ahmed narrates how jury elders would take a case. They would ask the person who is alleging that he was wronged, 'Is your case a murder/injury or marriage/property case?' If the person says it is a blood-related case, the elders would ask him (or her, the same system applied to women) whether it is a murder case or an injury case. If the person is complaining about non-blood-related aggression, jury elders would ask whether the crime is related to marriage or property.[18] As Ahmed contends, the Somali legal system of *Heer* was the source of Somali culture and religion. Since there was no fixed parliament, Ahmed explains, elders decided on legislation; when an event occurred that was new to them and to the *Heer*, people, including the elders, would come together for a meeting (*shir*) in a place that had water to discuss the issue. After careful deliberation the elders would pass legislation and would name it after the place where they met: for example, the law of Akaaro or the law of Yaaqle.[19]

While it is true that Somalis once had a traditional legal system that legislated matters relating to disputes between members of clans and between clans, Ahmed does not address the fact that Somalis did not have police, courts or prisons. So, however elaborate the traditional legal system was, it was still informal. If a given member of society rejected a decision, pressure through his kin group was the best way to convince that person to accept such a decision. Lewis writes that Somali men were 'divided amongst political units without any administrative hierarchy of officials and with no instituted positions of leadership to direct their affairs'.[20] Perhaps this is why conflicts occurred frequently.

FUNCTIONS OF CLAN IDENTITY

As outlined above, clan identity is the salient identity for the Somali people. One might then wonder: what is it that has made this identity dominant for so long? Four explanations are often given in response to this question. First, for Somalis, clan identity is the main characteristic that they use to recognize each other. Since almost all Somalis are Muslim, they generally believe clan identity is necessary for identification. The Holy Koran says, 'We made you into nations and tribes so you recognize each other' (Surah 49:11).[21] Recognition is an obvious function that identity brings with itself. Lewis agrees with this argument and writes, 'what a person's address is in Europe, his genealogy is in Somaliland'.[22] While I was at the Somali Studies conference in Djibouti in December 2007, a Somali intellectual rose to comment on a presentation and said, 'If you send a mail through DHL and write my three names, my clan and sub-clan and the city, the mail will be delivered to me safely.'[23] This is absolutely true. When members of the Somali Diaspora send remittances to a family member back home, many Hawala (money transfer) companies ask them to provide only the clan, the sub-clan, and the place that he or she lives.

A second and related point, as many scholars argue, is that identity is a human need.[24] Some of the individuals I interviewed for this book pointed out this fact. For instance, an Islamist said, 'Identity is dear to the hearts of many and they consider that it tells about their origin. When someone attacks your origin, strong emotions are evoked.'[25] Another Islamist agreed with him about the intrinsic importance of identity in general, and clan identity in particular. He said, 'Clan identity is a very important identity among the Somalis. Somalis are inter-connected along clan lines. This identity will be strong for a long time to come because it is an important identity for the individual.'[26] Many Somalis took this particular line of thinking.

Third, clan identity is similar to life insurance; members of clans come together during both happy and difficult times. When one of their members is getting married they provide assistance. Similarly, when one of them is killed or injured or dies from a natural cause, members of that clan come together and support each other. Traditionally, nomadic contexts such as the one in Somalia lack an authority that can enforce agreed-upon laws or common-sense requirements. Such a situation makes clan identity the last refuge that one uses in order to safeguard one's life and property. Explaining this fact, Lewis notes that 'in Somali lineage politics, the assumption that might is right has overwhelming authority and personal rights, rights in livestock, and rights of access to grazing and water, even if they are not always obtained by force, can only be defended against usurpation by forces of arms'.[27] Moreover, after the Somali state collapsed in 1991, the use of clan identity as an insurance policy became normal. Many Somalis were forced to leave their home cities due to another clan's claim to be there. Those Somalis had to resettle in areas in which members of their clans live. For instance, many Somalis who lived in Mogadishu were forced to flee to northern, central and eastern Somalia. And when the Hawiye sub-clans started to fight among themselves, a large number of these clans' members moved to the outside regions.

Within Somali culture clan identity is not always viewed negatively. The Dia-paying group does not only come together when a member of a given group kills a person or one of them is killed. As Lewis notes, and it is apparent in Somali culture, Somalis who consider themselves related as one Dia-paying group or one agnate (*Tol*), will help each other in a variety of ways: they collaborate when watering large numbers of livestock, when someone becomes poor, or when a group needs to dig a well. A new phenomenon in recent times is that clans, sub-clans and Dia-paying groups together have held fundraising events to open schools and universities in their cities.[28]

One of the most destructive elements of Somali culture is the act of 'collective punishment'. When someone kills a member of another clan, the victim's clan will kill someone from the criminal's clan, whether or not the person they kill is associated with the criminal. All they ask is to which clan the murderer belonged. Commenting on this fact, Samatar writes, 'in the Somali lineage system one literally gets away with murder, because the actual murderer may escape and never see punishment, while an innocent kinsperson of his may fall to a flying spear of vendetta'.[29]

Fourth and finally, most interviewees I talked to identified clan identity as a major tool for politicians who are trying to achieve or keep political positions. Taking advantage of the many grievances that Somalis have against each other, politicians use clan identity as a Trojan horse to achieve their aims. One Islamist pointed out several examples where clan identity was used by leaders. He said, 'Clan identity was used in order to commit aggression. Siyad Barre used nepotism and he gave significant political and economic opportunities to the people who were closely related to him clan-wise. He also used the central government's institutions such as the military and police against clans in order to punish them. He committed gross injustices in the name of clan identity.'[30]

This is a very important function as tribal entrepreneur politicians use and abuse clan identity for their own political gain. Many warlords became prominent simply because they identified with some of the real or perceived grievances of the members of their clans. This is true both for the many politicians who founded Somalia's rebel movements and for the many freelancing Somali politicians seeking political posts.

CLAN IDENTITY AND THE SOMALI CIVIL WAR

It is obvious that clan identity serves several functions for Somalis. However, scholars disagree in their explanations about the role this identity plays in the Somali civil war. The contestation is whether clan identity is a 'root' cause or a 'contributing' cause to the conflict. In other words, are Somali clans and militia groups fighting because of clan differences, or are they fighting to achieve other aims while using clan identity as a mobilization instrument? The various explanations that are provided can be grouped into two views. First, those who have a primordial view of identity argue that clan identity and the clanism that is often associated with it, are the main culprits for the initiation, escalation and perpetuation of the conflict.[31] In contrast, those who have an instrumentalist view of identity contend that identity is used in order to obtain resources or achieve power objectives.[32] Although clan identity is important, and it has elements that cannot be explained materially, the latter view is supported by the examples of socially constructed clans.

In general, as Deborah Britzman argues, merely the 'eugenic differences' among human beings cannot explain violent behaviour that is sometimes associated with those differences.[33] There are many examples that support this argument, as many nation-states in the world consist of heterogeneous groups and many of these groups live in harmony. Even in Africa, countries like Ghana and Tanzania are very peaceful, and yet they too are made up of different tribes. Dan Smith in 'Trends and Causes of Armed Conflicts', agrees with Britzman that identity difference in itself does not cause violence. However, Britzman concedes that the simple act of joining a group consciously or unconsciously is an exercise of engaging in a love-and-hate relationship.[34]

Consistent with Britzman and Smith's position, differences in clan identity among Somalis did not cause the civil war. One reason is that clan identity changes with prevailing circumstances, relative to the actors involved and the stakes contested. Like any other human being, a Somali has multiple identities. Depending on the person and to whom he or she is relating, one can be a Somali, Hawiye, Habar-Gidir, Sa'ad or Hilowle, and so on, in descending order.[35] In fact, the Somali civil war has other substantive political, economic and psychological causes.

The general conclusion that can be drawn from the above analysis is that most Somalis are homogeneous ethnic-wise, but plural clan-wise. This means that ethnic homogeneity is not sufficient to save a country from civil war. As Britzman argues, people, regardless of where they are, will always find differences that make sense for them.[36] In Somalia, given that resources are scarce and clan differences and rivalries have deep roots within the psychology and culture of Somali society, clan identity has played a significant role in the initiation and perpetuation of the recent civil war. However, that role was and still is instrumental. Clan identity, in itself, is not the cause of the conflict; it is a mobilization instrument for other objectives, albeit it has elements that cannot be quantified.[37] Moreover, the above arguments are based on John Burton's human needs theory which argues that conflict results from unmet needs, and identity is one of the basic human needs which is not negotiable. In simple terms, people want to reduce uncertainty because they do not want to lose control of their world.[38]

IMPACT OF CLAN IDENTITY ON PEACEBUILDING

In discussing the nature of clan identity and its functions within Somali culture, I show that clan identity is an indigenous identity that influences reality on the ground. Now the challenge becomes, how does this identity affect peacebuilding in Somalia? Before exploring the impact analysis, however, some definitions should be clarified. First, my analysis is based on Johan Galtung's (1975) distinction of concepts of peacekeeping, peacemaking and peacebuilding. For Galtung, peacekeeping occurs when, for example, neutral United Nations forces separate enemies and safe-guard a ceasefire; peacemaking, on the other hand, is the effort of bringing hostile groups together to end their differences at the negotiating table.[39] I use the term peacebuilding as defined by former UN Secretary General Boutros Boutros-Ghali in his 'An Agenda for Peace' (1992). For Boutros-Ghali, peacebuilding is the 'process that facilitates the establishment of durable peace and tries to prevent the recurrence of violence by addressing root causes and effects of conflict through reconciliation, institution building and political as well as economic transformation'.[40] Moreover, according to Taisier Ali and Robert Matthews peacebuilding consists of four pillars: the creation of a secure environment, the establishment of political systems, the reconstruction of economic development, and attention to issues of justice.[41] Based on the above definitions and on the themes that emerged from the data I collected, the following four areas of peacebuilding activity can be identified.

First, those who have sponsored peace conferences in Somalia have faced the difficult task of identifying and bringing stakeholders together. At one level the conflict has clan identity undertones. At another level there are ideological differences, differing interests, and external actors. Clearly, most militia groups were organized along clan lines and a warlord of the same clan commanded them. Thus, when a peace conference was being organized, warlords were considered as primary stakeholders in the Somali conflict. For example, at the first conference in Djibouti in 1991, six factions (representing six clans) were brought together to agree on a power-sharing formula. Fifteen clan-based factions participated in the next conference in Addis Ababa in 1993. Subsequently, more factions appeared and 28 factions were invited to the Cairo conference in 1997.

The above shows the fluid nature of clan identity. It is very difficult to determine who is to be included and who is to be excluded in both peacemaking and peacebuilding activities. Several warlords of sub-sub-clans such as the Daud and Sa'ad sub-clans, which belong to Hawiye, have participated in peace conferences, while bigger clans who were not armed were excluded. For example, the then leader of the Banadiri group, Mohamed Rajis, was not allowed to participate in the Djibouti conference as his clan was unarmed. He reportedly said, 'We were excluded because of the "crime" that we did not kill.'[42] A close observation reveals that whenever a peace process was being organized clashes among clans increased as each wanted to show its relevance by using force to occupy a new district or town. In other words, the fluidity of clan identity makes it difficult for those who are hosting a peace process to identify relevant stakeholders. This is further complicated by the emergence of Islamist forces that have a trans-clanic agenda and membership.

Second, while bringing proliferated groups together was and remains problematic, implementing peace accords is even more challenging. Interestingly, once Somalis come to a peace conference they are often able to arrive at and sign some form of a peace deal. But so far no agreement has been implemented. One of the biggest factors that causes the collapse of those arrangements has been the use of clan identity as a tool for spoilers seeking political positions. Indeed, whenever a new peace process is initiated, militia groups that are organized along clan lines start new conflicts in order to show organizers they matter. Utilization of clan identity in this way becomes problematic because it becomes a divisive and manipulative means for acquiring power, further correlating power of clan identity with distrust. And even after an agreement is signed, clan conflicts tend to increase for one reason or another, affecting the security component, which is a prerequisite for other political, economic and justice pillars.

Third, clan identity strongly affects the legitimacy of governments as it has a strong impact on the perception of representation of the general public. An individual Somali is not often a citizen of a geographical district, town or region, but is a member of a social group – clan or a sub-clan. For example, if government seats are divided among geographic localities and the city of Jowhar gets five parliamentary seats, some of the residents of that city might still perceive that the government does not represent them if one of the members of their clan is not selected or elected. In other words, the common person feels represented when a fellow clan member is in the government. This is further complicated by the fact that clan identity is very fluid and relative – a person who shares many identities with a given member of parliament might still believe his sub-sub-sub-clan is not represented. This is a very difficult problem, as the legitimacy of any governmental institution is extremely sensitive for Somalis.

Fourth, clan identity affects territorial ownership. Normally every citizen should be able to claim the whole or a part of the country, and each person should feel he or she has all the rights including political rights – the right to vote or compete for political positions – in every part of the country. The popular perception among Somalis is that each clan owns the traditional areas that it inhabits. So only that clan would have a say in the political and economic issues that are related to that part of the country. This perception has a negative impact when establishing a state wherein all groups share its ownership. This is further complicated by rapid urbanization and clan migrations; many people left central and northern and even some southern regions and moved to new areas where they traditionally did not live. For example, a large number of the Habar-Gidir clan and the Marihan clan moved from Galgadud and settled in Lower Shabelle and Lower Jubba respectively. Generally, such a migration by the citizens of one nation-state should not be a problem as long as it is within a legal framework – in fact, mobility right is enshrined in the Somali constitution. But, since the Somali state collapsed, these migrating clans have their own militia groups that are stronger than the militias of the clans that lived in those regions. These migrating militia groups have also committed atrocities against civilians of local populations. The reaction from local clans has been that these invading clans must move out of their regions. Currently these issues remain completely unresolved and they will haunt peacebuilding and peacemaking efforts in the future.

ANALYSIS AND OPTIONS FOR ADDRESSING CLAN IDENTITY IN SOMALIA

Scholars of identity conflicts have developed various strategies for addressing the political and social problems that stem from identity. One strategy involves completely ignoring and/or suppressing collective identity and focusing on the individual. This approach provides universal citizenship rights to every individual in the given nation-state while ignoring or suppressing communal or other collective identities. At the other extreme, a second strategy partitions countries along competing identity-based groups. Because clan identity is the main divisive identity in Somalia, this strategy would divide the country among clans and sub-clans. A third strategy is the establishment of some form of power-sharing formula among different identities; of course, this would mean clan identity in Somalia. A fourth strategy involves identifying an overarching identity and then thickening it so that divisive identities are replaced with an inclusive one.[43] The responses given by the individuals I interviewed regarding how to address clan identity in Somalia can be classified into the above four strategies.

One businessman whom I met in Djibouti was adamant in his dislike of clan identity in Somalia. Before I even officially interviewed him he started talking about the destructive nature of clan identity: 'All the ills that our nation faces are rooted in clan identity and clanism,' he said firmly. He argued that if we want to survive we need to drop this identity. He quoted a Hadith (a saying from the Prophet Muhammad): 'Leave clanism (tribalism), it is dirty.'[44] Although he confused clan identity with clanism, this businessman advocated clan-blind policies.

In the early 1970s Somalia's military tried the clan-blind strategy of ignoring and/or suppressing clan identity; the leadership of Somalia's revolutionary council called for the elimination of clanism. There was a lot of fanfare. Indeed, the Somali media (*October Star* newspaper and Radio Muqdisho) condemned the use of clan identity and reported the commitment of the leadership to eradicate it. The military leaders held a big event attended by thousands of people at which they formally buried clan identity and clanism, or so they thought. Also, the military-led government introduced laws that prohibited and at times criminalized the use of clan names and adjectives. In the Somali tradition if someone is a close agnate one can address him/her as 'cousin' (*ina-adeer*). This, too, was prohibited. The revolution popularized use of the word *Jaalle* which means 'comrade'.[45] The government's line was that in order to develop, Somalis needed to shelve this traditional identity system which was responsible, the government argued, for the persistent conflicts and backwardness of the country and its people.

While official rhetoric banned any use of clan identity in public places, the leadership practised it in its worst forms. One Islamist leader said that, as early as 1975, government agencies that dealt with security were using the clan system even though the same people were calling on the general public to forget about clan identity.[46] I also met a former senior military officer, Omar, who is now a member of the Diaspora community in Europe. In Somalia he had once been the head of a department responsible for security. Omar reflected on the idea of burying clan identity in relation to his work during that time. He said, 'When determining those who opposed the government, the military regime used clan classification.'[47] He explained further by talking about individuals (mostly from the Majeerteen clan) who the Somali government had arrested simply because of their association with clans that were classified as anti-regime.

The biggest challenge to the first strategy of ignoring or burying clan identity is that most Somalis are illiterate. Demanding that they forget in a few days what they have known all their lives is, at best, impractical. Traditionally, when two Somalis meet it is normal for them to ask each other about their respective clan identities. Somalis also use a traditional method for the issue of inter-clan marriages. For instance, depending on which clan one belongs to, a number of advantages or disadvantages might come with it. Some clans are small and are considered as belonging to a 'lower caste' (e.g., Madhibaan, Yibir and Jareer). Somalis from stronger clans discriminate against these clans and they do not often marry into them, even though urbanization has been changing Somali society. Benefits can be drawn from being a member of a clan that controls resources one way or another.

During the brief six months in 2006 when the Islamic Courts controlled southern Somalia, they made several declarations about the position of Islam in regard to these oppressed clans' identities. Like the military leaders, Sheikh Sharif Sheikh Ahmed condemned discrimination against these Somalis, calling it un-Islamic. I met with one of the pioneers (an Islamist) who was actively involved with the Union of Islamic Courts (UIC). This Islamist (himself a member of these discriminated clans) told me about a number of cases involving these clans which the Islamic Courts had addressed successfully. He said, 'The best system that can end discrimination (*takoor*) against us is Islam. Nobody can come to me and say I have a monopoly over the Islamic identity, but one can say you are not clan X because your lineage does not conform to that clan's lineage system.'[48] I am told by several Islamists that a few well-planned marriages involving women from discriminated groups and men from the bigger clans took place – the motive here was to challenge popular perception.[49]

With only a few exceptions, all my other interviewees rejected the approach of ignoring or suppressing clan identity. They believe that identity is a pertinent issue and ignoring it will not help – after all, earlier efforts failed and they think such an approach might lead to even more corruption. Moreover, one academic argued that there are areas where the Somali clan system can help. For instance, he thinks that governments should use the clan system for social welfare issues.[50]

The second strategy in dealing with identity conflict would involve partitioning Somalia along clan lines. This strategy was unanimously rejected by all the interviewees. Such complete rejection is obvious as clan identity is based on 'segmentary lineage', which is very fluid. If Somalia were to be divided along clan and sub-clan lines, there would be hundreds of governments within this small and poor country. Thus Chaim Kauffman's argument, that when people fight along identity lines the international community should divide the country along the competing groups, cannot reasonably be applied to Somalia. After all, the identity that Kauffman had dealt with was ethnic identity. For him, if different ethnic groups are separated the chances of these groups fighting would be reduced significantly. Even if the argument were used in the case of Somalia, as the overwhelming majority of Somalis belong to one ethnic group, they would form one nation-state. In other words, dividing the country along clan lines is virtually impossible.[51]

Most of the interviewees for this book prescribed strategy three (power-sharing) and strategy four (identity reconstruction). A clear divide was evident between business people and Islamists. Almost all business people argued that clan identity is here to stay. For the Somali people, clan identity has persisted for hundreds of years. It flourished under Somalia's democratic regime (1960–69) and resisted the repressive military regime (1969–91). One businessman said, 'We should not ignore this reality. The problem now is that bad individuals within the clans became leaders. We need to get a way that we can put the good people of the clan in leadership.'[52] Another businessman agreed and said that 'merchants from different clans own shares of most big companies in Somalia. If they can share business (profit and loss) Somalis can also share power too.'[53]

Somalia's current transitional government is based on the third strategy of power-sharing; the four major clans control 122 seats each, and the conglomeration of smaller clans control only 62 seats. This formula is called the 4.5 formula. The rationale for this is based on the assumption that in order for the political system to be representative, clan identity has to be the basic constituency. This originated from the Sodere (Ethiopia) conference in 1996. The leadership (warlords and faction leaders) of the Somali Salvation Alliance met there and agreed to use this formula. One of those faction leaders explained it to me by saying, 'We discussed this issue for a few days. The delegates from Darod and Hawiye clans could not agree on how to share power. After a long discussion the two groups came up with this formula. Each clan thought, by providing an equal share to the other two clans, it can get the support of those two clans against its competitor.'[54]

However, many, particularly from Islamist and intellectual groups, vehemently rejected the current 4.5 formula of clan power-sharing. For them, the 4.5 formula does not only produce an illegitimate system; it also empowers warlords and it strengthens clan identity – an outcome they want to avoid. There are three problems with the 4.5 formula, according to its opponents. First, they questioned how such a decision was reached. 'The assumption that there are four clans that are equal in number is not warranted,' one Islamist said. Second, even if there are four clans that are equal in number, according to this Islamist, the way members of parliament are selected is inconsistent with the traditional system.[55] In the current system, warlords and politicians select their supporters to become MPs.[56] Finally, Islamists argue that providing half for the so-called smaller clans and calling them a 0.5-clan adds insult to injury. 'The idea of calling some clans full (1) and others half (0.5) is simply not acceptable in Islam,' I was told.[57]

Although the grounds for rejecting the 4.5 formula are plausible, one cannot ignore the use of clan-based formulae. The idea of power-sharing among clans in Somalia is based on what is often called the consociational model. According to Arend Lijphart, consociationalism achieves stability by relying on four principles: it encourages building grand coalitions; it protects minorities by providing a minority veto; it guarantees the representation of all groups by employing proportional representation; and it provides segmental autonomy, particularly if there are religious or language segments. Lijphart, who is considered the pioneer of this model, identifies nine favourable conditions that, if they exist on the ground, would help the consociation model to succeed. These conditions are: absence of a majority group; segments of equal size; a small number of segments; small population; external threat; overarching loyalties; tradition of elite accommodation; socio-economic equality; and geographical concentration of segments.[58]

While several factors identified by Lijphart are present in the Somali context, the country still lacks segmental autonomy, which is the most important condition for this model. The consociation model is for plural societies, yet Somalis cannot be considered as such. The Somali people are homogeneous. However, the ethnicity factor needs further clarification: The overwhelming majority of Somali groups involved in the fighting are ethnic Somalis. The social segmentation is along clan lines. Although all Somalis share overarching cleavages (i.e., inclusive identity), the culture emphasis of the lineage system of clans and sub-clans is strong. A general conclusion that can be drawn from this is that Somalis are homogeneous ethnic-wise and religious-wise, but plural clan-wise. Although clan differences and rivalries have deep roots within the psychology and culture of Somali society, the plural nature of Somalis in terms of ethnicity and religion is questionable.

With respect to the other factors or conditions necessary for the consociational model to work, there is no one clan in Somalia that has a clear majority in terms of number. In addition, there is no reliable data available that precisely compares the population size of Somalia's clans, and estimations provided are based on perceptions of the writer in question. For example, if one reads material written during the Siyad Barre era or produced by Darod intellectuals, one would find that Darod is the largest clan. In contrast, material written by leaders and intellectuals of other clans such as the Hawiye, Isaaq, and Digil and Mirifle claims that those clans constitute a majority. Moreover, Somalia is a relatively small country (the size of Texas). The population is about 10 million people, all with similar socio-economic status.

Another relevant factor is that some clans are concentrated in one geographical location (Digil and Mirifle, Isaaq) while others are not (Darod, Dir and Hawiye). As for the number of Somali segments, one can argue that the clans and factions are too many. As George Downs and Stephen John Stedman point out, the greater the number of warring parties, the more difficult it becomes to reach or implement a peace accord: 'Strategies become less predictable, the balance of power becomes more tenuous, and alliances become more fluid.'[59] This seems to be the case in Somalia. In the last peace conference in 2004 the number of warlords and faction leaders had increased to the extent that it became impossible to invite all of the political groups to join the peace process.

With regard to the tradition of Somalia's elite accommodation, one has to answer the prior question of whether Somalis have political elites. There is a significant problem in this area. Although factions are organized along clan or sub-clan lines, the question of who represents the clan remains controversial. Traditional leaders have always been the legitimate clan leaders. But, colonial powers and successive Somali governments marginalized these traditional leaders and created an alternative leadership. Former cabinet ministers, generals and senior officials who worked with these foreign regimes became de-facto clan leaders. These new groups considered themselves as representing clans. While most of the traditional leaders have the respect and support of clan members, new elites control the militia groups, money, and guns. These new elites create problems because most of them also have outside backers such as Ethiopia, Eritrea or Libya. And since the so-called new political elite has perpetuated conflict, it would be necessary to include them in the political process regardless of their legitimacy, albeit they do not have the culture of compromise, and thus cannot be considered an elite. Thus far they have not cooperated in building a successful broad-based coalition to save the country.

Several scholars criticize the consociation model. D.L. Horowitz, for instance, argues that this model is motivationally inadequate. According to Horowitz, Lijphart's statesmanship is not sufficient to motivate politicians; rather, Horowitz believes, self-interest should be reason. In addition, he contends that the assumption that the elites of a divided society are more tolerant than the general public is unwarranted. Horowitz also rejects the consociation model on the grounds that there are always counter-elites who are driven by self-interest and who would politicize the ethnic factor. Finally, he criticizes the timing of the compromise between elites. In the conso-ciational model the elites are expected to build a grand coalition after the election. He argues that such an expectation is not realistic.[60] On the other hand, Timothy Sisk identifies three drawbacks of the consociational model: 'Reliance on elite accommodation, reification of ethnic identity, and a tendency toward anti-democratic and inefficient decision making.'[61]

Some of the above shortcomings of the consociational model are relevant to Somalia. First, as Horowitz argues, elites are not always more tolerant than the general public. And even if that was the case, in any context there are counter-elites that want to politicize identity. In Somalia, there are cases that illustrate this. For example, when General Mohamed Abshir Muse of the Somali Salvation Democratic Front signed the Cairo accord, Abdullahi Yusuf, who is from the same organization and clan, rejected it and in fact used this occasion to accuse Mohamed Abshir of selling out the cause of the clan. There are similar examples among all Somali clans. The most recent example is when Sheikh Sharif Sheikh Ahmed, a charismatic and popular Islamist leader, emerged, many former politicians and warlords who belong to the same Muddulod sub-clan as Sheikh

Sharif, including former prime minister Ali Mohamed Gedi and former president Ali Mahdi, started to present Sharif as though he represents other clans' interests.

All in all, the above analyses lead me to conclude that some form of power-sharing among clans and other actors will be necessary for the short term. Use of the clan system can bring to a newly established system some legitimacy because it deals with the question of representation in a way that average Somalis understand. This does not mean, however, that the current 4.5 formula has to be kept. It can be changed and the number of clans that participate in the political process can be increased to six or seven. That said, the use of clan identity formulae will also have a negative impact on the functionality of any new system. One way of reconciling the contradictory dimensions of clan identity is perhaps by using political representation and dividing seats among clans in the parliament while subordinating the use of clan identity to the other value of competency for the cabinet, senior bureaucratic positions and other important posts. Another way is to create a bicameral system where one of the houses represents clans while the other represents the population using geographical formulae. The challenge here is to design a temporary legitimate and representative system that can also function on the ground.

The fourth strategy for dealing with identity conflict is what is often called identity reconstruction. This involves identifying an inclusive identity that all combating groups share. For instance, the conflict between the groups in Ireland is based on different religious orientations. But they share the same Irish nationality or ethnicity. Those who want to address the problem of Ireland through identity reconstruction would adopt strategies that thicken Irish identity while thinning all other exclusive identities.

In Somalia, the Islamists and most intellectuals I interviewed openly endorse this strategy. One Islamist told me, 'Islam is both a religion and an identity that we all Somalis share. During the six months we were in power we have achieved a lot because of the Islamic faith and identity. Many people moved out of properties that they had occupied, even before the owners took the case to courts.'[62] In addition, another Islamist intellectual explained the difference between liberal democracy and Islam with respect to managing clan identity. He said, 'Liberal democracy presents a universal citizenship that is too abstract for the common Somali person. Second, it is based on material issues as it divides benefits to citizens. Islam, unlike liberalism, is based on faith. People believe it and want to get intrinsic rewards. Islam easily resolves problems that stem from clan identity while liberalism cannot do that.'[63]

There is more to this strategy, though: although identity reconstruction can help address identity-related problems, there are two major challenges. First, besides Islam most people share the Somali identity. Islamists are not clear on how they want to deal with this identity. For many years Islamists have been trying to thicken the Islamic faith and identity. In so doing, a good number of them rejected, at least in theory, both clan identity and Somali national identity. For them a universal Muslim nation is their dream and they work toward that goal. On the other hand, I came across some Islamists who argued that Somali national identity entails many characteristics of Islam and therefore it cannot be separated from Islamic identity – in Somalia, Islam and Somali identity can be used interchangeably. Interestingly, most Islamists did not use Somali nationalism rhetoric when they were fighting against Ethiopian occupation; they use Islamic terminology.

Second, unlike Islamic identity, there is no group that works toward thickening Somali national identity. Many members of each clan focus on emphasizing clan identity. At times security has been attached to clan identity and subsequently made this identity more important than all others. As such, Somali national identity is basically an orphan. Even earlier governments that used and abused Somali nationalism did not construct this identity through education or the justice system. The weakness of this identity, therefore, complicates the search for a Somali solution because clan identity is exclusive and it cannot replace national identity. However, Somalia's Islamic identity is not acceptable to external and powerful actors. Ethiopia and Kenya, next door neighbours, are dominated by Christians, albeit they have large Muslim populations. As they did in 2006, the governments of the neighbouring countries will do all they can to undermine any effort that thickens Islamic identity in Somalia. Moreover, because of the United States's 'war on terror', these two hostile neighbours have the support of the world's superpower. A combination of these two challenges might prolong a realization of identity reconstruction that employs Islamic identity.

In short, identity reconstruction could be the long-term solution to resolving Somalia's clan identity. Two overarching identities that can replace clan identity are Somali and Islamic identities. Since Somali Islamists have been working toward the goal of creating an Islamic state for decades and Islam has a faith component that resonates with the people, Islam has a better chance than the

Somali identity, at least for now. However, that does not mean that the Somali identity cannot recover. It has a large vocabulary that most Somalis are familiar with through literature and songs. Moreover, there was a historical period during which this identity was dominant and as a result of that Somalis got their independence from colonialists. If Somalia's education and justice systems are used, the Somali national identity can rise again.

CONCLUSION

Somalis are divided along clan families and sub-clans that are based on 'patrilineal segmentary lineage'. Clan identity is fluid in nature; one's identity depends on whom one is communicating with at the time. As some argue, clan identity contracts and expands depending on the situation.[64] Clan identity is important for Somalis, functioning both as an insurance system as well as fulfilling a psychological and emotional need for belonging. In the Somali civil war, clan identity acts as a mobilization instrument, one that affects the effort of building durable peace in Somalia. The system of governance that Somalis have adopted and the management of ever-proliferating group identities has been a major challenge for peacebuilders. Among the four strategies used to deal with identify conflicts, power-sharing (for the short term) and identity reconstruction (aiming for the long term) might be best suited to resolving the conflict in Somalia. Between the two overarching identities in Somalia, nation (Somali identity) and Islam (religious identity), Islamic identity has the better chance, at least at present, of functioning as an inclusive identity in identity reconstruction, as various groups have been promoting Islamic identity for a long time. The idea of re-invoking Somali nationalism, however, also has potential for the future.

4
Making Sense of Islam and Islamic Awakening in Somalia

The Islamic mind knows no pair of contraries such as 'religious-secular', 'sacred-profane', 'church-state' and in Arabic, the religious language of Islam has no words for them in its vocabulary.

Ismail Ragi Faruqi, *Sources of Islamic Thought*

Islam is a complete way of life and it cannot be separated from politics.

Sheikh Mohamed Moallim Hassan[1]

Islam has a long history in Somalia. As some scholars argue, Islam came to Somalia through peaceful means long before it reached Medina, the first capital of Islam. It is said that some of the companions of the Prophet, who were fleeing persecution in Mecca, visited the city of Zaila and shared the message of Islam with the people there. As a result, Somalis are considered to be 100 per cent Sunni Muslim. Somalis also largely follow the Shafi'i school of thought, one of the four jurisprudence schools of thought in the Sunni sector of Islam. However, 'Islamism' is a new phenomenon in Somalia. It was first introduced by scholars who returned from the Arab world in the 1960s; in fact, 'Islamism' arose with the modern political consciousness of Somalia's newly independent state.[2] This chapter looks at both Islam and 'Islamism' within the Somali context by examining the history and role of the Islamic faith in Somali society; the concept of 'Islamism' and its origins and growth in Somalia; and the challenges that Islamist forces, and the values they stand for, pose to Western efforts to build a liberal peace in Somalia. In other words the chapter will address the following questions: How did Islam arrive in Somalia and what role does it play in the lives of the Somalis? How did the Islamic awakening, or 'Islamism', evolve as a concept and a practice in Somalia? What methods of social transformation do Somali Islamists use? What role did the Islamic Courts play in Somalia? How does the presence of Islamists affect peacebuilding efforts? Finally, the chapter concludes with the key question: What is the future of the Islamic awakening or 'Islamism' in Somalia?

ISLAM AND ITS ROLE IN SOMALIA

Islam has deep roots in the Somali people. Some scholars, such as I.M. Lewis and Enrico Cerulli, note that Muslims who were running away from persecution introduced the Islamic faith to the Somalis through peaceful means before the Prophet Muhammad (PBUH) emigrated from Mecca to Medina, the Muslim capital.[3] That migration, termed *Hijra*, was around the fourteenth year after the birth of the Islamic religion (about 622 CE). According to this account, Muslim migrants arrived in the city of Zaila in northern Somalia. The people in Zaila accepted the Islamic faith peacefully and began propagating it to people in the Horn of Africa. This historical account is largely based on Somali oral history; the best evidence cited for its accuracy is the geographical proximity of Zaila and northern Somalia to Muslim centres at the time.[4]

Other scholars, such as Ali Abdirahman Hersi and Mohammed Haji Mukhtar, present a different account. For these authors the Islamic religion did not come to Somalia through the north a few years after the birth of Islam. In particular, Mukhtar argues that the north was too close to places from which immigrants were fleeing, and that part of Somalia did not have any major towns. Moreover, Mukhtar contends that the north was not attractive for immigrants because it did not have what he calls 'natural harbours' and its economy was as poor as the places Muslim migrants left.[5] Using a number of historical documents, both Hersi and Mukhtar claim that several boats from Arabia and Persia arrived at the southern part of Somalia during the era of Abu-Bakar (the era after the death of Prophet Muhammad).[6] Mukhtar writes, 'thus, there is a good reason to believe that the earliest wave of Muslim immigrants to the Somali coast occurred as early as the period of Abu-Bakar, the first Kalif of Islam'.[7] Both Mukhtar and Hersi argue that the name of the district of Mogadishu, 'Shingani', and the name of the Shanshi clan are both Farsi, which means that members of this clan emigrated from Persia.

As a country, Somalia did not have a single authority at the time. As such, it is not clear whether the north was part of the land of Sinji. It is also possible, and perhaps historically probable, that individuals who fled persecution came to the north, particularly Zaila, while groups that migrated settled in the south.[8] Although the exact time Islam arrived in Somalia is contested, it is clear that Somalis accepted Islam peacefully. Moreover, Somalis are Sunni Muslims. Ironically, although historians have documented strong evidence that suggests an early presence of Shi'a groups in southern Somalia, Shi'ism rarely exists in Somalia today. Prior to the Islamic movements, one can safely argue that most scholars in Somalia were Ash-aris[9] with respect to *Aqida* (theology). Moreover, in terms of the four schools of jurisprudence (*fiqi*), Somalis practised the Shafi'i[10] school. From the spiritual (*Tasawuf*) side, the Sufi tradition was dominant in Somalia for a long period of time.

There are three main Sufi *tariqas*[11] (brotherhoods) in Somalia: Qadiriya, Ahmadiya and Salihiya. The tariqa of Qadiriya was founded by the great Muslim scholar Sheikh Abdulqadir Jilani. In Somalia, this tariqa has two major sections: Zaiyli'iya and Uwaysiya. The followers of this tariqa are in the majority and are found in every region in Somalia. On the other hand, the tariqa of Ahmadiya was founded by Sheikh Sayid Ahmed Ibn Idiris Al-Fasi (1760–1837) who lived in Mecca.[12] But it was Sheikh Ali Maye from the city of Merca in the Lower Shabelle region of Somalia who introduced the tariqa of Ahmadiya to the Somalis.[13] The followers of this tariqa are concentrated in several regions such as Lower Shabelle, Banadir, and some places in the southern part of the country. The final tariqa of Salihiya was founded by Sheikh Mohamed Ibn Salih, who was a student of the founder of Ahmadiya and who also lived in Mecca. Although other scholars, such as Sheikh Mohamed Guled,[14] brought this branch of Sufism to Somalia, Sayid Mohamed Abdulle Hassan popularized the tariqa of Salihiya to the Somalis when he came back from the pilgrimage (*Hajj*) in the late nineteenth century.[15] Sayid Mohamed Abdulle Hassan was the leader of the Darwish[16] movement and is considered to be the father of Somali nationalism.[17] This tariqa is strong in northern Somalia.

Islam as a religion has played a significant role in the lives of Somalis. It was and still is a strong identity that competes and at times replaces clan identity for individual Somalis. Commenting on this fact, Hersi writes, 'Islam as a religion and a system of values so thoroughly permeates all aspects of Somali life that it is difficult to conceive of any meaning in the term Somali itself without at the same time implying Islamic identity.'[18] Moreover, Islam informs many facets of everyday activities. It is common to see Somalis observing prayers. Fasting during the month of Ramadan is also common for the average Somali. If one listens to a Somali individual talking, one would hear many Islamic concepts and Islamic vocabulary even though that person is not conducting a religious ceremony – this shows the extent to which Islam is present within Somali culture. This is not to say that Somalis do not commit actions that are un-Islamic. Were that the case, Somalis would not have fought the un-Islamic civil war that killed tens of thousands of Somalis.

Besides in everyday life, Somalis have used Islam to resist not only colonial forces, but also any transgression (*zulm*) among themselves. Imam Ahmed Ibrahim fought a long religious war against the Abyssinians in the fifteenth century. Somali clans were also involved in these wars.[19] Moreover, Sayid Mohamed Abdulle Hassan used Islam to mobilize Somalis against the colonialist Great Britain, Italy and Ethiopia. Sayid Mohamed was a capable leader and a great poet.[20] Many verses of his poems show the integral role that Islam played in his struggle.[21] Even the later nationalist movements adopted both nationalist and Islamic rhetoric when they were mobilizing Somalis against colonial forces. Examples are the verses of the late Ali Hussein as well as poems by the modern poet, Abdulahi Moallim Dhodan, in which he calls on people to fight against the Ethiopian government.

As mentioned, Somali clans also use Islam when resisting what they consider to be transgressions from other clans. Using Islamic terminology and vocabulary, clans develop a collective feeling of injustice and organize militia groups in order to defend themselves against the more dominant clans. There are many examples of this rhetoric, such as the series of Guba[22] poems. In addition, during the recent civil war many poets who wanted to justify their struggle used both clan and religious rhetoric in mobilizing people against the Siyad Barre regime. Poets such as Khalif Sheikh Mohamud of the Majeerteen sub-clan, Ga'amay of Habar-Gidir clan, Elmi Barrow of Hawadle clan, Mohamed Gandal of Ogaden clan and Ali Banfas of Isaaq clan among many others, mixed their clannish agenda with religious rhetoric when they were fighting against Siyad Barre's military regime.

ISLAMIC AWAKENING: WHAT IS IT AND WHY IS IT POPULAR?

Naming the emerging phenomenon that combines religion and politics in the Muslim world is highly contested. Some call it 'Islamic fundamentalism'. Others call it 'Islamic-fascism' (Islamofascism), while many more describe this phenomenon as 'Islamism' or 'political Islam'. As Bobby Sayyid argues, fundamentalism is not the appropriate term when one wants to make sense of modern

Islamic movements in the Muslim world. The concept of fundamentalism was coined to understand a movement that appeared in a different context and in a different era.[23] In fact, David Harrington Watt rightly argues that when we characterize someone as a fundamentalist, 'we are saying nothing more than X seems to have something in common with people such as Curtis Lee Laws and Jerry Falwell'.[24] Moreover, Sayyid takes a critical look and examines the factors that are associated with the concept of fundamentalism: control of women's bodies and the mixing of religion and politics. He concludes that the concept of fundamentalism that has often been associated with Protestant movements in the nineteenth century cannot explain modern Islamic movements.[25] Others come to a similar conclusion.[26] Therefore, I will not use the concept of fundamentalism for this book when explaining or analysing Islamic movements in Somalia.

Many on the right of the political spectrum have increasingly begun using the term 'Islamofascism' when talking about Islamic movements. Stephen Schwartz argues that the aims of Islamic movements and the methods they use in order to achieve those aims are similar to those of fascists in the early twentieth century.[27] David Horowitz, another conservative writer, has toured many American universities trying to raise the awareness of the American public regarding what he calls the dangers of 'Islamofascism'.[28] In agreement with these journalists, President George W. Bush added his voice in openly using this terminology when speaking of alleged terrorists from Great Britain in 2006: 'The recent arrests that our fellow citizens are now learning about are a stark reminder that this nation is at war with Islamic fascists who will use any means to destroy those of us who love freedom.'[29] Many Muslims and non-Muslims condemn the use of this term and argue that it unfairly equates Islam with fascism. I will not use this term as I believe it is not only an inaccurate and Islamo-phobic, but also an insult to Islam and Muslims.

There is some disagreement among experts as to the definition of 'Islamism' or 'political Islam'. Graham Fuller argues that Islamists are those who believe that 'Islam as a body of faith has something important to say about how politics and society should be ordered'.[30] Guilain Denoeux defines 'Islamism' as a 'form of instrumentalization of Islam by individuals, groups and organizations that pursue political objectives'.[31]

While the latter definition is more useful in explaining Islamic movements in the Muslim world, Muslim scholars who are the pioneers of these movements disagree with the labels of 'Islamism' or 'political Islam'.[32] For instance, Sheikh Yusuf Al-Qaradawi rejects these labels and calls for Muslims to reject them as well. He argues that those who use 'Islamism' or 'political Islam' labels against Islamic movements do so in order to 'scare people from its [Islam's] content and sincere, true men who call people to comprehensive Islam, which encompasses faith, Sharia, religion and state'.[33] Sheikh Al-Qaradawi believes Islam has a lot to say about not just politics but also many other areas of life, so restricting it just to politics is at best a partial characterization.[34] Keeping this contestation of language in mind, I will use the terms Islamism, political Islam and 'Islamic awakening' interchangeably in this book.

With respect to its origin, the Islamic awakening is a new phenomenon in the Muslim world. The often-identified founder, Jamal-al-din al-Afghani, lived in the nineteenth century (1838–1897). He was concerned about the decline of Muslims and the rise of Westerners in the Muslim world. He called on people to use their religion to resist the then-colonialists or imperialists. However, Mohamed Abdouh, the student of Jamal-al-din al-Afghani, developed the concept of Islamic awakening further. As a revivalist, Abdouh also called on Muslims to return to their religion and resolve pertinent issues among themselves by using Islam.[35] Rashid Rida, editor of *Al-Manar* newspaper, played a significant role in advancing the Islamist discourse. The issues that these scholars were trying to address included the underdevelopment of Muslim nations. One scholar at the time wrote a book called *Limada Ta'akhara'l Muslimun walimada taqaddama gheyruhum* (Why have Muslims regressed while others progressed?).[36]

After the collapse of the Ottoman Empire in the 1920s, Imam Hassan Al-Banna began to mobilize Muslims around the principles that were laid down by earlier scholars such as Jamal-al-din al-Afghani and Mohamed Abdouh. Imam Hassan Al-Banna created the Muslim Brotherhood organization. He wrote a number of works for the organization, including the Risalatu-Ta'alim in which he explains the objectives of the organization and how they are to be achieved. Later, Sayyid Qutb joined the Muslim Brotherhood and developed revolutionary ideas. For instance, he argued that for Muslims to liberate themselves they need to reject all forms of *Jahiliya* (ignorance). He contended that, as had others before him, Islam is the solution to all problems. Islam, according to Qutb, espouses major political views such as the idea of establishing an Islamic state. Islam is not only *Din* (religion), but also *Dowla* (state). The centre of the development of this orientation, known as Ikhwan,[37] was Egypt, even though Ikhwan has branches in most of the Muslim world. In addition, Abul-Ala Al-Mawdudi has written a number of books that have contributed significantly to the idea of an Islamic awakening: *Nazariyad Siyasi Fil-islam* (Political theories in Islam); *Islamic State*; *Let Us Be Muslims*; and *This Religion*.

The Salafi orientation of Islam runs parallel to the Ikhwan orientation.[38] In its current form, the Salafi movement was founded in the late eighteenth century by Sheikh Mohamed Abdulwahab. This orientation originally focused on improving the understanding of Islam. The Sheikh rejected excesses and some superstitions that many Muslims practised such as visiting graveyards and venerating people who died by believing that they can help. Sheikh Mohamed Abdulwahab's major work is *Kitab al-Towhid* (The book of unity of Allah). Another often-used book, in the Somali context, is *Usulu-Talata* (Three fundamental principles). Islamic movements that have a Salafiya tendency use several other texts including *Aqi-datul-Wasitiya* (The creed of people of moderation) by Sheikh Ibn Taymiya. Overall, Salafi groups have focused their activities in the area of *Aqida* (faith) while those with an Ikhwan orientation have placed emphasis on the area of politics. In contrast to Ikhwan, the centre for the Salafi orientation was and still is in Saudi Arabia.

There are similarities between these two major orientations: the establishment of an Islamic state, a positive perception of the early history of Islam, and the use of the Koran and Sunnah as two sources of legislation.[39] However, the two schools differ in their emphasis. While the Ikhwani approach focuses on politics the Salafi orientation emphasizes the purification of society. Moreover, according to Abdelwhab El-Affendi, when interpreting the Koran and Sunnah, the Salafi orientation tends to use a literal interpretation while other schools attempt to go beyond literal meaning and engage in some form of a textual analysis. For El-Affendi, this difference comes down to the assumptions that these two schools have about the capacity of human nature. The Salafi school does not trust the capacity of human beings and argues that people have to stick to the obvious meaning while other schools, including some Sufi traditions, would go beyond that meaning.[40]

With respect to the reasons that Muslims are attracted to Islamist political activism, many authors point to the failure of secular leadership, a lack of development, and the West's domination of Muslims.[41] In fact, Mohammed Ayoob classifies the factors that are behind Islamist popularity into those that are 'inherent in Islam' and those that are external to Islam. Those factors that are inherent to the religion include the 'simplicity' of the Islamist message.[42] For Ayoob, Islamists can readily explain why Muslims have declined and how they can more easily recover than secularists. Moreover, Ayoob contends that the fact that many Muslims are familiar with the Koran and its vocabulary helps the advancement of Islamic movement groups.[43] Regarding the factors that are external to Islam, Ayoob identifies the repressive practices of authoritarian Muslim regimes, US policies toward the Muslim world (support for the hated dictatorships), and America's unqualified support for Israel. Any combination of these internal and external factors, according to Ayoob, benefits Islamic movements in their activity.

EVOLUTION OF ISLAMIC AWAKENING IN SOMALIA

The two major orientations (*itijah*) of Islamic awakening, Ikhwan and Salafi, which are found within Islamist groups all over the world, are also present in Somalia. The first school, Ikhwan, is the one that Imam Hassan Al-Banna established in 1928 in Egypt. Several Somali Islamic movements identify with the Muslim Brotherhood (Ikhwani) orientation: Islah, Tajamu-Al-Islami (formally called Ikhwan-Al-Muslimun) and Wuhdatu-Shabab Al-Islam. Islah is the official branch that represents the Muslim Brotherhood movement of Egypt in Somalia. The second school, Salafi, was represented by Al-itihad al-Islam in the 1980s and early 1990s. This organization was disbanded in 1997. Now the Al-Itisam Al-Islami movement represents the Salafi orientation in Somalia. There are also other groups that have a Salafiya orientation such as Al-Shabab, Hizbul-Islam and Salafiya Jadida. Many notable individuals who are not members of these organizations but who are in line with the principles of one of the two orientations can be found in Somalia as well.

The Salafi and Ikhwani orientations are not mutually exclusive, particularly in Somalia. There are two reasons for this. First, the Somali context is different from that of the Arab world. One Islamist I interviewed commented on how members from different orientations worked together to defeat Somali warlords: 'The Salafis in Somalia are not the same as those in the Arab world and the Ikhwan groups are also not the same as the brotherhood groups in other countries.'[44] Many Islamists who explain the disparity think that the major difference between Somali Islamists and others in the Muslim world is that the average Somali Islamist knows more about the basic sources of Islam than his counterparts. Second, most of the leadership and key scholars in Somalia have a history with both orientations.

There are several accounts of how the origins of the Islamic awakening in Somalia emerged. In fact, there are various explanations, as each movement narrates its own history. For instance, some Salafiya groups argue that the Islamic movements first began in Somalia in the 1950s[45] when Sheikh Nur Ali Olow came back from Saudi Arabia. Sheikh Nur started to teach this orientation at mosques in Mogadishu. According to this school, the religious establishment at the time rebelled against Sheikh Nur by calling him a Wahabi. But he persisted. Moreover, according to this view, late in the 1960s and early 1970s many Somalis went to the Gulf countries either to work or to study. When these individuals came back they reinforced the ideas that Sheikh Nur Ali Olow had previously introduced in the Somali context.

Unlike the Salafiya movements, Islamic movements that associate themselves with the Ikhwan orientation narrate three different accounts of Islamic awakening in Somalia. Members of Islah, the official representative of the Muslim Brotherhood International, argue that the Ikhwani approach was brought to Somalia by Sheikh Mohamed Nur Garyare and others who returned from Saudi Arabia in 1964. Sheikh Garyare was a student in Saudi Arabia when he joined the Muslim Brotherhood and he is one of the founders of Al-Islah.[46] The Al-Islah movement also claims that Sheikh Abdiqani, the former minister of justice in the 1960s, was part of the group that pioneered the Ikhwani approach in Somalia. The Islah activists note that these scholars created the Nahda political party in 1968 in order to participate in the 1969 elections.

A second account of the emergence of Islamic awakening in Somalia is through the Wuhdatu-Shabab movement. The Wuhdatu-Shabab, like Islah, was associated with the Ikhwan orientation but was established in the northern part of Somalia (Somaliland), particularly in the capital, Hargeysa. The youth group that started the movement did not get their ideas from major Somali towns in the south such as Mogadishu. Instead, since the north is closer to the Arab world, Somalis there have had a long relationship with Arab people. Through contacts with people from the Arab world at the height of the *Sahwa* (awakening) period in the 1960s, many young and Arabic-speaking individuals were influenced by books written by leaders and intellectuals of the Ikhwan movement in the Arab world, and intellectuals such as Sayyid Qutb. Some of the prominent activists I met told me that the Islamic movement in the north was separate, and it emerged in 1969. The 1969 election triggered this movement to organize along the Ikhwan orientation.

The Tajamu (Ikhwan) group provides a third account. It argues that Sheikh Mohamed Moallim Hassan introduced Islamic awakening in Somalia when he came back from Egypt in 1969. Sheikh Mohamed studied at Azhar University. He completed his undergraduate and graduate (MA) degrees, specializing in philosophy and Aqida (faith), and a postgraduate degree in education at Ain-Shamsi University. When Sheikh Mohamed was a PhD candidate at Azhar University he was writing his dissertation on 'Iman wa atharuhu fi xayatil-fardi wal-mujtama' (The faith and its consequences on the life of the individual and society). He returned to Somalia in 1969 before he completed his doctoral work. When Sheikh Mohamed Moallim came back from Egypt he established good relations with the religious establishment in Somalia and started teaching *Tafsir* (interpretation of the Koran) at the Maqaamka Sheikh Abdulqadir mosque in downtown Mogadishu, centre of the Qadiriya Tariqa.

It is possible that all the above accounts are accurate. But most Islamists, Salafi and Ikhwan alike, consider Sheikh Mohamed Moallim Hassan to be the father of the Islamic awakening in Somalia, as he had the greatest impact on the youth of the time. He is largely respected by most of the groups. Sheikh Mohamed spent twelve years in prison during Siyad Barre's dictatorship era.[47] While in prison he was attacked and severely wounded. Although all groups respect Sheikh Mohamed Moallim, he is often associated with the Tajamu or Ikhwan group. In fact, Sheikh Mohamed was the spiritual leader of that group for many years.

Sheikh Mohamed had taught Tafsir (interpretation of the Koranic sciences) while using many different authorities on this area of knowledge. Among them, according to his students, was Sayyid Qutb's Tafsir, *The Shade of the Qur'an*. Moreover, besides the popularity of these lessons, the first organized movement appeared in the early 1970s and was named *Al-Ahli* (an Arabic term meaning 'the relatives'). This name was chosen as a means of concealing the activities of the organization from the repressive military regime. Although secret at the time, Abulkadir Sheikh Mohamud led this movement at its inception.

Sheikh Mohamed Moallim and many other scholars were arrested in 1975 (others fled the country over subsequent years, including Sheikh Mohamed Garyare, the leader of Islah). As a result of the arrests and of the regime's killings of ten religious scholars, the

Al-Ahli movement divided into two groups, Jama'a Islamiya and Islah. These groups immediately started to compete for the loyalty of the members of Islamist movements. Another group, the Takfir wal-Hijra, emerged in the late 1970s. The members of this group asserted that those who do not rule according to Allah's revelation were apostates and those who do not call them infidels (*Kafirs*) were also infidels. So the Takfir deduced from this reasoning that since the regime was socialist, those who led Somalia were not Muslims, and since Somalis did not rebel against the regime, against the killings and abuses that the regime committed against Muslim activists, Somalis were thus infidels by default. This movement paralleled the Takfir movement in Egypt.

As time progressed many more splinter groups appeared. For instance, a majority wing of the Jama'a Islamiya and a wing of the Wuhdatu-Shabab agreed to unite calling their movement the Al-Ittihad al-Islami (AIAI). AIAI became the most powerful Islamic movement in Somalia during the late 1980s and early 1990s. After fighting several wars and losing them, the AIAI disappeared in 1997. The remaining wing of Jama'a Islamiya retained the same name and later became the Ikhwan Al-Muslimuun, which, in 2001, named itself Tajamu Al-Islami. Interestingly, two movements with separate orientations (Tajamu and Al-Itisam) merged in May 2008 and called their newly found organization Jama'a Al-Wafaq Al-Islamiya.[48] Some considered this merger a political necessity, not an ideological shift of the groups. Al-Islah kept its name since its inception in the 1970s although it has used the name Harakal Islamiya (Islamic Movement) and Ikhwan Al-Muslimuun (Muslim Brotherhood). However, Al-Islah split up into two movements when the Islamic Courts emerged in 2006.[49] Both groups, however, still claim the name Al-Islah. To distinguish these two groups among the Islamists one of the factions is called the 'New Blood' while the other is called Al-Islah (the Old Guard).

ISLAMIC MOVEMENTS AND THEIR METHODS OF SOCIAL CHANGE

Islamist groups in Somalia clearly want to transform Somali society and its institutions. For all Somali Islamic movements, a primary goal is the establishment of an Islamic state in the country. All want Sharia to become the basis of all legislations and all aim to make Somalia a society that observes Islamic requirements. However, although these groups have similar objectives, they differ in their approaches and in their methods of social change. Initially, all of the Islamic movements in Somalia argued that the best way to transform Somali society was through propagation (*Da'wa*). Therefore, before the state collapsed, members of Somalia's different Islamic movements informally propagated the Islamic awakening project in schools and mosques. During the Siyad Barre era such a movement was considered illegal. As a result of this ban, members of these movements had to conduct their work discreetly and recruit new members secretly.[50]

During Siyad Barre's dictatorship, there were several instances where Islamists and the military regime clashed. First, when the state introduced the family and inheritance legislation, religious clerics, including traditional scholars in Somalia, such as the *fuqaha* (jurists) and Sufi scholars, resisted the state and began to challenge that law. The state suppressed this group and arrested hundreds of its followers. And, as mentioned above, the military authority killed ten scholars who led the resistance and arrested Sheikh Mohamed Moallim and many of his students. As a result of this crackdown many young Islamists fled the country, mostly to Arab countries in the Gulf region. A similar event occurred in 1983 when many Islamists were imprisoned. Ten of those jailed were sentenced to death. Sheikh Hassan Dahir Aweys, one of the leaders of the Islamic courts, was among these. The death penalty was not carried out because President Siyad Barre pardoned these scholars.

In July 1989 when the Roman Catholic bishop Salvatore Colombo was killed, Siyad Barre arrested some well-known religious leaders and scholars. Among the scholars who were arrested were Sheikh Ibrahim Mohamed Dhaqane (Suuley), Sheikh Shariif Sharafow and Sheikh Abdirashiid Ali Sufi. As a result, Islamist groups decided to show their support for the arrested scholars by resisting state repression. The young leaders of the Islamic movements organized a demonstration after Friday prayer on 14 July 1989. The state received tip-offs about these demonstrations and brought a large number of soldiers to the streets of Mogadishu. After Friday prayer, the Islamists clashed with the military and police who used excessive force killing many protesters that day. The military also killed many other civilians over the following days.

Generally the debate that relates to the method of change focuses on two options. One camp argues that meaningful change can only come about when force is used. The other camp, while not dismissing the possible use of force, rejects this argument and contends that a combination of political involvement and *Da'wa* (propagation) can result in meaningful political change. Both camps use evidence from sources of Islam and from the history of Muslims. In Somalia, both camps exist within the Islamic movements. Most of Somalia's Islamic movements claim that they will use peaceful means, particularly *Da'wa*, for social transformation. In fact, some Islamists openly announce that they would be willing to participate as a political party in a democratic competition.

Prior to the collapse of the Somali state in 1991, almost all Islamists used peaceful methods. There is no Islamist group that took up arms against the Somali state before 1991. But as soon as conditions changed and the all-out civil war began a group within Al-Ittihad al-Islami decided to take up arms against the factions that overthrew the government. This created a heated debate amongst Islamist groups. Those who supported the use of force in order to fight against the warlords argued that prevailing conditions necessitated this strategy. Their argument was largely based on self-defence grounds, that is, protecting innocents from the militias. This group first fought against General Mohamed Farah Aideed's United Somali Congress (USC) at the Arare Bridge in 1992. General Aideed defeated the Islamists. But, the Al-Ittihad al-Islami group moved to the northeast and to Ras Kamboni. Again, Colonel Abdullahi Yusuf's Somali Salvation Democratic Front (SSDF) fought with the Al-Ittihad movement in the northeast regions. Abdullahi Yusuf defeated the Al-Ittihad al-Islami movement once again.

Although the AIAI lost the battle to the SSDF, they left a positive impression with the general public during the time they managed Bosaso city and its port in 1992. They were less corrupt than the SSDF faction and thus earned the support of the people.[51] In 1994, Al-Ittihad again captured the Gedo region in the south. This time they controlled the region for months and created a secure environment.[52] The Ethiopian-supported Somali National Front then fought against the Al-Ittihad. This time Ethiopia's forces and airplanes took part simply because the Islamists were stronger than the Somali National Front faction. This blatant Ethiopian intervention resulted in Islamists who were not part of the AIAI joining the fight. Several scholars including Sheikh Sharif Abdinur and Sheikh Mohamed Moallim Hassan produced a legal ruling (*fatwa*), calling on all Somali Muslims to fight against the Ethiopians. A group of young Islamists from the Tajamu movement joined the AIAI in the fight against Ethiopia in the Gedo region.

While the AIAI was fighting these wars many Islamic scholars in the rank and file criticized the idea of taking up arms against the Somali Muslim clans. Some of them even condemned the act of using violence against Somali clans and left the movement altogether. This necessitated many members of Al-Ittihad to revisit its strategy. In 1997 the organization decided to abandon the idea of using force in order to change the status quo. But, the AIAI still endorsed the fight against Ethiopia because it was considered a legitimate cause; Ethiopia had colonized Somali territories ('Ogaden' region). The majority of Al-Ittihad members adopted this position with the exception of a few groups, among them the Raskambooni group, Hisbul-Islam and Al-Shabab. Ideologically, these latter groups are the only ones to say that they would use force in order to change the situation.

With respect to the other Islamist groups, some within the Tajamu movement (which has an Ikhwani orientation) joined the war against Ethiopia in the Gedo region in 1996. Their spiritual leader, Sheikh Mohamed Moallim Hassan, issued a fatwa stating that fighting against the Ethiopian invading forces was legitimate and that it served the Islamic cause. In fact, at the time Sheikh Mohamed argued that it was religiously mandatory to fight against the invading Ethiopians. Many other scholars such as Sheikh Sharif Abdinur also called on Mogadishu residents to help fleeing civilians, many of whom had returned to Mogadishu, even though in 1991 they themselves had been forced to flee because of their clan identity. The position of Tajamu (Ikhwan group) and the majority of Al-Ittihad (Salafiya group), with respect to using force, was that it was obligatory to fight against the invading Ethiopians, but participating in the civil war was not permissible. The Al-Islah movement maintained its position of non-violence throughout history.

However, a new phenomenon emerged after 11 September 2001. First, a group of warlords who worked with the Ethiopian government and American intelligence agencies began to hunt down individuals across Somalia whom they labelled terrorists. This action forced many leaders of Islamic movements to revise their original strategy of non-violence. A question asked many times was: Can Islamist groups fight against Somali warlords from the Sharia perspective? Some Islamist leaders became convinced that they needed to take up arms against the warlords. In late 2005 and early 2006, Al-Shabab, Tajamu, a faction of the Islah (New Blood), a faction of Ictisam along with many independent individual Islamists and some clans joined forces and began to wage war against the warlords. The Umbrella of Somali Scholars in Mogadishu, led by Sheikh Mohamud Sheikh Ibrahim Suley and Sheikh Nur Barud, issued a fatwa stating that it was incumbent on them to fight against Somali warlords.

These Islamist groups, operating in the name of the Islamic Courts, defeated the warlords and stabilized Mogadishu and southern Somalia. But, the Ethiopian government, with the support of the United States, invaded Somalia and removed the Islamists from power. Most Islamist movements in Somalia were fighting against Ethiopian occupation. Islamists used the religious rationale that when a Muslim state is invaded by a non-Muslim state, Jihad becomes *Fard Eyn* (mandatory). So with the exception of Salafiya Jadida (New Salafis), one faction of Islah and the one faction of Ictisam in Bosaso, other Islamic movements have taken up arms against Ethiopia. There is a fatwa signed by more than seventy scholars that calls for Somalis to resist against Ethiopian occupation and those who are supporting them.[53]

As a result of the events that have unfolded in the last few decades, Islamic movements in Somalia enjoy the support of many people.[54] The reasons for this support are manifold. Among them is that Islamists offer social services. Islamic movements, or individuals with Islamist tendencies, run almost all the schools and health centres in Somalia. Islah is a leader in providing these services. Islamists also help in the areas of security and the private sector, particularly in business. General Jama Mohamed Ghaleb, whom I interviewed for this book, said 'these groups cannot be ignored anymore because they have many supporters. They have a large constituency.'[55] The above events lead me to conclude that Somalia's Islamists are interested in transforming Somali society and most of them would revert to non-violent means if conditions allowed it. While some Islamists do reject the idea of taking up arms, most of them do not consider Islam a pacifist religion. They believe that if conditions necessitate, force can be employed particularly in case of defensive Jihad. Moreover, most Islamist members interviewed for this book say they do not intend to use force in order to capture power. Instead, they claim that they want to liberate Somalia from the invading forces of Ethiopia and its warlords. Moreover, even minority groups – which, in principle, endorse the idea of changing the Somali situation through the use of force – have focused on the warlords and their Ethiopian backers for some time, albeit this is changing. Al-Shabab is the main protagonist that propagates this view. Moreover, a wing of Hizbul-Islam is not clear on their political agenda flip-flopping between the two views.

At the time of writing, no group has publicly declared war on the West or on America. Even the Shabab leadership, which claims to have similar goals and objectives to Al-Qaeda and professes some ideological commonalities, did not officially call Jihad against the West or America. That said, it is becoming clearer now that Al-Shabab has an internationalist Jihadist agenda and that it condemns America's policies towards the region. Regarding the link between Al-Shabab and Al-Qaeda, what is clear so far is that these two groups admit they have collaborated for their common objectives and they are proud of that cooperation. Abul-Yazeed, the Al-Qaeda leader in Afghanistan, recently gave an interview and admitted that they supported Al-Shabab and one of the Al-Qaeda leaders, Abu-Dalha al-Sudani, was killed in Mogadishu. Similarly, former spokesman of Al-Shabab, Sheikh Mukhtar Robow Ali (Abu-Mansur) and the current spokesman, Sheikh Ali Mohamud Rage also admitted that they have similar objectives and enemies as Al-Qaeda. Both Al-Qaeda and Al-Shabab rejected the idea that the two organizations are united under one movement.

ISLAMIC COURTS IN SOMALIA: A VEHICLE FOR SOCIAL CHANGE

The first time an organized group attempted to introduce Islamic courts in Somalia was in the immediate aftermath of the state collapse in 1991. As mentioned in the above section, the militia which succeeded in deposing Siyad Barre began to hunt down innocent civilians living in Mogadishu simply because of their clan identity. At this time, several well-known scholars such as Sheikh Sharif Sharafow, Sheikh Ibrahim Suley and Sheikh Mohamed Moallin Hassan established a Sharia court in order to control the situation and to rescue innocent Somalis from the attacks of militia groups. Prior to organizing the court system, these Sheikhs created an organization called the Majma'a Al-Ulama Al-Somal (Council of Scholars of Somalia) and secured some politicians' support, initially including that of Ali Mahdi Mohamed, interim president of Somalia at the time. According to the leaders and soldiers who worked for the first Islamic court, those in power at the time undermined and then destroyed the efforts to create a lasting court. When the courts began to punish criminals, General Aideed and Ali Mahdi, who otherwise were enemies that competed for power, collaborated to destroy the courts. One young Islamist told me the following story that relates to the first Islamic court in Mogadishu: 'I was one of the Horseed [court] soldiers, and I was told to be on duty in the area of Taleh [in Mogadishu]. At around 2:00 p.m., one day, one of my fellow soldiers notified me that a militia group had taken four men who belonged to the Darod clan out of their homes. It was a very difficult process for us but we finally freed these innocent elders from their captors.' He added, 'I met those I helped free that day in Kenya later on, and they helped me with my business.'[56]

Parallel with this first court in Mogadishu, Sheikh Mohamed Haji Yusuf and Sheikh Mohamud A. Nur established a new Islamic court in the Luq district of Gedo region in 1992. This court was more successful than the one attempted in Mogadishu. These scholars succeeded in creating a secure environment in the area, and for a while, from 1992 to 1997, Luq district was the safest area in Somalia.[57] Ethiopia and the local Somali National Front faction collaborated to destroy the Gedo Islamic court. As a result, chaos increased and intra-clan warfare proliferated. Then in 1994, a form of Islamic courts reappeared in Medina district. One of the warlords, Muse Sudi, helped a group that wanted to create a court in his district. But the major defining move came when the Muddulod clans of northern Mogadishu decided to establish their own Islamic court in 1994, often called the Sheikh Ali-Dhere court. The scholars, elders, business leaders and politicians collaborated in establishing this court because their part of the city had become a very dangerous place to live. There are many sayings that became popular prior to the creation of the Islamic court in northern Mogadishu. One was 'Siraadka Qiyaama iyo Siisii Allow na mooti' (Oh God, save us from the troubles that are associated with the day of judgement and those of the Siisii street).[58]

Interestingly, after the Sheikh Ali-Dhere court was established, peace returned to the northern part of Mogadishu. Sheikh Ali-Dhere showed no mercy toward convicted criminals, and there are videos recording hands being amputated or people being killed for murder. One interviewee told me that 'the Siisii, the most dangerous street in the city became safe'. For instance, he added, 'Two thieves stopped a civilian man one night. They wanted to rob him. But, each of the thieves asked the other to search the person. Each refused because the one who held the gun may be punished by a few lashes but the one who searches would lose his hand or a hand and leg. For fear of Ali-Dhere's punishment, the two thieves finally let the man go unsearched.'[59] Other clans followed the Muddulod clans and created their own courts. In particular, two Islamic courts were created in 1996 in the Hiran and Bay regions. The popular slogan became 'If you want peace, establish an Islamic court.' Wherever a security need existed, Islamic courts appeared, but they were never sustained.

Besides politicians' concerns for their power base, external actors such as human rights groups showed concern about the way Sheikh Ali-Dhere was implementing Sharia. Abdinur N. Hashi notes that the representative of the European Union (EU) to Somalia at the time, Sigurd Illing, visited northern Mogadishu and met with politicians there. According to Hashi, Mr Illing told politicians to do something about the human rights issue as it might affect the presence of humanitarian agencies. Hashi writes, 'to the Western world, anarchy is more tolerable than the Islamic ways of restoring law and order'.[60]

However, regardless of the Westerners' position there were legitimate criticisms against Islamic courts coming from within Somalia at the time. First, many people thought that petty criminals, for example, those who stole something in order to eat, were being punished while powerful gangs and warlords were left to operate freely. This became a significant issue among Islamists and the general public as well. The question of partial implementation of Sharia (punishing petty criminals and impunity of warlords) was put to Sheikh Omar Faruq while he was delivering a lecture at a conference. He responded by saying one cannot steal another person's property under any circumstances. 'If you need help,' he said, 'you need to ask for it.' Sheikh Mohamed Moallim, who was participating in the same programme, argued that, from the Islamic perspective, it was permissible to enforce Sharia laws in the conditions that prevailed in Somalia. His answer was 'if you cannot get all you want you do not leave all'. For him, whatever was possible under the circumstance has to be implemented. Sheikh Ibrahim Suley and Sheikh Nur Moallim agreed with these scholars too. Regardless of the scholars' rejection of the all or nothing argument, many Somalis are still uneasy about the presence of warlords, remembering the severe punishment Sheikh Ali-Dhere handed out against petty criminals. The argument, 'a criminal is a criminal whether small or big' and 'we will go after whoever we can, based on our strength' did not convince many people.

The creation of a secure environment aside, Sheikh Ali-Dhere was also accused of becoming a power-hungry individual. Because he was so popular and powerful he began to challenge political leaders of the Muddulod clan. A war of words ensued between Ali Mahdi and Sheikh Ali-Dhere. Ali Mahdi used force and succeeded in destroying Ali-Dhere's court in northern Mogadishu. Chaos returned to the northern part of the city because those who destroyed the courts were unable to come up with an alternative security system. Even current Islamist groups distance themselves from Sheikh Ali-Dhere because of his past records.

Wherever Islamic courts were created some form of stability returned and the courts became popular among Somali clans in southern Somalia. In particular, in 1998, communities of clans in southern Mogadishu started to create Islamic courts; the first that appeared was created by the Saleman sub-clan of Habar-Gidir. One intellectual who lived in the city at the time the court was created, told me: 'Many of the gangsters in the city belonged to this clan and whenever these gangsters commit a crime against the members of other clans, those clans targeted the innocent individuals of the Saleman clan and their property. This necessitated that they [elders and businessmen of the clan] find a way to control their criminals and that is why they created the court'.[61] After the Saleman clan established its own courts, other clans, such as Ayr, Duduble, Sa'ad, Jareer, Murusade, as well as sub-clans of Muddulod (Wa'aysle), joined them and created their own Islamic courts. Immediately, this phenomenon expanded to the Lower Shabelle region too.

THE ISLAMIC AWAKENING AND ITS IMPLICATIONS FOR PEACEBUILDING IN SOMALIA

Islamists as a force and Islam as a value system can have a significant impact on building durable peace in Somalia. For the sake of time and space I will limit my discussion to two factors that relate to peacebuilding and two that relate to state-building.

Peacemaking and peacebuilding in Somalia entail a number of challenges. First, in any meaningful peace process, it is necessary to include all the forces that are on the ground, which means that Somalia's Islamic movements, along with other groups, have to be accepted and included. But this poses a very significant challenge. The international community does not yet seem ready to really allow Islamists at the negotiating table, although this is now changing.[62] The American government has argued that some of Somalia's Islamists harboured terrorists.[63] In addition, Ethiopia and many warlords have taken advantage of the US war on terror and deemed all Islamic movements in Somalia as being organized by terrorists. Thus far the powers that influence and control the peace processes, particularly the United States and Ethiopia, are reluctant to tolerate powerful Islamists.[64]

Second, even if the recent rhetoric of inclusion by the international community is to be believed, Islamists will come up with many issues that may complicate the peace process. There are two levels of challenges. First, Islamists are expected to discuss openly their intentions and agendas regarding the US war on terror and Ethiopia's regional interests. The Islamists' conception of the war on terror is that it is against Islam and Muslims. Most Islamists I interviewed were not even interested in using this 'war on terror' terminology saying that the practice shows the United States is against all Muslims. One Islamist said, 'Americans are not after a few criminals who destroyed their buildings and embassies; they want to destroy Islam and Muslims. For them, Islam replaced communism.'[65]

Moreover, there are issues that relate to Ethiopia and its regional interests. Most people interviewed for this book acknowledged the meddling of Ethiopia as one of the key challenges. 'Ethiopia wants to keep Somalis in the current situation,' one Islamist told me. In fact, at issue is more than the current meddling by the Ethiopian government. There have been two wars between Somalia and Ethiopia and the root of the problem was the 'Ogaden' region. Pessimistic about the long-term relationship between Ethiopia and Somalia, one Islamist leader noted, 'The war between the Somalis and Ethiopians has been going on for centuries and religion was driving it. I think it will continue for many years to come.'[66]

Domestically, Islamists in Somalia are largely dominated by southerners. If one looks closely at the makeup of the Islamic courts – the dominant Islamist movement – the overwhelming majority of Islamists are from the Hawiye sub-clans. Even if one looks beyond the Islamic courts, most Islamic movements were born in Mogadishu and therefore clans in the south dominate them; some argue that this was the result of the movements' natural growth. This clan imbalance creates a problem, as many clans might not be included in the Islamist movement. Dealing with such perceptions of exclusion is not an easy problem to solve because there needs to be a formula that can accommodate contradictory realities. For instance, as clan identity is very strong among Somalis, so this has a significant impact on how people perceive political representation. Clan wars affected the composition of Islamic movements because many clans fled metropolitan areas and sought refuge where they traditionally inhabit. While the Islamic identity cuts across all Somali clans, the Hawiye clans' dominant position within the Islamist movements disproportionately affects Somali politics. Many Somali clans have opposed the domineering Hawiye for the last two decades.[67]

While Islamists openly call for an Islamic state and the Sharia rule, the international community, Western governments in particular, want a state based on liberal democracy and a market economy.[68] There is a clear mismatch here. The external powers' wishes and the main domestic actor's agenda are at loggerheads. The Islamists I talked to repeatedly said that they want to work for a Sharia-based Islamic state. One of them clearly said, 'This is a basic Islamic principle and we cannot compromise our principles at all.' And he told me, 'You now live in the West and you have to follow the rules and the regulations of the country you live in. But, they, the Westerners, have to accept that we have the same rights that they have when we are in our countries. They have to respect us and our Sharia.'[69]

Domestically, the Islamist agenda involves many aspects of state-building, yet certain questions must be addressed, such as: the specific model of governance (federal, unitary, decentralized state, or consociation); the type of government (presidential vs. parliamentary); the role of Sharia in the state; what to do with the warlords (peace partners or criminals); the role of democracy; and how to deal with issues of transition including the creation of a secure environment and the rebuilding of the economy.

Most Islamists I talked to reject a federal system and the 4.5 clan formula that was endorsed in the Kenyan-hosted peace process in 2002–04. Because of Ethiopia's manipulation, Islamic movements were not invited to participate in that peace process. Thus Somalia's current charter, parliament and government, according to Islamist groups and many intellectuals, reflect Ethiopian interests. One Islamist said, 'We rejected federalism and we reject the 4.5 system because we think this is a deliberate move of Somalia's enemies to weaken and divide us.' He added that, 'There is a way in which we can allow administrative systems where communities can choose their leaders, while keeping the country together.'[70] Although the Islamist did not use the exact terminology, the system he is endorsing is a decentralized unitary state. Such a system allows a unitary state that, through legislation, provides powers to regions while leaving ultimate power in the hands of the national legislators.

Although many Islamists, intellectuals and civil society members I interviewed, rejected a federal system, some business leaders, civil society members and intellectuals disagreed with that rejection. A businesswoman said, 'I have legitimate concerns about the unitary system because the powerful clans will use it against the unarmed clans. That can result in another civil war. I want the country to be federal, and I would like to keep the 4.5 system.'[71] A businessman told me, 'A federation is necessary since people do not trust each other. So let each clan build and develop its own territory.'[72]

Jama Mohamed Ghaleb, a well-respected police general and a member of Somali civil society, has also voiced concerns about a unitary state. He argued that the idea of a federal system was first introduced in Somalia by Abdirahman Ahmed Ali, 'Tur'. Abdirahman Tur was the first president of 'Somaliland', the region that intends to secede from Somalia. Tur reconsidered his position and decided to rejoin the south, but only through some form of federal arrangement. General Ghaleb favours a federation but it has to be between the north and south.[73] Others who agree with General Ghaleb prefer a federation that is beyond the south and north. In particular, Somalis from Puntland and from the Bay and Bakool regions, perhaps with the exception of Islamists, tend to prefer a federation that is based along clan lines.

Another controversial point is how to deal with the warlords. Islamists and intellectuals I interviewed agree that warlords should be excluded from positions of power. However, Islamists express completely different policy prescriptions. For instance, one Islamist says: 'A general amnesty for the crimes that are against the state is necessary. But, no one can forgive the specific crimes that warlords committed against individuals. Only those individuals can forgive them.'[74] Another Islamist said that warlords have to be punished wherever they are found, while some Islamists called for a complete amnesty. Members from the business community and intellectuals were similarly divided between those who said warlords have to be punished and those who said they have to be given a blanket amnesty. A civil society member told me that 'the crimes they committed cannot be forgiven'.[75] Several intellectuals suggested that some form of lustration, such as removing warlords' political rights, is necessary while allowing them to live peacefully; in fact, providing warlords immunity in order to get peace would be an option for these intellectuals.

In short, Islamist movements and the values they propose will have a significant impact on peacebuilding activities. The Islamic movements want to install a Sharia-based Islamic state. This proposal clashes with the liberal ideals that are embedded within the international community's peacebuilding efforts. Moreover, the current American-dominated unipolar world is not ready to accept an Islamic state. On the domestic front, Islamist movements want to implement proposals that might challenge some of the accepted norms and interests within Somali society.

THE FUTURE OF THE ISLAMIC AWAKENING OR 'ISLAMISM' IN SOMALIA

In general, Islamic awakening or 'Islamism' has been on the rise. Because of some factors that are inherent in Islam and some that are external to it, as Ayoob argues, Islamic movements have been gaining in popularity. Authoritarian regimes that have allowed Islamists to participate in the competition for power realized that they cannot easily defeat Islamist movements in Algeria, Turkey (several times), Palestine, Jordan and Egypt. As Ayoob states, 'political Islam as the quintessential anti-hegemonic ideology will continue to thrive as long as this remains to be the case'.[76] Ayoob goes further and writes that the ideology of 'Islamism' 'may even become the voice of the vulnerable and the weak in the international system regardless of religious affiliation'.[77] Similarly, the Islamic movements in Somalia have been growing for the past two decades. The outlook of every Somali city reveals a heavy presence of what the Islamists call signs of the Islamic awakening (*Sahwa*). Culturally, both women and men dress according to interpretations of Islamic requirements. Islamist-run schools and health institutions are sometimes the only services that many Somali civilians have seen for the past two decades.

Yet, there are two major challenges to this growth: one domestic and the other external. First, the salience of clan identity within the Somali people has proven that it can resist the overarching Islamic identity. Today, most Islamist movements are dominated by one or two clans. This often creates a trust deficit; the mere fact that some communities are absent makes some feel that they are excluded and marginalized. Although there is no rule that discourages or prevents members of all clans joining a given Islamist organization, there are systemic practices that result from the de-facto centres of the organization. For instance, Wuhdatu-Shabab was founded in Hargeysa and most of its members were from Hargeysa from as early as the 1970s. Moreover, Islah, Tajamu, Ictisam and Shabab were first founded or headquartered in Mogadishu. For each of these movements, clans that settle in Mogadishu and the south dominate. In the late 1980s and early 1990s Al-Ittihad had been the most multi-clan Islamist movement. After the disintegration of Al-Ittihad in 1997 and the emergence of Salafiya Jadida, the movement split into three distinct centres along clan lines: Mogadishu, Bosaso and Hargeysa. On the other hand, the Al-Shabab movement is the most recent one and is perhaps the most organized and diverse (multi-clan) of all Islamist movements at this time.

Since these movements work in secret most of their practices are based on trust between members. Clan identity can be considered a source of trust among individuals. If individuals are Islamists and belong to the same clan, this might further enhance the trust between them while negatively affecting the trust of members from other clans. Any way one looks at it, clan identity remains one of the most important challenges that the Islamist movements face today.

The second major challenge is the role of external actors. Time and again, Islamists have proven that they can dominate their domestic competitors. Islamists defeated their domestic opponents several times (Gedo region in 1996 and southern Somalia in 2006). In each of these cases, external actors reversed the situation. Even if Ethiopia did not send troops to Somalia in 1993, it has supported the Somali Salvation Democratic Front (SSDF) with military weapons. In addition, Ethiopian troops directly attacked the Islamist organization Al-Ittihad in both the Gedo region and in southern Somalia. Based on these past experiences, the only force that can contain Islamist groups is Ethiopia and its Western backers. This is further complicated by the weakness of the Somali state.

Based on the practices of the United States since the 1979 Iran revolution, different administrations in Washington have adopted 'accommodationist rhetoric' and 'confrontationist policies' when it comes to Islamic movements in the Muslim world.[78] According to Fawaz Gerges, the United States suspects the irredentist intentions of the Islamists, and seeks stability in the oil-producing region of the Middle East. During the post 9/11 era, the Bush administration confirmed this, although this seems to be changing. In 2008 Condoleezza Rice, then US Secretary of State, wrote in *Foreign Affairs* that, 'Although we cannot know whether politics will ultimately de-radicalize violent groups, we do know that excluding them from the political process grants them power without responsibility.'[79] If anything, the Somalia case confirms that Washington would prevent radical Islamists from taking power in Mogadishu. For example, the United States provided political and military assistance to Ethiopia in order to weaken the Islamists in southern Somalia.

On the other hand, Somalis who fought against colonial forces, such as Sayid Mohamed Abdulle Hassan, used Islam (albeit not in the current Islamist form) to resist them. Islamic movements have clearly shown that the Islamic awakening or 'Islamism' is a potent ideology today. Moreover, Islamist movements developed a way to thrive during the military regime and during Somalia's civil war. What is obvious now is that Islamic movements of different brands, both mainstream and radical, are a permanent feature of Somali politics.

It is also clear that external actors can no longer keep Islamists at bay. As long as corrupt politicians, warlords such as Abdullahi Yusuf, Mohamed Dhere, Abdi Qeybdid, Yusuf Hagar, or clannish Diaspora members represent secularist views and forces in Somalia, Islamists will have a field day. Islamists are more credible than warlords and faction leaders. Most schools in Somalia are run by Islamist members. When one observes the business sector, the health sector and the security sector, Islamists also dominate. This leads me to the conclusion that Somalia's Islamic movements are enduring realities for the foreseeable future. If elections are allowed, Islamists will surely win as they do not have any credible domestic competitor. If peaceful options are denied, Islamist hardliners that are determined to use force to achieve power will dominate Islamist movements. They might also succeed, as they have defeated domestic clan militias several times in the past.

CONCLUSION

Islam is both an identity and faith to Somalis. Of significance to understanding the Somali conflict is the evolution of Islamist movements in Somalia over the past fifty years. There are both limitations and opportunities for Islamist movements in Somalia. Islamist movements are present realities. Strategies used in order to contain Islamists have backfired as Islamists return each time more experienced and more committed. As long as Islamists are challenged by external actors and hated warlords, they will enjoy the support of the Somali people. This makes Islamist rule basically inevitable in Somalia.

5
Understanding the US Policy toward Somalia

I would prefer that we lead from behind, and what I mean by that is pushing the Somali people first, pushing the sub-region next, and then mobilizing the resources of the international community.

Jendayi Frazer, former Assistant Secretary of State for African Affairs[1]

During the Cold War, the United States supported Somalia's military government that had led the country into its protracted civil war. After the regime was overthrown and the state collapsed, US interest in the country was sporadic. However, after the attacks of 11 September 2001, the Bush administration showed a keen interest in Somalia and argued that Somalia's collapsed-state environment constitutes a security threat to the United States and its interests. This chapter examines US policy toward Somalia, with particular emphasis on US policy after 9/11. It argues that the US approach toward Somalia has often been flawed and counter-productive, contesting that the United States's containment policy has dealt with the symptoms but has not addressed the statelessness problem that the Bush administration used to justify its limited and negative involvement in Somalia. Moreover, the chapter analyses the Bush administration's decisions to designate Al-Ittihad and Al-Shabab Islamic groups as terrorists and to freeze the assets of Al-Barakaat money transfer and telecommunication companies. It also explores how individuals, particularly the Islamists, perceive US policies and actions in Somalia. The chapter concludes with a brief discussion on the Obama administration's efforts to change the US policy toward Somalia.

CONTEXT

In general, the liberal values and institutions that the United States and its allies promote are dominant drivers and engines of world events. Somalia is no exception: Western policy influences the events that affect the already difficult process of peacebuilding in Somalia.

The following section will elaborate on US policies toward Somalia. US geostrategic interests in Somalia have undergone quite dramatic changes, from Cold War military support of Somalia to indifference in the immediate aftermath of the Cold War, to full intervention followed by a long period of disinterest, to renewed interest after the 9/11 terrorist attacks on New York and Washington, DC. During the Cold War the US provided significant military and developmental assistance to Somalia's military regime, including the training and equipping of Somalia's army. Lyons and Samatar write: 'Between 1983 and 1990, the US committed almost a half billion dollars in military assistance to the Somali government.'[2] When the Somali state collapsed in 1991, however, the United States left the country because of security concerns.

But a combination of civil war and drought resulted in tens of thousands of Somali deaths from starvation and, subsequently, the US led an international intervention into Somalia in early 1992. Although the US-led United Nations mission (UNISOM) did not end the conflict or reestablish the state, the intervention did prevent starvation for millions of Somalis. However, despite public support for the mission, a violent conflict broke out between the UNISOM forces and those of Mogadishu warlord General Mohamed Farah Aideed. On 3 October 1993, General Aideed's faction killed 18 American soldiers and wounded another 74. That day alone, the US forces killed or wounded more than one thousand Somalis in a deadly conflict in Mogadishu.[3] Soon after the Clinton administration decided to withdraw troops from Somalia, the US appeared to adopt a 'wait and see' position.

Following 9/11, US national security interests in Somalia shifted to a focus on terrorism, and specifically on the ways in which so-called failed states may provide a 'conducive environment' in which terrorist cells may organize, allowing them and illicit resources to cross borders undetected. Washington established the Combined Joint Task Force-Horn of Africa (CJTF-HOA) and dispatched troops to Camp Lemonier in Djibouti as a headquarters for the region. The CJTF-HOA, which consists of about 1,800 soldiers and administrators, works with governments in the Horn of Africa region to fight terrorism. According to the US Naval Forces Central Command, the CJTF-HOA would focus on 'detecting, disrupting, and ultimately defeating transnational terrorist groups operating in the region'.[4] Moreover, according to William Pope, Deputy Coordinator for Counterterrorism, the Bush administration committed $100 million through the East Africa Counterterrorism Initiative in June 2003, for the purpose of strengthening the governance capacity of several countries including Ethiopia, Uganda, Djibouti, Tanzania and Eritrea.[5]

With respect to the Somalia context in particular, in 2001 the Bush administration added Al-Ittihad al-Islami, a major Somali Islamist organization, to the US list of terrorist groups. The US also froze the assets of Al-Barakaat, the largest money transfer and telecommunications company in Somalia, and then listed some twenty Somali companies and individuals as 'terrorists'.[6] In March 2008, the Bush administration added the Al-Shabab Islamic movement to its list of terrorist organizations. Moreover, after it expelled the Taliban from Afghanistan in 2002, the Bush administration seriously considered attacking Somalia, arguing that the statelessness in Somalia may give terrorist movements an opportunity to organize and attack American interests in the region.[7] Although the US did not take military action against Somalia at the time, Somalia remained on the State Department's watch list.[8] In addition, the US was heavily involved in toppling the Union of Islamic Courts (UIC) from power in December 2006. To contain the Islamists' growing rise, Washington first supported Mogadishu warlords; but when the UIC defeated Somali warlords the US then collaborated with the Ethiopian government.

From the beginning (i.e., since 9/11 and the subsequent 'war on terror'), the US government has believed that there are terrorists operating from Somalia. Former Acting Assistant Secretary of State Charles Snyder stated in a speech he gave in November 2003 at UCLA's James S. Coleman Center for African Studies that 'there is an active Al-Qaeda cell that we have our eye on in Somalia. If we have to we'll take it out.'[9] In May 2005 US Marine Maj. Gen. Samuel Helland, commander of the CJTF-HOA, said, 'Somalia is a safe haven, it is ungoverned space.'[10] Moreover, former US Assistant Secretary of State for African Affairs Jendayi Frazer repeatedly asserted that the US government believes there are some terrorists in Somalia.[11] In fact, Frazer stated that three men who participated in the 1998 bombing of American embassies in Kenya and Tanzania were hiding in Somalia. Thus, in the Bush administration's view, the combination of widespread poverty and a lack of a functioning state in a predominantly Muslim country made Somalia a potential 'breeding ground' for terrorism.[12] The US has also become concerned with the rise of Islamist movements and their attempts to install an Islamic state in Somalia, groups which the US repeatedly targets as harbouring terrorists.

WAR ON TERROR: DEFINITIONS, PRINCIPLES AND GOALS

Both the 2003 US National Strategy for Combating Terrorism (NSCT) and the earlier 2002 National Security Strategy of the United States of America (NSS) define terrorism as 'premeditated, politically motivated violence perpetrated against innocents'.[13] In the 2003 NSCT President Bush said, 'we must use the full influence of the US to de-legitimize terrorism and make clear that all acts of terrorism will be viewed in the same light as slavery, piracy, or genocide: behavior that no respectable government can condone or support and all must oppose'.[14] This broad definition does not distinguish among all the actors who commit acts of violence in order to achieve political goals. In other words, it does not matter whether those who use terrorism are religious fanatics, national liberation movements, states, or warlords. Moreover, the victims of those actions also are not differentiated.[15] For the purposes of US national security, all acts of terrorism are the same and will be treated with the same response, meaning that the administration aims at discrediting the various tactics of terrorism.

The above two national security documents and senior administration officials insist that failed states pose a security threat to US vital interests because, like in Afghanistan, failed states might harbour non-state terrorist agents. One aim, then, is to prevent 'another Afghanistan'. According to the 2003 NSCT, the US will 'ensure that efforts designed to identify and diminish conditions contributing to state weakness and failure is a central US foreign policy goal'.[16] Moreover, in August 2004 Secretary of State Colin Powell announced the creation of the State Department's Office of the Coordinator for Reconstruction and Stabilization (S/CRS), which is tasked to deal with failing and fragile states.[17] Former US Ambassador to the Ukraine, Carlos Pascual, was nominated to serve as Coordinator of the new office. In 2006 Secretary of State Condoleezza Rice appointed Ambassador John Herbst as the new Coordinator. The United States Agency for International Development (USAID) also created a parallel office that works with the Department of State, which is intended to address the problems of fragile states.[18]

US strategies to prevent or deal with failing states in Africa, according to Walter H. Kansteiner, former US Assistant Secretary of State for African Affairs, include building democracy, increasing trade and investment, assisting Africa with HIV/AIDS, protecting the environment, and ending wars through conflict resolution.[19] Policies toward Somalia are, however, somewhat different. Kansteiner argues that goals that are unique to Somalia guide the administration's policies. The US policy objectives relating specifically to Somalia include 'removing the terrorist threat extant in Somalia and ensuring against Somalia's use as a terrorist base; preventing developments in Somalia from threatening regional peace and stability; and overcoming the long-term governance challenges that terrorists exploit to make Somalia a base'.[20] In addition, Kansteiner notes that the State Department has adopted five goals to guide policy efforts in Africa. Of these five, the US places most emphasis generally on the first: promoting democracy throughout Africa.

In a speech delivered by US Secretary of State Condoleezza Rice at the American University of Cairo on 20 June 2005, she stated, 'for 60 years, my country, the United States, pursued stability at the expense of democracy in this region here in the Middle East – and we achieved neither. Now, we are taking a different course. We are supporting the democratic aspirations of all people.'[21] But when it comes to Somalia, the US focuses on dealing with the terrorist threat and containing the problems of Somalia within its borders. In short, these are the principles that inform US strategies in pursuing the war on terror in Africa, and in Somalia in particular.

POLITICS OF ADDING AL-ITTIHAD AND AL-SHABAB TO THE TERRORIST LIST

As mentioned above, the Bush administration added Al-Ittihad al-Islami (AIAI) and the Al-Shabab movement to the terrorist organizations' list. The AIAI was an Islamist organization that was established in the 1980s. It claimed to be working toward the creation of an Islamic state in Somalia. Most of its members were students, teachers and professionals.[22] Since the military government of the day did not allow opposition parties, the organization operated in secret. However, in 1989 when the military regime became weak, the AIAI became public.[23]

Like most other Somali opposition groups, Al-Ittihad did not anticipate the quick disintegration of the Somali state. It expected, perhaps naively, that a democratic government would replace Siyad Barre's military regime. When Mogadishu fell to the United Somali Congress (USC), the Somali conflict quickly turned into a clan civil war. Confusion resulting from the complete chaos led the AIAI to take up arms. Members of the AIAI first fought against General Mohamed Farah Aideed of the USC, at the bridge of Arare near the port city of Kismayo. The AIAI lost this battle and moved to the north-eastern region's capital city of Bosaso. The people of that region welcomed them: Al-Ittihad was given authority to manage Bosaso's port and other important facilities because it was less corrupt than the Somali Salvation Democratic Front (SSDF) leadership.[24]

At that time, Abdullahi Yusuf, former chair of the SSDF who was released from Ethiopian imprisonment, was trying to take a leadership role in Somalia. Although there are only anecdotal reports on who started the conflict, many Somalis believe the SSDF leadership was not happy with the increasing influence of the Islamist organization. Thus they provoked a conflict and, with the help of Ethiopia, eventually defeated the Islamist organization, forcing its members to move to the south. AIAI members subsequently captured the city of Luq and several other smaller cities in the Gedo region in the south between 1995 and 1996. This time, Al-Ittihad made the area they controlled more peaceful and less corrupt. But, once again the leadership of the Somali National Front, particularly Omar Haji Mohamed, decided to fight against the AIAI. With the help of Ethiopian direct military intervention, Al-Ittihad was defeated once again. In 1997 the organization abandoned the idea of using force to achieve its goals and closed most of its military training camps; Al-Ittihad has since disappeared.[25]

Unlike Al-Qaeda, Al-Ittihad was an Islamic movement that had a local Somali agenda and as such it fought against warlords for control of Somali regions and cities. Yet, when it failed, as in 1997, Al-Ittihad laid down arms and retreated from violent politics. Scholars provide three possible explanations for such a decision.[26] First, the organization was defeated on all three occasions that it captured a city or an area militarily. It lost some of its finest and most dedicated members in the wars in which it participated. The leadership of the organization also became convinced that capturing and holding an area was not politically and militarily feasible for it.[27] Second, the idea of taking up arms became controversial and divisive among Islamist organizations and within the ranks of Al-Ittihad. A debate on whether there were religious grounds to use force within Somalia ensued among Somali Islamists in the 1990s. Those who opposed the use of force argued that since the people who were fighting were all Muslims, AIAI should not contribute to the suffering of Somali people. As an alternative those members proposed that the organization should be involved in peacemaking not in the war machine. Other religious groups also rejected AIAI's strategy of using force in Somalia. Al-Islah led what many AIAI members saw as an opportunistic campaign to discredit Al-Ittihad. It was common to hear the leadership of Al-Islah from the BBC Somali section and other media outlets condemning AIAI's decision to take up arms. In addition, other groups and religious scholars called for AIAI to lay down arms and contribute to overall peacemaking efforts.

The third explanation for the AIAI's decision to abandon the use of force, according to Menkhaus, was that the nature of the Al-Ittihad membership had become problematic. When Al-Ittihad captured a city the local clans became concerned about the incoming armed individuals from hostile clans. Al-Ittihad's rivals took advantage of this and mobilized the clans against Al-Ittihad. Menkhaus notes, 'the presence of outside clansmen was seized upon by the secular Marehan faction in the region, the Somali National Front, to claim that Al-Ittihad was a "foreign front" taking control of Marehan land'.[28] In fact, both Colonel Abdullahi Yusuf and General Omar Haji Mohamed openly argued that the Hawiye clan, which expelled people from their homes in Mogadishu, was using Al-Ittihad to create security problems in these regions. In 1996 the BBC Somali section aired a debate between Sheikh Hassan Dahir and General Omar Haji Mohamed regarding this issue. The latter asserted that the Gedo region belonged to his Marihan clan, and that Sheikh Hassan Dahir and the members of Al-Ittihad should leave the area. Sheikh Hassan Dahir rejected the idea of clan ownership of regions and territories. Interestingly, while some Darod faction leaders accused AIAI of being a Hawiye movement, supporters of General Aideed and other Hawiye warlords characterized it as a Darod front because they (AIAI forces) fought the United Somali Congress militias in 1992.

Al-Ittihad's Ogaden wing was spared the criticism that the main organization faced in Somalia. Since Al-Ittihad was fighting against the Ethiopian regime, most Somalis sympathized with this cause. Al-Ittihad fought alongside the Ogaden National Liberation Front for the same cause that Somali government leaders fought two wars and many skirmishes over the 'Ogaden' region. The idea of a greater Somalia was and still is alive among many Somalis. 'Ogaden' was under Ethiopian occupation for many decades. Unfortunately, the region remains underdeveloped. Moreover, Al-Ittihad first registered itself as a political party in Ethiopia. While this move suggests that the organization may participate in competitive politics, Addis Ababa banned Al-Ittihad and then fought against it.

Since giving up the armed struggle in 1997, most members of AIAI have become part of civil society groups working to deliver public goods such as education and health. If this is the case, then why did the US list AIAI as a terrorist organization with links to Al-Qaeda? As Ted Dagne writes, the link between AIAI and Al-Qaeda was exaggerated by the warlords and the Ethiopian regime. He notes:

some observers are skeptical that Al-Ittihad is an international terrorist organization or that there is a strong link between Al-Qaeda and Al-Ittihad. They argue that there are no credible reports that Al-Ittihad ever targeted innocent individuals, U.S. interests in Somalia or Africa. Some observers assert that Al-Ittihad does not have a regional reach let alone a global reach. Moreover, some Somalis credit Al-Ittihad for its social services and for restoring law and order in areas where it has maintained presence.[29]

Similarly, Menkhaus contends that the 'allegations of extensive and intimate ties between AIAI and Al-Qaeda have never been supported by any "smoking gun" – no Somalis appear in Al-Qaeda's top leadership, and until 2003 no Somali was involved in a terrorist plot against a Western target outside of Somalia'.[30] Menkhaus further notes that the focus of Somali Islamists, such as Al-Ittihad, Al-Islah and others, was on Somalia. In other words, the agenda of Al-Ittihad and other Islamic movements reflected on Somali issues in the Horn of Africa.[31] John Hirsch and Robert Oakley argue that from 1992 to 1993 some Somali warlords were attempting to take advantage of the US army's presence in Somalia. The warlords exaggerated the strength and motives of Islamists in the country. The leadership of the Operation Restore Hope mission, for its part, took all potential threats seriously. Hirsch and Oakley write,

In the beginning, Aideed, Ali Mahdi, SSDF leaders Abshir Musa and Abdullahi Yusuf, and other faction leaders were keen to tell Oakley and UNITAF commanders of the threat from the Somali National Islamic Front (NIF), which was reportedly receiving substantial support in training, weapons, and money from Iran and Sudan. Each claimed to be ready to take the lead in actively combating these Islamist radicals.[32]

Hirsch and Oakley conclude that the four warlords mentioned above provided wrong and misleading information in order to get

American support to further their political interests. In the opinion of many regional experts, Al-Ittihad focused on Somali issues where the only political process available was the use of guns.

Similarly, in 2008, the Bush administration added to the terror list the Al-Shabab movement, which had become public only in 2006. Washington argued that some of Al-Shabab's leadership were trained in Afghanistan and that they had ties with Al-Qaeda[33] because they provided sanctuary to three wanted men in Somalia. However, many Somalis disagreed with Washington at the time, and considered this group an idealist Somali Islamist movement with objectives similar to those of other Islamist groups. The Al-Shabab movement was instrumental in defeating Somali warlords. Although this seems to be changing, thus far most of Al-Shabab's military operations were against Ethiopian troops, transitional government militias, and warlords. Other Islamist movements also adopted similar strategies, with the exception of suicide bombings that Al-Shabab carried out against Ethiopian military bases and transitional government leaders.

Regarding Al-Shabab's link to Al-Qaeda, Al-Jazeera TV interviewed Sheikh Mukhtar Robow, the former spokesman for the movement about this issue. Sheikh Robow argued that although Al-Shabab is not directly under the command of Al-Qaeda, they share many ideological objectives and they benefit from the movement. For Robow, there is nothing wrong with that since Al-Shabab has been resisting occupation. In other words, idea wise, the global Jihadist agenda is expressed in Somalia through Al-Shabab, albeit they have not yet fought beyond Somali borders. That said, the rhetoric of Al-Shabab changed as the leaders said openly that they would send fighters to Yemen[34] and attack Kenya.

In contrast to Al-Shabab, Ethiopia and its proxy warlords have exaggerated and at times fabricated stories to link Al-Barakaat and Al-Ittihad to Al-Qaeda. The Commission investigating the 9/11 attacks could not find a link between Al-Barakaat and Al-Qaeda.[35] Moreover, and as mentioned above, Al-Ittihad has been a non-existent entity since 1997.

US SUPPORT FOR SOMALI WARLORDS AND THE ETHIOPIAN OCCUPATION

In addition to the US listing Al-Ittihad as a terrorist organization and shutting down the Al-Barakaat bank, the US also worked with some warlords to hunt down alleged terrorists in Somalia. Suleiman Abdalla Hamed, for example, was captured in Somalia with the help of Somali warlord Mohamed Omar Habeb.[36] The US also maintained that other terrorists who were involved in the bombing of the American embassies in Kenya and Tanzania were hiding in Somalia.[37] The Bush administration used this as a justification to give support to the hated warlords. The US has also conducted routine air surveillance over Somalia and patrolled its coastline.[38]

US strategy has been to contain any potential problem within Somali borders. Commenting on US strategy, former Acting Assistant Secretary of State Charles Snyder acknowledged that the Bush administration's policy toward Somalia was to contain the problem, not solve it. In 2003 Snyder noted, 'we [the US] have too much baggage... This is a problem right now that we're managing, not solving.'[39] At that time Snyder rejected the idea of the US leading a nation-building or even peacebuilding process in Somalia, arguing: 'we don't want to be the bus driver. We'd like to sit in the third row on the bus. We don't want to sit all the way in the back of the bus, but we don't want to be the bus driver.'[40] Jendayi Frazer, then US Assistant Secretary of State for African Affairs, agreed with Snyder, arguing that Washington would not openly lead the Somali peacebuilding agenda. Commenting on the Ethiopian invasion in 2007, she stated, 'we will lead from behind'.[41] This approach was interesting as Washington wanted to be involved but did not want to be blamed if things went wrong.

The International Crisis Group (ICG), the only Western think tank in East Africa, reported in July 2005 that US-backed counter-terrorism groups, Ethiopian-supported groups, and a Jihadist group have been fighting a 'dirty war' in the streets of Mogadishu for over a year. The ICG warned the West that its terrorism strategy was isolating the Somali people and thus the US war on terror was losing the hearts and minds of the general Somali public: 'unidentified surveillance flights, the abduction of innocent people for weeks at a time on suspicion of terrorist links, and cooperation with unpopular faction leaders all add to public cynicism and resentment. Without public support, even the most sophisticated counter-terrorism effort is doomed to failure.'[42] Although the ICG warned Washington about the potential danger of supporting Somali warlords, nothing has changed.

THE US ROLE IN DEPOSING THE UNION OF ISLAMIC COURTS

On 18 February 2006, a group of warlords announced the creation of an alliance called Counter-Terrorism and Pacification of Mogadishu. They told the media that about seventy international terrorists were hiding in Mogadishu and that Somalia's Islamic Courts were protecting them. Bloody war started within hours of the creation of the alliance.[43]

Hundreds of civilians died as a result of this clash and thousands were displaced. The Union of Islamic Courts (UIC) mobilized the Mogadishu people and defeated the warlords one by one. Mohamed Qanyare Afrah lost his airport in February 2006. He fled from Mogadishu in June 2006, and sought refuge in Jowhar. In addition, Bashir Rage lost Cisiley airport, El-Ade port, and a key checkpoint in Galgalato. Another warlord, Muse Sudi Yalahow, also lost a number of important locations including the city of Bal'ad (30 km north of Mogadishu). Other warlords such as Abdirashid Shire Ilqeyte, Abdi Nure Siyad, Botan Alin, Abdi Qeybdid and Mohamed Omar Habeb were also defeated. All of these men fled the country. Moreover, Yusuf Hagar and Barre Hirale lost the Hiran and Lower Jubba regions to the UIC.

The United States was implicated in these Mogadishu clashes because some of the warlords and merchants supported by America were involved in the conflict. The UIC openly blamed Washington for masterminding the attacks. The US Department of State, responding to these allegations through the BBC Somali Service, reiterated its support for the newly created transitional government and its concerns regarding terrorist figures in Somalia. The State Department did not say whether the United States actively sought the creation of the alliance.[44]

The chairman of the Union of Sharia Courts, Sheikh Sharif Sheikh Ahmed, told the media that Mogadishu warlords were involved in the kidnapping of about fifty religious scholars and that they handed them over to American and Ethiopian authorities. In one of his interviews he said, 'the danger is that when the US military leaders in Djibouti return religious scholars, the warlords kill them in the airports they controlled because they do not want people to find out what happened. Thus as many as fifty individuals have disappeared, and we suspect the number is even more than fifty.'[45] Islamists I talked to repeatedly recalled many atrocities that warlords such as Mohamed Qanyare, Bashir Rage, Abdi Waal and Abdi Qeybdid committed against innocent religious leaders. In particular, they spoke of the ruthlessness of Mohamed Qanyare and Bashir Rage.

When the UIC evicted warlords from their bases, they also removed all the checkpoints in the areas warlords controlled. They opened Mogadishu's international airport and sea port – an accomplishment that had proved elusive for several transitional governments.

The UIC also started cleaning the streets with the help of local people and school children. After the UIC's victory, warlordism piracy and political assassinations ended. Overall, women, children, the elderly, unarmed clans, and civilians appreciated and welcomed this change.

However, internationally, the Union of Islamic Courts' victory raised the profile of the Somalia case. Major US and Western media outlets carried articles and editorials regarding the Somalia issue. Several leading American newspapers, including the *Los Angeles Times*, *New York Times*, *Washington Post* and *Chicago Tribune*, criticized how the Bush administration was handling Somalia by supporting warlords.[46] Chairman Sheikh Sharif Sheikh Ahmed sent a letter to the Western embassies clarifying his groups' position with respect to international terrorism.

The US called for an international conference on Somalia. The Assistant Secretary of State for African Affairs, Jendayi Frazer, led this conference in New York in June 2006, and one of the outcomes was the establishment of the International Contact Group for Somalia.[47] Moreover, the Bush administration was not interested in moderating, or cooperating with the UIC. The US sponsored several Security Council Resolutions that clearly showed its intentions toward the UIC. Senior officials in Washington, such as Assistant Secretary Frazer, began to call on the UIC to halt its expansion into other Somali regions. Most importantly, the US argued that it was concerned with a small group within the UIC: the Al-Shabab movement.

In December 2006 after the Union of Islamic Courts expelled the notorious warlords from Mogadishu and surrounding regions, the Ethiopian government declared war on Somalia and ordered thousands of its troops to invade. Prime Minister Meles Zenawi asserted that the UIC was a threat to Ethiopian security.[48] As the *New York Times* reported, the Bush administration endorsed, if not masterminded, the Ethiopian move by providing the Ethiopian government with financial, diplomatic, intelligence and sometimes direct military support.[49] On a number of occasions US warplanes bombed targets in Somalia.[50] At the time of writing this chapter, things are changing quickly and it is very difficult to predict what will happen next. What is clear though is that the Ethiopian army has occupied Somalia for two years and the UIC, Al-Shabab movement, and several clan militias have waged a guerrilla war against this occupation. The US has also sponsored another Security Council Resolution (1744) which authorizes the African Union (AU) to send regional peace support forces – about half of the 8,000 soldiers have already been deployed. Although Ethiopia withdrew from Somalia, many Somalis believe the Ethiopian meddling haunts the state-building efforts in Somalia.

Ironically, Ethiopia's official rhetoric claims that it supports the transitional government, yet in reality its policies and activities point to the opposite. Ethiopia supports factions, clans and former warlords, at times under the banner of a religious name – that is the Ahlu-Sunna Wal-Jama'a. Those Somali politicians that have political ambitions frequent Addis Ababa in order to consult with the Ethiopian authorities. Several pro-Ethiopian and clan-based political parties are expected to emerge very soon. All these Ethiopian activities suggest that Addis Ababa does not want to see a stable and united Somalia.

The foregoing analysis begs the question as to whether Washington's containment policies address the challenges that Somalia poses and the statelessness in the country. It is obvious that the US response to Somalia does not address the conditions that produced the statelessness problems in the first place. Although the US argues that without a functioning state Somalia could be a breeding ground for terrorism, it has shown little or no interest in addressing the statelessness problem in the past. After 9/11, the United States adopted a strategy of identifying and destroying specific targets in Somalia. For instance, it carried out several high-profile military attacks in Dobley and Dusamareb in which Adan Hashi Ayro, the military commander of Al-Shabab, and another senior officer were killed in April 2008 by an American missile. The US commandos also killed Salah Ali Nabhan, whom Washington considered Al-Qaeda's Horn of Africa leader, on 14 September 2009.[51]

As stated above, the US opened a military base in Djibouti; it conducts routine surveillance on Somalia's coastline; it closed down Al-Barakaat Bank; and it listed Al-Ittihad and Al-Shabab as terrorist groups. Moreover, the US has supported some of Somalia's warlords and sponsored the Ethiopian occupation. All of these efforts did not end statelessness in Somalia – the root cause of insecurity in the country. Because of the 'war on terror' project, thousands of Somalis have been killed and more than a million displaced. Although one of the three men that Washington was seeking, Salah Ali Nabhan, was killed, many non-Somali radicals joined extremists in Somalia. Even worse, because of the Ethiopian occupation, anti-American sentiment has increased and the Al-Shabab movement has become a very powerful organization. The strategy of 'detecting, disrupting, and ultimately defeating' Somalia's Islamists has not worked well for Washington.

SOMALI PERCEPTIONS OF THE US ROLE

When I asked about peacebuilding challenges, many Islamists responded by saying that the main reason for the absence of security in Somalia is external and that Ethiopia and the global superpower are responsible for that. Responding to a follow-up question of the motives behind external actors' meddling, Somali Islamists and some of the country's intellectuals provided four reasons for the US involvement in Somalia. First, Islamists say the 'war on terror' is basically a war on Islam and since Somalia is a Muslim country, the United States is against the 'universal Islamic awakening'. According to one Islamist, the United States is in a modern 'crusade war' against Islam and Muslims.[52] Another Islamist said 'even George W. Bush admitted that', referring to President Bush's statement after the 9/11 terrorist attacks: 'this is a new kind of – a new kind of evil. And we understand. And the American people are beginning to understand. This crusade, this war on terrorism is going to take a while.'[53] Although the Islamists often articulated this view that the US was in a crusade-like war against Islam, it is a widespread belief as even average Somalis repeated this sentiment to me many times.

Second, another local interpretation of previous US policies toward Somalia is that the Bush administration adopted a 'hostile' attitude toward Somalia because it wanted to take revenge for the 1993 killings of the 18 American Rangers. Because the supporters of General Aideed, who was one of Somalia's main warlords, dragged dead American soldiers' bodies through the streets of Mogadishu, some interviewees asserted that the United States felt it needed to punish Somalis.[54] Even some intellectuals expressed this view, saying that this event had a deep psychological impact on the American leadership and policymakers. Interestingly, around the time the American soldiers were killed, the US intervention in Somalia was popular with most Somalis because it ended a deadly famine that had killed more than 300,000 people. However, the political aspect of the mission failed because General Aideed did not like the direction in which the US-supported United Nations mission was heading. He provoked the United Nations Somalia Mission (UNISOM) by killing 24 Pakistani soldiers during an inspection of a Somali arms weapons storage site on 5 June 1993. In response, the UN issued an arrest warrant against General Aideed. He fought back, and as a result, on 3–4 October his supporters killed the 18 American soldiers and dragged their bodies through the streets.

Third, other interviewees mentioned the rich resources that Somalia has, notably oil. One Islamist told me, 'Because of the current energy problems, the United States wants to make sure it has unlimited access to Somalia's resources, particularly the oil.'[55] Another agreed and said, 'Previous Somali governments gave concessions to the United States, and now China has persuaded some African countries such as Sudan to revoke previous concessions given to America. So the United States does not want this to happen again in Somalia.'[56] Similarly, several Western writers questioned the motives of the United States when it earlier intervened in Somalia in 1992. The *Los Angeles Times* published a series of articles arguing that the United States was more interested in oil than the protection of starving Somalis. For example, in one article, foreign correspondent Mark Fineman wrote:

> That land, in the opinion of geologists and industry sources, could yield significant amounts of oil and natural gas if the US-led military mission can restore peace to the impoverished East African nation... [and] whether the oil concessions granted under Siyad Barre will be transferred if and when peace is restored... it's potentially worth billions of dollars, and believe me, that's what the whole game is starting to look like.[57]

Most interviewees I spoke with did not hesitate to say that Somalia has vast oil resources. Perhaps one reason for this widespread belief is that, during the military regime, Somalia radios used to broadcast frequently about the country's God-given rich resources, promising that Somalia would easily satisfy its own needs when these are exploited.

Finally, the issue of Somalia's strategic location and how world powers have continued to compete for control of this area has been raised as a motive that drives external actors' intervention in Somalia. Amina Said, an activist Somali intellectual, contends that 'Somalia is still where it was when superpowers competed for its allegiance. It is strategic and they want to control it.'[58] Robert Weil agrees, and argues similarly that Somalia remains an important strategic country for the United States:

After all, Somalia is still where it was when the United States armed the dictator Mohammed Siad Barre to help win his allegiance away from his former Soviet backers. Situated at the bottom of the Red Sea, on the Gulf of Aden, right across from Yemen and Saudi Arabia, the Horn of Africa remains critical to the stability of the oil-bearing region which the United States defines as most vital to its interests, and over which it so recently fought the Gulf War. Chaos in this area of the world, no matter what its cause, is a matter of concern to those who believe that Middle East petroleum belongs to the United States and its imperialist allies. With Islamic fundamentalism now dominant in nearby Sudan, and having small but significant followings among some Somalis, and with neighbouring Kenya to the south in increasing turmoil, the country can hardly be left to its own purposes, whatever they might be.[59]

In an interview with Himilo Somali Newspapers, the late Mohamed Said Samatar 'Ga'aliye' also asserted that the major objective of the American intervention in 1993 was to control the Horn of Africa and the Red Sea in order to influence what was happening in the Arabian Peninsula, especially in Iran and Sudan.[60] In addition, even if the geostrategic argument is not as relevant as it was during the Cold War era, Somalia is still a strategic country for the US war on terror because various Islamic movements are active in Somalia. The issue of rising piracy in Somali waters and on the high seas further shows the strategic significance of the country.

THE OBAMA ADMINISTRATION AND SOMALIA: IS THERE ANY CHANGE OF POLICY?

When Barack Obama came to power in early 2009, a new sense of optimism filled the streets of the Muslim world and Somalia was no exception. President Obama quickly moved to dispel widely held negative perceptions against the United States. He gave an interview to the Al-Arabiya television channel and tried to explain to Muslims that the United States was not targeting them. He also visited Turkey and Egypt and delivered historic speeches in Ankara and Cairo. Regarding Africa, President Obama visited Ghana and addressed African leaders and populations on governance and HIV Aids.

From the start, Obama considered Somalia as one of the major challenges. His Secretary of State visited the region and met President Sharif Sheikh Ahmed in Nairobi, pledging support for the newly established transitional government, and calling it the 'best hope we had for some time'.[61] The Obama administration has also ordered an inter-agency policy review on Somalia. For now, it seems that the Obama administration's policy toward Somalia will be different from its predecessors', but the direction it will take is still unclear. Al-Shabab's increasing military power and its open endorsement of the other international extremist groups, the humanitarian crises, the government's weakness and the region's volatility will all contribute to how Washington approaches Somalia again.

Rhetoric aside, the Obama administration has not articulated a comprehensive policy towards Somalia. What is clear is that the United States is determined to support the transitional government. As some media outlets reported, Washington provided limited financial and military support to the Somali government.

CONCLUSION

The above analysis reveals the gap between the understanding of American policymakers and the perceptions of some of the important stakeholders, particularly Somali Islamists. The United States considers Somalia as a front on its 'war on terror'.[62] Based on its information, largely from Ethiopia and its allied warlords, the United States added Al-Ittihad and Al-Shabab to its list of terrorist groups. The US military bombarded Somalia several times and on the last attack killed Aden Hashi Ayro, one of the leaders of the Al-Shabab movement. The United States froze the accounts of Al-Barakaat.

Moreover, the US helped to destroy the Union of Islamic Courts by supporting the Ethiopian occupation of Somalia. The Somali Islamists internalized these actions using religious terminology. They say the United States is fighting against them because it does not want to see Muslims using their religion to solve problems. They also think that the United States wants to install a regime that gives Washington unlimited access to Somali resources. Finally, most Somali Islamists, intellectuals, and business groups I interviewed think that the United States is punishing the Somali people for the 1993 events when Aideed's supporters killed 18 American Rangers.

6
The Role of Regional Countries and Organizations in the Somali Conflict

At independence, Somalia was claiming parts of Djibouti, Kenya and Ethiopia and initiating armed conflicts to try and realize this dream. Its neighbours feared that a reunited and prosperous nation might resurrect Somalia's territorial claims.

Daniel Arap Moi, former president of Kenya[1]

Although post-Cold War conflicts occur largely within and not among states, neighbouring countries and regional organizations play a significant role in initiating or perpetuating these violent encounters. Scholars put forward various motives for the actions of regional countries. Some argue that since civil wars result in humanitarian disasters, neighbours intervene for benign, humanitarian motives. Others contend that civil conflicts can affect neighbouring countries by producing refugees and destabilizing the border regions, arguing that the neighbouring countries' intervention is for self-defence.[2] As Michael Brown argues, countries often intervene in their neighbours' affairs for opportunistic reasons or for pursuing their own geopolitical interests.[3] Of course, there are many motives behind any given conflict. This chapter examines the role that Somalia's neighbouring states, Ethiopia, Kenya, and Djibouti, and two regional organizations – the African Union (AU) and the Inter-Governmental Authority on Development (IGAD) – play in Somalia's conflict. The intimate involvement of these actors has been a continuing factor in the Somali crisis and one that needs to be addressed.

First the chapter examines the historically hostile relationship between Somalia and Ethiopia, analysing events between these two countries over three periods: pre-Somalia statehood (prior to 1960), during Somalia's statehood (1960–91), and after the collapse of the Somali state in 1991, and how, since 1991, as Somalia's historical enemy, the interventions of Ethiopia have prolonged the conflict in Somalia. Second, it analyses Somali–Kenyan relations, contending that Kenya facilitated Ethiopia's hostile policies toward the reestablishment of Somalia, albeit Kenya implemented its policies in a less confrontational manner than did Ethiopia. The chapter also discusses the positive role that Djibouti has played during the Somali conflict. Finally, it examines the role played by the AU and IGAD in the conflict, how these organizations, because of their lack of capacity, have uncritically facilitated the hostile policies of Somalia's neighbours.

ETHIOPIA: HISTORIC ENEMY AND HOSTILE NEIGHBOUR OF SOMALIA

Religious and ethnic rivalries have characterized Somali–Ethiopian relations in the Horn of Africa for hundreds of years. As early as the fifteenth and sixteenth centuries, historians have documented religious wars between Muslims which included ethnic Somalis and Christian Abyssinians.[4] The Ottoman and Portuguese empires were involved in supporting Muslim and Christian parties, respectively. However, as of the eighteenth century, territorial ambition and access to a sea corridor became the dominant drivers of the conflict between Somalis and Abyssinians. As Charles Geshekter notes, from 1891 Ethiopia has been expanding to the east. Ethiopia's King Menelik, for instance, wrote a circular in 1891 to the European leaders who were planning to divide Africa among themselves and demanded his share, writing: 'Ethiopia has been for fourteen centuries a Christian island in a sea of pagans. If the Powers at a distance come forward to partition Africa between them, I do not intend to remain an indifferent spectator.'[5] Interestingly, European powers acquiesced to King Menelik's demands and gave him the 'Ogaden' region of Somalia to appease him.

As John Spencer notes, a long-time adviser to Ethiopian Emperor Haile Selassie argued that Ethiopia could not survive without access to a sea corridor. Spencer justifies this assertion, recalling the Second Italo-Ethiopan War in which Italy easily invaded Ethiopia simply because France denied access to the Djibouti port and there were no other ports available for Addis Ababa. Spencer writes, 'After all, Laval had closed it [Djibouti port] and the railway during the Italo-Ethiopian war, thereby guaranteeing to Mussolini the defeat of Ethiopia.'[6] According to Spencer, a search for secure ports became a priority: 'The acquisition of seaports remained the ultimate challenge.'[7] As result, Emperor Haile Selassie began a campaign to claim both Eritrea and Somaliland as part of Ethiopia. In what Spencer calls the 'Green Memorandum', Ethiopia drafted a letter to the London (1945) and Paris (1946) conferences regarding these two territories, claiming that they were both part of greater Ethiopia.[8]

On the Somali side, Sayid Mohamed Abdulle Hassan initiated a strong resistance against colonial forces from the late 1890s to 1921. Although Sayid Mohamed's long liberation struggle against Great Britain is well-documented, Sayid's Darvish movement also fought against Italy and Ethiopia.[9] Moreover, after Great Britain defeated Sayid Mohamed the Somali Youth League (SYL) resumed the resistance and expanded to Somalia's different regions. It is this movement that spearheaded the idea of 'Greater Somalia' or Pan-Somali nationalism in the 1940s and 1950s. The idea behind pan-Somali nationalism is based on the creation of a united Somalia under one strong nation-state. Colonial powers divided Somalis (a homogeneous ethnic group) into five regions: Great Britain took two parts, Italy colonized Southern Somalia, France controlled Djibouti, and European colonizers gave the 'Ogaden' region to Ethiopia.

Although Somali nationalists were fighting for the cause of liberating and uniting all Somali regions, Ethiopia was openly against these aspirations and worked to undermine them. During the 1940s Ethiopia tried to annex Somalia, calling the country 'lost provinces' of Ethiopia.[10] Although Ethiopia succeeded in keeping the 'Ogaden' region, it failed to subvert or undermine the independence of Southern Somalia and Somaliland. However, this development channelled the conflict between Somalis and Ethiopians into an international one, since both were by then sovereign states and members of the United Nations.

Between 1960 and 1990, Somalia and Ethiopia fought two major wars. The first took place in 1964 and ended quickly, although neither Somalia nor Ethiopia won. However, Somalia captured most of the 'Ogaden' region during the 1977–78 war. Interestingly, the United States and Soviet Union were involved in one way or another because the conflict occurred at the height of the Cold War between two strategic Third World countries. In particular, the Soviet bloc (including Cuba, Yemen and Libya) intervened militarily and held back Somali troops.[11] Then the conflict between Somalia and Ethiopia turned into frequent but low-intensity skirmishes. Moreover, each of these countries provided military and political support for the opposition groups of the other. For instance, Somalia supported the Eritrean People's Liberation Front (EPLF), the Eritrean Liberation Front (ELF), the Tigrayan People's Liberation Front (TPLF), and the Oromo Liberation Front (OLF). On the other hand, Ethiopia supported the Somali Salvation Democratic Front (SSDF), the Somali National Movement (SNM), the United Somali Congress (USC), and the Somali Patriotic Movement (SPM).

Ironically, both Somalia and Ethiopia were members of the Soviet bloc between 1975 and 1978. Yet, being clients of one superpower did not help improve relations between them; in 1977 Cuban president Fidel Castro attempted to mediate the conflict between these two states in Yemen, but his efforts ended without success.[12]

As a consequence of the wars and sustained hostility between Somalia and Ethiopia, the Somali state collapsed and the Ethiopian regime fell. The TPLF, which was a client of Somalia, dominated the coalition that took over power in Ethiopia, whereas several Ethiopian-client Somali factions became prominent in Somali politics. For instance, General Mohamed Farah Aideed of the USC, Abdullahi Yusuf of the SSDF, Ahmed Omar Jes of the SPM, and Abdirahman Ahmed Ali 'Tur' of the SNM controlled parts of Somali territories in the early 1990s.

ETHIOPIA AND POST-STATE COLLAPSE IN SOMALIA

Many expected that a new era would begin for the Ethiopian and Somali peoples once the military governments of these countries fell in May 1990 and January 1991 respectively. The fact that the coalition group ruling Ethiopia took a long time to consolidate its power increased social optimism. Somalis who fled the civil war sought refuge in Kenya and Ethiopia. Although most of the Somali-populated refugee camps were located in Kenya, people who went to these countries would complain more about Kenyan police treatment than about the Ethiopian authorities. But, after Ethiopian leader Meles Zenawi consolidated power, Ethiopia's policies toward Somalia changed significantly. As time progressed, Ethiopia's meddling increased: it sent weapons to its proxy factions; micro-managed and/or undermined Somali peace processes; it attacked and briefly occupied border regions; and finally, it invaded the country and captured Mogadishu in December 2006.

Both superpowers, the United States and the Soviet Union, armed the Somali regime from 1960 to 1990.[13] But, after Somalia's state collapsed in 1991, Ethiopia became the major source of weapons for Somali factions. During the 1991–93 famine in Somalia when food and water were scarce, weapons and ammunition were abundant.[14] There are two explanations for this. The first is that Ethiopia itself was experiencing security problems. Officers and personnel of the military organized by Ethiopian prime minister Meles Zenawi were selling arms and weapons to anyone who could buy them. This is probable because at the time Zenawi's regime was weak and had not yet consolidated its power throughout the country. This explanation would have been plausible had the flow of weapons stopped after the early years of Zenawi's regime, but, to the contrary, the flow of weapons continued. The second explanation is that Addis Ababa was sending weapons to its proxies in order to destabilize Somalia deliberately and thus eliminate or weaken a historic enemy. Many Somalis interviewed for this book expressed this second opinion.

In addition to sending weapons to Somalia, Ethiopia has been heavily involved in the Somali peace processes. Ethiopia convinced the AU and IGAD that it should be assigned to mediate between Somali factions, thus taking charge of Somalia's reconciliation file.[15] As early as 1993 Ethiopia hosted the Addis Ababa peace conference for Somali groups. Two Ethiopian ministers, Dr Abdi Aden and Dr Abdulmajid Hussein, who were from the Somali ('Ogaden') region, organized the conference. Dr Aden, who later defected from Ethiopia and sought refuge in Canada, presented a paper in a conference that took place at the University of Toronto in 2002. Dr Aden asserted that he and Dr Hussein were ordered to make sure that the result of the conference was consistent with Ethiopia's interests. For Dr Aden, Ethiopia was not interested in helping establish peace or a functioning state in Somalia.[16]

Besides the Addis Ababa conference, Ethiopia organized two others for the factions it supported. The first was held at Sodere city in 1996–97. About 15 Somali factions, under the umbrella of the Somali Salvation Army, met and agreed to hold an inclusive conference in Bosaso. But this meeting never materialized. Second, after thousands of Somalis met in Djibouti and formed Somalia's Transitional National Government (TNG) in 2000, Ethiopia once again organized a conference for its proxies in the city of Awase.[17] The participating groups formed the Somali Reconciliation and Restoration Council (SRRC). Again, Ethiopian-supported factions succeeded in undermining Somalia's TNG.

Finally, with the help of Kenya, Ethiopia pressured the IGAD regional organization to sponsor yet another reconciliation conference in Kenya. During the 2001 IGAD summit in Khartoum, the Ethiopian delegation argued that Somalia's peace process was not complete, claiming that some of the key players were not yet included.[18] As a result, the Kenyan-hosted, IGAD-sponsored, and Ethiopian-dominated conference began on 15 October 2002. After two years the conference concluded with Ethiopia imposing a charter, parliament, and government on Somalia.[19] Nearly all of Ethiopia's proxies became parliamentarians. Moreover, these parliamentarians chose Abdullahi Yusuf, Ethiopia's long-term warlord and spoiler, as president.

Ethiopia complemented its strategy of undermining peace conferences it did not control and/or imposing its own peace processes with direct military attacks on Somalia's border regions; the Ethiopian military first started to openly invade Somali regions in 1996. Using the pretext of the Al-Ittihad al-Islami (AIAI), the Ethiopian military and air force attacked the Gedo region.[20] At the time, this region was a stronghold for the AIAI Islamic movement, one of the main Somali Islamist movements. The AIAI defeated the local Somali National Front (SNF) and imposed Sharia rule in the region. Ethiopia argued that the AIAI group was a threat to its security as it was assisting an Islamist group that was fighting in the 'Ogaden' region.[21] Moreover, by assisting the Rahanweyn Resistance Army (RRA) to re-capture the city of Baidoa in June 1999, the Ethiopian troops evicted Hussein Aideed's militias from the Bay and Bakool regions.[22]

When Somalia's TNG was formed in 2000, Dr Ali Khalif Galaidh, who was a prime minister in that government, waged an international campaign against the Ethiopian military presence in Somalia. Although this campaign forced the Ethiopians to withdraw troops to the border temporarily, Addis Ababa sent its forces occasionally to the Gedo, Bakol and Bay regions. After 1999 it became clear that where Ethiopia's proxies were powerful enough Ethiopia simply sent weapons, and where they were not as powerful the military got directly involved, thus changing the balance among Somali groups.

In 2006 the Union of Islamic Courts (UIC) emerged and defeated most of Somalia's warlords. They pacified most of the country and opened Mogadishu's international airport and port. Moreover, they evicted several warlords from regions outside Mogadishu, such as Lower Shabelle, Hiran, and Middle Shabelle. The fact that these Islamists defeated Somali warlords made the movement very popular among Somalis. Again, Ethiopia reacted to this development and claimed that what was happening in Mogadishu was a threat to its national security.[23] It sent thousands of troops to Somalia and captured Mogadishu for the first time in history. A combination of violent and sustained Islamist-led resistance and negotiation between the Djibouti-based Alliance for the Re-liberation of Somalia and the Transitional Federal Government convinced Ethiopia to withdraw its troops from Somalia in January 2009.[24]

In summary, the Ethiopian government has been involved both militarily and politically in Somalia's internal affairs since 1991. Each time an interim government has been established, Ethiopia has changed sides with warlords and supported the destabilizing side. Commenting on this pattern, Elmi and Barise write,

> When Ali Mahdi was chosen to head an interim government in 1992, Ethiopia supported his main rival, General Aideed. When Aideed became stronger and created his own administration in 1994, Ethiopia supported Ali Mahdi and his groups. When all Somali groups signed the Cairo Accord, Ethiopia recruited Abdullahi Yusuf and Adan Abdullahi Nur. When Somalis formed the TNG, Ethiopia organized all the opposition, helped them create the SRRC (Somali Restoration and Reconciliation Committee) and provided military aid to subvert the TNG.[25]

As Michael Brown argues, countries often intervene in their neighbours' conflicts for self-serving purposes.[26] Ethiopia has been doing this in Somalia for a long time. Addis Ababa contributed significantly to the collapse of the Somali state, as Ethiopia either created or supported factions that destroyed the Somali state. Ethiopia also perpetuates the conflict by undermining legitimate peace processes and imposing its own solutions on the Somali people. A case in point is that Ethiopia's opportunistic invasion resulted in thousands of deaths and the displacement of 1.5 million people, forcing UN officials to argue that the Somali conflict is 'worse than Darfur'.[27]

Ethiopia has released a document it calls 'Ethiopia's Policy Toward Somalia', in which it articulates its interests and goals as they relate to Somalia.[28] Ethiopia acknowledges its hostile attitude toward Somalia during the Siyad Barre era, arguing that Somalia was a source for many of Ethiopia's problems. Moreover, Ethiopia justifies its actions by claiming that pan-Somali-nationalism and Islamist projects are threats to its national security interests. Finally, Ethiopia acknowledges in the document that Somalia's ports could help Ethiopia's development. Based on these objectives, Ethiopia asserts that it wants to promote peace and security in Somalia, and as such it supports Somaliland and Puntland. A critical reading of this document reveals that Ethiopia wants to install a weak, friendly and divided Somali government that it could micro-manage.

KENYA: FACILITATOR AND BENEFICIARY OF THE CONFLICT

Historically, unlike Ethiopia, Kenya is a young state that has not had past hostile relations with the Somali people. Like Somalis, Kenyans themselves also lived under colonial rule. But in the early 1960s when Great Britain granted independence to Kenya it forcibly put together people of many different tribes. In fact, Great Britain appointed a commission that was to report on public opinion of Somalis in the Somali region. The commission reported that five of the six Somali districts in Kenya favoured unity with the Somali republic. But, Great Britain went ahead with its decision and made the Somali region the seventh province of Kenya. Initially the Somali Republic and Somalis in the region protested this decision. The Somali Republic broke off diplomatic relations with Great Britain and openly renounced the move. Somalis in the region mobilized to fight for their independence during the 1960s.[29]

In 1963 Kenya and Ethiopia signed a 'mutual defence-pact' against Somalia.[30] The rationale for this agreement was that the Somali Republic was irredentist and was seeking to unite all Somalis in the region. For Ethiopia and Kenya, this meant that they could lose the Somali regions under their control. Moreover, Ethiopia and Kenya collaborated diplomatically against Somalia, particularly at the Organization of African Unity (OAU) level. Ethiopia and Kenya capitalized on the idea that they faced a common enemy. Even though there was never a major war between Kenya and Somalia, the Kenyan government sided with Ethiopia in the 1964 and 1977 wars between Somalia and Ethiopia. Like many other black African countries, Kenya perceived Somalia as the aggressor state when Somalia and Ethiopia fought over the 'Ogaden' region.[31]

After several rounds of negotiations, the question of the Somali region in Kenya was finally settled in 1967 in Arusha, Tanzania. Although Somalis in Kenya have had their grievances against the Kenyan government, their situation is far better than the Somalis in the 'Ogaden' region. Somalis in Kenya have significant influence in the political direction of that country. That said, although Kenya is not as confrontational as Ethiopia, this background informs Kenya's policy toward the Somali Republic. While it shares common goals with Ethiopia, Kenya follows a different strategy.

When the Somali state collapsed in 1991, Kenya's policy toward Somalia followed Ethiopia's policy. Although hundreds of thousands of Somalis fled to Kenya, it shared the objective with Ethiopia that it did not want to see a strong Somalia re-emerge. President Daniel

Arap Moi openly admitted this in 2002 when he visited the United States Navy Academy in Washington. Kenya and Ethiopia feared another revival of the 'Greater Somalia' concept. Second, many Somalis, particularly business groups, moved to Nairobi and began to contribute effectively to Kenya's economy. Finally, almost all of the international organizations and non-governmental organizations that worked in Somalia began to operate from Nairobi, Kenya. When I was doing my field research I visited Nairobi and it seemed to me that this city had become Somalia's de-facto capital. I met with and interviewed Somali intellectuals, politicians, and officials, foreign diplomats that deal with Somalia issues, and the representatives of the United Nations agencies for Somalia in Nairobi.

With respect to Somalia's conflict, Kenya sponsored three of the 17 conferences (two small conferences and one major one) held for Somali groups over the past 17 years. Moreover, Kenya was actively involved diplomatically in the Somali conflict as its capital city hosted diplomats and officials involved in Somali politics. Although several factions accused Kenya of militarily supporting some Somali groups, the only conflict in which Kenya was openly involved was the military campaign against the Union of Islamic Courts in late 2006 and early 2007.[32] The Kenyan government used the pretext of the 'war on terror', meaning that while the United States provided air and naval support, the Ethiopian military did the fighting on the ground. Kenyan troops closed the border with Somalia and arrested many people who were fleeing the conflict. However, unlike Ethiopia, there is no evidence that Kenya has been sending weapons to Somalia. Moreover, all of Somalia's political groups, clans and warlords regularly have gone and continue to go to Kenya for political and business reasons.

DJIBOUTI: PEACE PROMOTER IN SOMALIA

In the late nineteenth century when colonial forces divided Somalia, France took control of Djibouti. Somali and Afar ethnic groups constitute the two largest ethnic groups in Djibouti, although Somalis are the dominant power there. During the liberation struggle Somalia's government and the Somali people played a significant role in efforts to gain independence in Djibouti. Moreover, Somali governments never considered Somalis in Djibouti as foreign citizens. Indeed, many Somalis from Djibouti moved to the Somali Republic and some even held important positions within the ruling party.[33] During the era of the Somali state (1960–91), Djibouti was largely an ally, although it had good relations with Ethiopia as well.

When the Somali state collapsed there was no evidence of Djibouti sending weapons to Somalia or supporting the warlords there. Instead, Djibouti sponsored the first two peace conferences that took place in June and July 1991.[34] Six factions met in Djibouti and selected Ali Mahdi Mohamed to lead an interim government. Both of these attempts failed because of domestic and external factors that were present at the time, including lack of will on the part of Somali faction leaders. In addition to these meetings, Djibouti organized another major conference in one of its cities in 2000: the Arta Peace Process. Based on the capacity and resources of Djibouti, according to Dr Ali Khalif Galaidh, organizing such a successful peace conference was a miracle.[35] More than three thousand Somalis, mostly civil society members, and the Somali Diaspora met and discussed the contested issues of their country. After four months of talks, Somalis enacted a Transitional National Charter (TNC), and formed a Transitional National Government (TNG) and Transitional National Assembly (TNA). Tens of thousands of people welcomed TNG leaders and it became the first government, since the Somali state collapsed, that received broad support from the Somali people.[36]

Although the peace process held in Djibouti was transparent, most warlords refused to participate in the talks. Moreover, Ethiopia rejected the outcome, arguing that the Arta peace process was incomplete. The reason for Ethiopia's hostile attitude was because most of its Somali client-warlords did not participate in the talks. Ethiopia organized its proxy warlords and undermined the outcome of this conference. Although Ethiopia and warlords were the two main spoilers when it came to the outcome of this effective and transparent peace process, the leadership of Somalia's Transitional National Government also contributed to its failure. Most of the members of the government had been senior officials in the military government. For instance, President Abdikassim Salad Hassan and Prime Minister Ali Khalif Galaidh were both cabinet ministers for Siyad Barre's military government. Moreover, within the first year, internal conflict marred their administration, and this eventually led to the removal of Dr Ali Khalif Galaidh from the premiership. In short, in Djibouti Somalia's peace process failed one more time.

In 2008 Djibouti again sponsored several rounds of peace talks among the Somali groups. The first took place in May, the second in June, and the third phase took place on 30 July. These talks eventually led to the formation of the Government of National Unity in February 2009. Although the record of the outcomes of the past Somalia reconciliation conferences is not encouraging, many Somalis are optimistic and they hope that it leads to peace in their country. Yet, it is safe to say that Somalis do not consider Djibouti as an enemy with its own agenda; they perceive this country and its activities positively. In fact, I met many of my interviewees in Djibouti. Some of them openly expressed their gratitude toward Djibouti, saying it has a positive influence and is doing what is expected from a brethren country. One Islamist summarized a conversation he had with some leaders of Djibouti, saying how they repeatedly mentioned how the existence of a strong and united Somalia benefited them during the 1980s.[37]

REGIONAL ORGANIZATIONS: INSTRUMENTS USED BY ETHIOPIA AND KENYA TO PERPETUATE SOMALIA'S CONFLICT

Somalia is a member of several regional organizations, including the Arab League (AL), the Organization of Islamic States (OIS), the AU and IGAD. For the last two decades the activities of the AL and OIS have been limited to passing resolutions calling for Somalis to end their conflict. However, the AU (from 1963 onward) and IGAD (from 1991 onward) have been heavily involved in the Somali conflict, either with neighbours or with Somalia itself. Moreover, Kenya and Ethiopia are also members of the AU and IGAD. For the purposes of this book I will discuss the AU's positions with respect to Somali peoples' interests during the past four and a half decades and will limit my discussion to the major events that occurred in the Horn of Africa during this period. I will examine how the IGAD reacted and contributed to the Somali conflict. I argue that Ethiopia and Kenya have effectively used these two organizations against Somalia since their inceptions.

When the OAU was established in 1963 the organization was mainly dealing with newly independent African countries and many African liberation organizations. The charter of the OAU recognized existing borders as colonialists left them, arguing that if Africans were to revisit them this would open up a Pandora's box.[38] Initially, Somalia's president, Aden Abdulle Osman, rejected that position, contending that it simply condoned colonial policies and led to a 'defeatist' conclusion. The president clearly stated his intentions by saying that 'the Somali government has no ambitions or claims for territorial aggrandizement. At the same time, the people of the Republic cannot be expected to remain indifferent to the appeal of its brethren. The Somali government, therefore, must press for self-determination for the inhabitants of the Somali areas adjacent to the Somali Republic.'[39] As such, Somalia's policy toward Somali regions under Ethiopia and Kenya was that they should become independent and then unite with the main republic, as Somaliland (a former British protectorate) did in 1960.

In addition to endorsing a position that Somalia's government perceived as serving the interests of its hostile neighbours, the OAU refused to recognize Somali movements that were fighting against the Ethiopian and Kenyan governments as 'liberation movements'.[40] This move had a significant impact on the definition of the conflict between Somalia and its neighbours. Subsequently, during the 1977–78 war between Somalia and Ethiopia, the OAU considered Somalia as the aggressor state. In other words, the OAU accepted Ethiopia and Kenya's argument uncritically: Somalia was pursuing an expansionist policy that was based on the concept of 'Greater Somalia'.[41] John Spencer, who was an adviser to Emperor Haile Selassie for over 35 years, acknowledged the advantage that Ethiopia enjoyed within the OAU, contending that Somalia had more friends in the United Nations General Assembly since many Arab and Muslim countries supported the idea of uniting all Somalis. To combat this, according to Spencer, Ethiopia always favoured the issue being referred to the OAU because Addis Ababa had more support than Somalia within the OAU.[42]

After the Cold War, global politics significantly changed, and the OAU had to adjust. The organization that many earlier called the 'dictators' club' now had to project a different image, one that promoted democracy among other things.[43] A number of articles of the OAU Charter were revised, among them article 4. Although the new African Union is still committed to the principle of non-interference, the Constitutive Act, particularly articles 4h (humanitarian crises, genocide and war crimes) and 4j (regime security), allows for situations where the organization can intervene in African states' internal affairs. Interestingly, the African states included article 4j of the Constitutive Act, which protects African regimes. If a government was overthrown, according to this article, the new AU would support the overthrown regime and it would not accept the opposition as the government.[44] Moreover, members of the AU created a new Security Council organ for the security of the continent. This consists of 15 countries from the five regions of

Africa, with three countries representing each region.[45] Ethiopia and Kenya represent East Africa, and they have effectively used the African Peace and Security Council (PSC) against Somalia. Most of the resolutions that support the Ethiopian agenda were passed at the PSC, and then the AU, and to a large extent the UN, followed suit.

IGAD, on the other hand, was created in 1986 by countries in the Eastern part of Africa. Originally the organization was established to help these states collaborate when dealing with natural disasters.[46] Between 1986 and 1994, IGAD was limited not only in terms of capacity but also in terms of mandate. However, in 1994 these countries revised the organization's charter and changed its focus to development. However, even after IGAD's mandate was revised, the organization did not have balanced and consistent policies toward its member states; particularly, IGAD did not articulate its approaches to conflict resolution.[47] Moreover, in 1994 Somalia did not have a government that could enter into an international treaty, as the country had disintegrated into small regions controlled by warlords. When Somalia's Transitional National Government was formed in 2000 it reoccupied its IGAD seat, but that government did not follow proper procedure: Somalia's Parliament at the time did not debate the issue of rejoining IGAD nor did it revisit the organization's changed mandate or the new charter.[48] The current Transitional Federal Government (TFG) followed a similar pattern.

When Somalia collapsed, both the AU and IGAD provided Ethiopia in 1992 with the mandate to assist in the reconciliation of Somali groups.[49] This was a careless decision on the part of these regional organizations as it did not take into account past animosity and conflicts between Somalia and its neighbours, Ethiopia and Kenya. El-Affendi writes, 'from 1992 Ethiopia was designated by the IGAD and the Organization of African Unity (OAU) as the main coordinator of the Somali peace process, a supreme irony given the history of conflict between the two neighbors'.[50] In agreement with El-Affendi's assessment, Barise and Elmi argue that expecting Ethiopia and Kenya to mediate between Somali groups is like 'putting the fox in charge of the henhouse'.[51] What many close observers warned against did materialize: Ethiopia capitalized on this opportunity and made sure that Somalia remained a collapsed state.

ANALYSIS AND IMPLICATIONS FOR PEACEBUILDING IN SOMALIA

Peter Wallensteen and Margareta Sollemberg observed that the role that neighbouring states play is significant in ending civil wars.[52]

As it happened in Mozambique, Guatemala, El Salvador, and to a large extent Cambodia, if surrounding states support and facilitate the peace accord of a warring neighbour it is likely that the conflict ends, whereas if neighbouring states undermine peace efforts, these efforts fail. Stedman writes, 'spoilers often exist because external patrons provide them with guns, ammunition, capital, and sanctuary. External patrons may also help internal spoilers survive by supporting their claims to legitimacy...'[53] This obvious reality exists in Somalia. Ethiopia, a very powerful and well-positioned state, is an avowed hostile neighbour that is determined to keep Somalia's status quo, as the above brief history of the relationship between the two countries and the analysis of Ethiopia's policies to undermine peacebuilding efforts in Somalia illustrates. Ethiopia largely controlled the Kenyan-hosted and IGAD-sponsored peace talks that took place from 2002 to 2004 in Nairobi. As such, Ethiopia deliberately excluded from the peace process the Islamists, business people, and nationalist intellectuals. In addition, members of these groups promote two issues that Ethiopia finds unacceptable, as its policy toward Somalia clearly demonstrates. First, Somalia's Islamist groups favour a strong and united Somalia where Islam is the main source of legislation. In other words, Islamists want to establish an Islamic state in Somalia. Ethiopia abhors this and is determined to block any efforts toward this end. Second, secular nationalist intellectuals would also prefer a strong Somali state, one based on Somali nationalism. Ethiopia is not interested in entertaining this idea either, as this might revive the concept of the 'Greater Somalia' or pan-Somalism.

Instead, as the practices of the Ethiopian government and its policies for the past 17 years suggest, Ethiopia is interested in establishing several clan-based regions that are hostile to each other but that have good relations with Addis Ababa. For instance, Ethiopia developed the building-block approach in 1997. According to this approach Somalia would be divided into four or five regions along clan lines. As a result, while capitalizing on the people of Puntland's dissatisfaction with never-ending bickering in Mogadishu, Ethiopia assisted Puntland Regional State in Garowe in 1998. Ethiopia openly supported this new state and Somaliland (which intends to secede from Somalia), arguing that the best and most practical approach in rebuilding Somalia would be a bottom-up approach in which regions form their own administrations.[54] Interviewees I spoke with, particularly Islamists, interpreted this move as an Ethiopian plot to divide the country into small and rival fiefdoms that would be under Addis Ababa's control. Furthermore, even though proponents of the building-block approach claimed it was bottom-up, in reality it was not. For example, local people did not elect their local representatives in Puntland. Instead, both first and second presidents, Abdullahi Yusuf Ahmed and Mohamud Muse Boqor, appointed regional governors and mayors of the cities of Puntland. In reality it was a highly centralized system that was just one level lower than the national government.

As one Islamist intellectual asserted, both Ethiopia and Kenya have large and active Muslim minorities. In fact, according to this Islamist, Muslims are now a majority numerically in Ethiopia even though they are a minority in terms of power.[55] He told me, 'Ethiopia, which historically considered itself a Christian island in an ocean of Muslims, is sensitive to this fact.'[56] Moreover, Ethiopia has portrayed Somali–Ethiopian wars as though they were motivated by religion most of the time. For instance, Somalia's military government in 1977–78 was far from Islamic or of any other religion. To the contrary, Siyad Barre promoted scientific socialism and suppressed Islamists. Yet, Ethiopian diplomats claimed that Siyad Barre waged 'Jihad' against Ethiopia.[57] Therefore, Ethiopia would not tolerate a powerful Islamic government next door. Kenya shares with Ethiopia this goal of containing the growth of Islamism. Although the Muslim population is a minority in Kenya, it is a vocal minority that wields significant power. Therefore, what happens in Somalia will have huge implications for both Ethiopia and Kenya. Such implications would threaten a status quo that is beneficial to the current Ethiopian elite.

Another benefit of the status quo relates to the fact that Ethiopia is land-locked. Access to a sea corridor and secure ports (or the threat of having no access) has been driving Ethiopia's policy toward its neighbours for the last two centuries. As Spencer notes, Ethiopian leaders believed that as long as they were land-locked the country's independence would not be fully achieved. In fact, according to Spencer the main reason that Ethiopia claimed ownership of both Eritrea and Somalia in the past was to get access to secure ports.[58] Ethiopia's current policy toward Somalia acknowledges the great need for ports. Mohamud Khalif, a Somali intellectual, put it succinctly: 'when Eritrea became independent in 1993, Ethiopia lost access to secure sea ports, thus finding itself in the same conditions that it has been in prior to 1951'.[59] As Spencer narrates, during the 1940s Great Britain offered Ethiopia the Zaila corridor provided that Addis Ababa gave up the 'Ogaden' region.[60] Ethiopia rejected this offer because, with the help of the United States, it secured the control of Eritrea in 1951. Since Eritrea is hostile and the Zaila corridor is not on the cards the only convenient option left for Addis Ababa is to install several client clan-administrations in Somalia.

In addition, there is a regional dimension to the conflict in Somalia. Eritrea is not only an independent country, but one that is now hostile to Ethiopia. Eritrea has also been a headquarters for Somali resistance groups that fought against the Ethiopian occupation, and it provided military and political assistance to Somali Islamists (both radical and moderate) and nationalists. For Addis Ababa, if Somalia is left to its natural forces, Islamists and nationalists might take control of the country, thus guaranteeing another hostile neighbour on its eastern border. Based on historical evidence, Ethiopia will not accept such an eventuality. For example, when Hussein Aideed collaborated with Eritrea in 1998–99, Ethiopia evicted Aideed's militias from the Bay and Bakool regions (Aideed's faction committed heinous crimes against civilian populations in these areas).

Ethiopia undermined Somalia's TNG and worked with Kenya to organize a peace process that they controlled together. This plan has worked as the Nairobi peace process resulted in a Somali charter, parliament, and government that reported to these hostile neighbours. After the conclusion of the Somali peace conference in October 2004, Somalia's sovereignty more or less fell into the hands of Ethiopia and Kenya. Whenever President Yusuf and Premier Gedi or Premier Nur Hussein wanted to take action they had to visit Addis Ababa and Nairobi. As a result, the worst came when Ethiopian troops invaded Somalia in December 2006. Whenever the Ethiopian military bombarded Mogadishu's residential areas, pro-Ethiopian politicians had to justify it by claiming that Ethiopians were fighting against terrorists even if the victims were civilians. A case in point is when Ethiopian troops entered the Hidaya mosque and brutally killed twenty clerics from the Jama'a Tablig in Mogadishu on 19 April 2008.[61] Although human rights agencies condemned this crime,[62] Somalia's prime minister Nur Hassan Hussein claimed that Ethiopians did this for self-defence.

Recently, two important events have taken place. First, in May 2008, the United States Senate passed resolution 541, calling for Ethiopia's 'responsible withdrawal' from Somalia and for an investigation into alleged human rights atrocities.[63] Moreover, in June 2008 the UN Security Council recognized Somalia's main opposition group, the Alliance for the Re-liberation of Somalia, and met its leadership in Djibouti.[64] These two events increased pressure on the Ethiopian government to withdraw its troops from Somalia. Subsequently, the Somali groups meeting in Djibouti agreed that Ethiopians would withdraw from Somalia within 120 days.

When Ethiopia realized it could not sustain a long-term occupation, it changed its strategy. As the United Nations Monitoring Group has reported, Ethiopia has begun to re-arm Somalia's friendly clans and notorious warlords, sometimes under the banner of Islamic names.[65] Somali media reported in the final fortnight of June 2008 that Ethiopian military leaders provided weapons to well-known Somali warlords such as Yusuf Hagar of Hiran, Muse Sudi (Mogadishu) and Abdi Qeybdid (Mogadishu).

In short, as the above analysis shows, Ethiopia and to a lesser extent Kenya have important stakes in either installing their own proxy government in Somalia or in perpetuating the Somali conflict for as long as they can. The strategies that Somalia's hostile neighbours adopt differ. At a time when the world would not allow an opportunistic invasion, Ethiopia sent weapons and created warlords from different clans. After 9/11, Ethiopia and Kenya capitalized on the 'war on terror' and used it to their advantage. As such, Ethiopia invaded Somalia as a part of a 'war on terror' campaign, albeit in pursuance of its own geopolitical interests. Kenya has also facilitated this invasion. This leads me to conclude that these countries are determined to block a viable and strong Somali state for as long as they can, as their perception is based on a zero-sum understanding of power.

CONCLUSION

Regional countries are important for either the continuation of the conflict or else building peace. Based on the above analysis, Somalia's neighbours and two major regional organizations have contributed to the perpetuation of violence in Somalia, mostly for self-serving reasons. Ethiopia has played a significant role in prolonging the Somali conflict by sending weapons to its proxies, undermining peace efforts, imposing its own solutions while using hated warlords, and eventually, by invading Somalia. Kenya to a lesser extent was involved in this saga, facilitating Ethiopia's hostile policies. Moreover, while it shares the objective of undermining the concept of 'Greater Somalia' with Ethiopia, Kenya also benefits from the status quo as well as shouldering a heavy burden: Many Somali businesses moved to Kenyan cities and most international organizations and NGOs that work in Somalia operate from Nairobi. On the other hand, Kenya now hosts hundreds of thousands of refugees. With respect to the AU and IGAD, these organizations became instruments in the hands of Somalia's hostile neighbours simply because these organizations lack the capacity and the understanding necessary for resolving the Somali conflict.

7
Peacebuilding Education: Contested Resource and Vehicle for Social Transformation

Kol haddaan garaad lagala harin, galabba sheeggeeda;
Inta maanku gaajeysanyahay, guuli waa weliye.

As long as people do not learn lessons from experience from daily events;
As long as the brain is thirsty and hungry, victory is far away.[1]

Mohamed I. Warsame (Hadrawi) 'Gudgude'

Although the Somali civil war destroyed most of the country's educational institutions, in its aftermath many non-governmental organizations (NGOs) and Somali individuals have been busy rebuilding the education system in Somalia. Two views are clearly present in the reconstruction efforts. On one side, Western NGOs and international organizations promote a secular education system that uses the Somali language as the medium of instruction. UNESCO (United Nations Educational, Scientific and Cultural Organization) and UNICEF (United Nations Children's Fund) are the leaders in this effort. On the other hand, Somali Islamists promote an Islamic-based education system that largely uses the Arabic language as the medium of instruction.

UNESCO and UNICEF, as well as Somali Islamists also teach the English language in their schools as a subject and occasionally use English as a medium of instruction. This chapter examines the level of destruction and the politics of reconstruction in Somalia's education system in the context of the collapse of the Somali state. It looks at the proliferation of private schools and Islamic schools, and also discusses the UNESCO initiative to help rebuild Somalia's education system. Interviews with educators and administrators from both sides reveal that there is negative competition between NGOs and Somali Islamists. Somalia's education system can play a role to advance peace through universal access to formal education, citizenship education, peace education and peacebuilding education.

For the purposes of this book, I use a general and inclusive definition of education that encompasses all types of learning in different contexts: formal, non-formal, and informal. Formal education consists of organized content and pedagogy that is delivered to students in schools with programmes that lead to certification. Non-formal education involves intentional planning but may not entail an assessment component. For example, the peace education component of citizenship education that is delivered to students but that may not lead to certification would be considered non-formal education. Informal education comes from everyday experiences from family, work, and other communal activities.

EDUCATION IN SOMALIA: BACKGROUND

Somalis have inhabited the Horn of Africa region for centuries. Compared to other ethnic groups in the region, the Somali language and culture did not only survive this long period but thrived. Earlier Somali generations passed attitudes, knowledge and skills to succeeding generations through the non-formal and informal systems of the local, indigenous Somali education system. Boys learned from their fathers how to herd livestock and protect their family and property, while girls learned from their mothers different context-appropriate skills such as sewing baskets, mats and other creations used for building a traditional Somali house (*aqal*).[2] Moreover, since most Somalis are nomads, and therefore do not have libraries and museums, they use their language, particularly proverbs and poems, to transmit to new generations what they have learned from life experiences. Some Westerners who have studied Somali culture and its oral tradition are amazed by the richness of the Somali language, calling Somalia 'the nation of poets'.[3]

Apart from language, Islam has served as a main source of learning for the Somali people. As discussed in previous chapters, the religion of Islam arrived in Somalia within thirty years after the birth of Islam.[4] Thus, historically Islam is a significant part of the Somali individual's identity. For hundreds of years, there have been many centres of Islamic knowledge which Somali scholars have visited in order to learn Islam. For instance, students of Islam have travelled to Mogadishu, Merca, Barave, Dinsor, Bardere, Harar and Jigjiga in order to learn the Arabic language, jurisprudence (*fiqhi*), Koran interpretation (*tafsir*), and other branches of Islam. As I noted in Chapter 4, Somali identity and Islamic identity go hand-in-hand for Somalis.[5] Thus, for this book both Islam on one hand and Somali culture and language on the other are considered to be the two main indigenous sources of knowledge for the Somali people.

Besides Islamic religion and Somali culture, many Somalis have also been exposed to the Western education system. Western powers have colonized Somalis since the nineteenth century. From 1884 to 1960 these colonial powers introduced formal schools to the Somali people.[6] In the north, Great Britain built the well-known Sheikh and Amoud secondary schools. Italian colonizers also introduced formal schools to the southern regions they colonized, while France did the same in Djibouti. These schools employed colonizers' languages as the medium of instruction and trained most of the Somali elites who later ruled the country when it became independent in 1960.[7] After gaining independence, particularly after the 1969 revolution, Somalia's military government built many schools, thus significantly increasing the number of students in formal education. For example, there were 20 secondary schools[8] in Mogadishu, the capital city, when Somalia collapsed in 1991.

ROLE OF EDUCATION IN THE SOMALIA CONFLICT

The correlation between school attendance and behaviour is a noted factor in conflict situations.[9] As school and curriculum help educators influence citizens' behaviour toward certain objectives, education can be both positive and negative in building peace or perpetuating conflict. According to Clayton Thyne the major reason for the positive relationship is that school attendance provides access to economic and political resources.[10] However, on the negative side, education is a valuable resource, which the group in power can deny to others, potentially resulting in conflict. Education can also be used as a tool for indoctrination, perpetuating conflict by teaching with one-sided hate curriculum books and history.[11] As Terrance Carson and David Smith note, in 1918 there was a strong movement in Europe that lobbied against the teaching of history. Education can be used to perpetuate certain politico-historical and racial biases; it can be used to transform conflicts by teaching key values of tolerance, respect, empathy, and other inclusive and useful values.[12] In general, the fact that one attends school and becomes literate can have a positive effect on the behaviour of individuals.[13]

In Somalia, education, particularly formal education, is largely seen as a positive force. Most interviewees I spoke with saw reason to encourage formal education, primarily because it increased economic opportunity, albeit this view has colonial roots. But such assertion needs to be qualified. The interviewees were commenting on opportunities that come with formal education, not on the other forms of non-formal and informal indigenous educational systems. In fact, no matter how much one knows about indigenous knowledge, little material value is attached to such knowledge systems. A minor exception might be knowledge of Islam. Although Somalis highly respect religious scholars, religious schools (i.e., Koran schools) compared to Western schools are different in terms of the buildings used, equipment employed, and dress codes. Furthermore, this qualification is necessary because many practices that are embedded in the Somali culture, such as collective punishment, a culture of vendetta, and negative clan competition,[14] fuel mistrust among Somali clans.

Although formal education is generally perceived positively in Somalia, prior to 1969 education was largely available only to those who lived in major towns and those who could pay for it. After the 1969 revolution, however, access to education improved. For instance, through the revolution's self-help programmes, hundreds of schools were built throughout Somali regions and towns, although the quality of education was compromised. Moreover, in 1972 for the first time a standard orthography or script of the Somali language was incorporated. The script, based on the Roman language was instigated by Siyad Barre's military regime, which also began an extensive literacy campaign in the country.[15] Yet, different regions and clans in Somalia have experienced regime implementations differently. That is, Somalia's regions and clans did not benefit equally from developments in education during the 1970s and 1980s. The formal education system in Somalia was still largely concentrated in urban centres. Somalis who traditionally settle in rural areas were disadvantaged in accessing all government services, including education. Yet, no violent conflict erupted between two clans or between one clan and the state because of lack of access to education.

Although the education system was available to Somalis in urban centres during the military revolution, it was used to advance socialist ideology, thus not strengthening Somali patriotism. Instead, the regime mandated schools to teach scientific socialism. I remember my early grades; we were introduced to Marx and Lenin and other socialist figures in a subject that was called 'revolution'. Students of schools in Canada and elsewhere usually sing their national anthem before the school day begins. In Somalia, we would sing a song that praised General Mohamed Siyad Barre: 'Gulwade Siyaad,

Aabihi garashada, geesigayagow' (Siyad, the pioneer of victory, the father of knowledge, our hero) every day before classes. This was contradictory behaviour on the part of the regime. On one hand the regime showed, more than any other Somali government, its commitment to expand the education system by building many schools and adding new faculties of the Somali National University. On the other, the quality and objectives of the education system suffered heavily.

Somalia's education policy, particularly regarding language, was inadequate, as the primary, intermediate and secondary schools did not properly prepare students for higher education. After the Siyad Barre regime wrote the Somali script, it changed the medium of instruction to the Somali language. It hastily ordered education experts to translate texts into the Somali language. Although such a decision appeared to support nationalistic aims, it had unintended consequences. Students graduated from secondary schools proficient only in the Somali language. The Arabic language was in the curriculum from grades 1 to 12, while the English language became a subject in grade 9. Ironically, English, Italian and Arabic were the mediums of instruction in the Somali National University. For example, most students that joined the university had to learn Italian within six months in order to get a higher education while a significant portion had to learn English on their own accord, through the Lafole College of Education at Somalia National University.[16]

Despite the poor quality of and limited access to education, this was not one of the major grievances that resulted in the Somali civil war. There were other political, security and economic problems that caused the fighting. Still, there was corruption in the education system. I came across many Somalis from different regions who complained that they were denied the scholarships they earned. But, this was both a corruption-related problem and a society-wide phenomenon. This, however, does not mean that education cannot and should not play an important role in building peace in Somalia.

POLITICS OF RECONSTRUCTION

After the collapse of the Somali state in 1991, most of the schools were destroyed or abandoned. Indeed, between 1991 and 1996, few schools were open in the whole country. Many people who lived in major cities were forced to leave their homes and flee to areas where their clans traditionally settled. Some displaced people lived in government buildings, including schools, and refused to vacate. Since there was no functioning state that had a monopoly over violence, some of the business warlords traded education and government institutions for money. For example, a gunman occupied a school in Mogadishu. After several years of the gunman living there, a group of Islamist educators came to him and asked him to vacate because they wanted to use the building as a school. The man refused and demanded money. I am told that in order to avoid bloodshed, the Islamists paid the man money and also employed him as a janitor and security guard at the school.[17] Similar cases happened in Mogadishu and other major cities after the civil war.

Destruction and occupation of schools, lack of textbooks and educational equipment, and the absence of a policy-making authority have greatly affected access to education in Somalia. For instance, UNICEF reported that as of 2006, there were only 393,856 students enrolled in schools and 12,787 teachers in Somalia and that most of these teachers were poorly educated and trained.[18] This is one of the lowest enrolment rates in the world. According to the 2007 Millennium Development Goals Report, more than 81 percent of school-age children do not have access to education. Moreover, about 81 percent of Somalis are illiterate.[19] The cost of such limited access to education is huge for Somali society. The UNDP writes:

> Due to the civil war, an estimated one-and-a-half million 'youth' missed out on any kind of educational opportunities so were unable to develop their potential for their own benefit, that of their societies or their country. In Central South Somalia, male youth without education, marketable skills and access to the labour markets have been enticed to make a living through the use of the gun by joining militias, even at a young age, not necessarily by choice but lack of other survival options.[20]

Despite this limited access, as early as 1993 many Islamist-led NGOs started private Islamic schools that used Arabic as their medium of instruction. UNESCO and UNICEF also decided to revive the Somali curriculum and rebuild or help set education policy throughout the country.

There was suspicion from both sides initially. Mohamed Abdulkadir, a well-respected educator and one of the owners of Imam Shafi'i Islamic School, considered the best school in Mogadishu, narrated a story about how UNESCO and UNICEF approached the reconstruction of the Somali education system. He told me:

UNESCO and UNICEF initiated their project in 1997. They divided the country into three zones: Somaliland, Puntland and South-Central. Then they organized a meeting in Galkayo in 1999 and brought experts, although it was not that beneficial. A decision to write textbooks from grades 1 to 8 was made. Interestingly, they asked us to write the books in English even though we could write them in Somali. Then they hired translators who translated them into Somali. After that they asked us to review how the translators did the job. I wrote math texts.[21]

While those on the UNICEF/UNESCO side would explain such a process as one that was intended to serve transparency, Somalis, particularly Islamist educators, interpreted such a move as serving the purpose of control by UNESCO since the education sector was heavily dominated by Islamists. Mohamed Abdulkadir added that in his view, 'the complete monopoly of UNESCO/UNICEF damaged the ownership of this project. Somalis call these texts the UNESCO texts and UNESCO officials do not like that. They would like Somalis to take the ownership.'[22] According to some interviewees, the Islamist-dominated Formal Private Education Network in Somalia (FPENS) decided to go its own way because the members of this organization wanted Arabic textbooks that had Somali content. Islamist groups drafted their own policy and started writing their own texts. They approached some Arab-based NGOs and international institutions. The Islamic Development Bank and the World Assembly of Muslim Youth helped print textbooks for grades 1 through 9 in six subjects (math, science, history, civics, Arabic language, and Somali and Islamic Studies).

The UNESCO/UNICEF and the FPENS curricula differ in three important ways. First, the medium of instruction for the UNESCO/UNICEF curriculum is the Somali language while FPENS uses Arabic. Second, UNESCO/UNICEF is based on Somalia's traditional education structure, which consisted of four years of primary, four years of intermediate and four years of secondary school. The schools under the FPENS umbrella adopted a different model, used in Arab countries: The primary school consists of six years, followed by three years of junior secondary school and three years of secondary school. Finally, the UNESCO/UNICEF approach includes social studies as a subject while the FPENS curriculum includes both history education and citizenship education.

UNESCO/UNICEF printed two different textbooks, one for Somaliland and one for the rest of Somalia. The reason for this decision is that Somaliland is interested in seceding from the rest of Somalia and the authorities in the Ministry of Education in Hargeysa refused to accept textbooks that contain similar contents to the rest of Somalia. Commenting on this, Paul Gomis, UNESCO's country director for Somalia, said, 'Printing the books was a politicized process. All stakeholders were there and it was difficult to convince them all. You can't produce books for each part. We don't want to entertain division.'[23] Save the Children's Toby Kay agrees with this politicization of the education system and expressed similar frustrations. Ironically, although they did not explain how they managed, the Islamist-led FPENS operate in all parts of Somalia. Yet, they did not print different textbooks for the different regions.

EDUCATION AND IDENTITY

Somalia has been categorized as a 'collapsed state' since 1991. The civil war destroyed most of Somalia's state institutions. As some scholars argue, in order to rebuild the country a comprehensive nation-building project is necessary. Andrea Kathryn Talentino defines nation building as 'the process of creating a stable, centralized, and cohesive state that represents a definable community'.[24] Often, such activities consist of state building and identity building. In Somalia, education is crucial for both. In particular, according to Talentino, reconstructing national identity is necessary in order to build durable peace for any recovering society. Talentino writes, 'ultimately, acceptance of, and commitment to, the processes of the state – belief in their legitimacy, a sense of ownership in their representation, and even pride in their development – are essential in building a sense of identity'.[25]

There are three important identities that are relevant to both the analysis of the conflict and exploration of possibilities for reconstruction in Somalia: clan identity, Islamic identity, and the Somali national identity. Two of these identities – clan and Islamic – have their own indigenous education systems that nourish, support, and thicken them. Clan identity is linked to the cultural and language sources of education. Although largely informal and non-formal, most Somalis get their knowledge of the clan system from family and society. As I.M. Lewis notes, clan identity is fluid and largely dependent on whom one is talking to.[26] Yet, most Somalis understand well how this complex identity functions, how each generation passes the required knowledge to the next.

Islamic identity also has its links to Islamic sources of education. Unlike clan identity, Islamic identity has a faith component to it in that people believe the knowledge it entails is from God. One reads the Koran, traditions of the Prophet Muhammad, history of Islam, and books on jurisprudence and spiritual education in order to understand behaviours and attitudes consistent with this Islamic identity. It is worth noting here that clan and Islamic identities do inform each other within the Somali context. Members of clans use knowledge and behaviour rooted in Islam while Islamic identity is sometimes overpowered by non-Islamic cultural practices.

Somali national identity is not linked to any meaningful indigenous education system. Although it has ethnic components, having a national identity is fairly new for the Somali individual. While explaining the achievements of the Somali Youth League (SYL), former prime minister Abdirizak Haji Hussein, remarked, 'When a Somali is asked who are you, he or she used to say I am clan X prior to the 1940s. SYL changed that habit because when asked, the members of SYL started to respond saying I am Somali.'[27] In other words, this identity is consistent with the concept of the nation-state, which in itself is foreign to Somalis. While Somalis may feel their ethnic identity when dealing with external ethnic groups such as the Oromo of Ethiopia, this is largely absent for most Somalis since they live in the hinterland and do not interact with non-Somali ethnic groups. In addition, between 1960 and 1991 the Somali state had not invested in constructing this identity simply because it took for granted that since the majority of Somalis shared ethnicity, and since Somali national identity was superior to clan identity, it would prevail over all other identities in Somalia. As a result, while both clan and Islamic identities are thick or strong within Somalis, the Somali national identity is very thin in Somalia (although this seems to be changing for the Somali Diaspora).

The lack of national identity creates a major challenge for nation building in Somalia. If Somalia is to become a functioning nation-state, either Somalia's national identity or its Islamic identity has to be constructed using both the state and the education system. In particular, citizenship education, peace education, and peacebuilding education programmes can be employed to this end. One reason for this argument is that clan identity is so divisive it has to be de-emphasized. In contrast, the Islamic identity is inclusive but it has external enemies. As the quote at the start of this chapter suggests, both Ethiopia and the West would not encourage such an identity becoming strengthened.

CITIZENSHIP EDUCATION IN SOMALIA

The conception of citizenship in any given state generally affects citizenship education. W.C. Parker argues that the purpose of citizenship education is teaching 'enlightened political engagement'.[28] He asserts that school and curriculum can be employed in order to produce enlightened citizens. While the state may seem to have a say in how it teaches the virtues of citizenship, this is particularly difficult in the case of Somalia because groups within the state disagree on the interpretation of the past, the role of heroes, sources of myths and ownership of literature.

The military government of the Sayid Barre era (1969–91) was aware of the importance of using education to influence the thinking of its citizens. As a result, the former ministry of education built many schools and designed a Somali-owned curriculum. Yet, subjects such as history and geography mostly focused on world history and Muslim world history. There was one subject called 'Somali Language' and another called 'Literature' (*suugaan*), which taught students Somali literature and a history of the country and its people.

After the civil war, some intellectuals questioned how literature and curriculum had been used. For instance, Ali Jimale Ahmed and Abdi M. Kusow argue that certain clans wrote their own literature and narrative of events while using the state to impose those same narratives on other clans.[29] Other groups, such as members of the Jareer Weyne tribe, felt that their history was not included in the formal curriculum and that the revised curriculum reprinted by UNESCO insults them. In addition, there are more and more voices discussing the role that education should take in rebuilding Somalia. For instance, Somaliland, the stable region that wants to secede from the rest of Somalia, has pressured UNESCO and other agencies to fund a unique curriculum that would teach its students the history of the struggle of the Somali National Movement. The SNM was controlled by the Isaaq clan that fought against the Siyad Barre regime.

Many Somalilanders desire such a curriculum because they believe their students should know about the struggle they carried out in order to get 'their independence' from the south. This surprised Paul Gomis (Country Director of UNESCO) who told me that 'the 4.5 clan formula [where four clans get 61 seats of parliament and several smaller clans get 31 seats] is a problem. Some clans want their history written in their own way.'[30] Furthermore, the two systems of education – Islamic-informed and secular – both different in nature, are at odds in Somalia. The FPENS curriculum emphasizes an Islam-informed education. Somalis consider Islam as both their faith and part of their indigenous identity. On the other hand, the UNESCO/UNICEF curriculum is expected to contribute to the objective of building a state that is based on liberal democracy and a market economy. Toby Kay of Save the Children, noted this fact and said, 'Harmonizing Islamic and secular schools is a major challenge.'[31] The presence of these two education systems and the different actors involved in them will have strong policy implications for Somalia's education system.

Interviewees from both secular and Islamist groups confirmed the current efforts of reconstructing Somalia's education system that include citizenship education. I was also able to take a close look at the books printed by UNESCO/UNICEF and FPENS. In the UNESCO curriculum, social studies textbooks for different grades entail sections that teach citizenship education. For instance, in grades 3 and 4, students learn appropriate and expected behaviours for responsible citizens such as obeying the law, helping people, and taking care of the environment. Moreover, students learn about different regions and the structure of local governments. Interestingly, when learning about these regions one cannot help but notice the difference between Somaliland and the rest of Somalia. UNESCO and UNICEF conceded to the authorities in Hargeysa and thus students in Somaliland, for example, do not learn about the southern regions whereas students in the rest of Somalia do learn about the Somaliland regions.

FPENS, however, adopted a different approach. From grade 1, students are required to take a citizenship education course (e.g., 'Tarbiya – Al-Wataniya'). I located three textbooks for grades 7, 8 and 9. Their contents shows that students learn about rights and responsibilities of citizens, universal human rights, human rights and Islam, the ethics of dialogue and debate, work ethics, issues of the security of the country, respect for law, and many other important and relevant values for citizenship. Clearly, with respect to citizenship education, FPENS' stated approach is more advanced and detailed than the stated UNESCO/UNICEF approach. Mohamed Abdulkadir was very happy to see this curriculum in Somali schools and said to me, 'FPENS brought experts together to write the content of this curriculam. For instance, we teach our students about the history of our heroes and our religious scholars.'[32] However, FPENS books are written in Arabic while

UNESCO/UNICEF books are written in Somali. Whether it is an unintended consequence or by design, students from FPENS often get their higher education from Arab countries, particularly Sudan, Yemen and Egypt. This is an interesting phenomenon because if one looks at the leaders and intellectuals of the Islamist organization, almost all of them graduated from universities in the Arab world.

PEACE EDUCATION IN SOMALIA

If education in general is important for reducing violence, then peace education is even more important in building peace. As discussed in the introductory chapter, this book utilizes Michael Wessels' and Susan Fountain's understandings of peace education. In Somalia, peace education programmes are rarely used. One reason for this is, as mentioned previously, formal education is not widely accessible to all Somalis. Second, both resources and experts in the area of peace education are non-existent. For instance, while UNICEF and UNESCO fund peace education programmes in other post-conflict contexts such as Liberia and Sierra Leone, they do not fund similar projects in Somalia to the same extent. There is only one programme, Geedka Nabadda (Tree of peace), that UNESCO funded from 1992 to 1993. This programme was a radio play in which several Somali artists performed. About 50 segments of the series were aired through the BBC Somali service. Since then, no other independent peace education programme has been funded.

In addition, both curricula (UNESCO/UNICEF and FPENS) do not explicitly or implicitly include peace education modules. This is not to say that there are no related topics within these curricula. In fact, FPENS' citizenship education course and the UNESCO/UNICEF social study subject have sections that teach relevant peace values. In other words, the few Somali students who access education are not directly taught peace or conflict resolution skills. Paul Gomis acknowledged this shortcoming and tried to justify it, telling me that 'We are all donor-driven. There is a donor disinterest in the area of culture of peace.'[33] Interview data from Somali educators reveals that they do not intentionally use peace education programmes in order to affect students' behaviour. Most educators I talked to have assumed that education, in general, has side benefits that contribute to positive behaviour. It was obvious to me that they did not think about specifically using peace education programmes in schools. Some of them were even open about it, saying that they did not try or it did not occur to them to try.

PEACEBUILDING EDUCATION IN SOMALIA

For Kenneth Bush and Diana Saltarelli peace education as a concept is too narrow for societies that are recovering from civil conflict. These authors call for peacebuilding education, which may include both citizenship education and peace education programmes. They say that a programme can be called peacebuilding education when war-torn societies own and drive it and when it corresponds well with the culture and experiences of the society. Moreover, for Bush and Saltarelli peacebuilding education programmes have to address concrete problems:

> Peacebuilding education – like peacebuilding itself – would be a bottom-up rather than top-down process, driven by war-torn communities themselves, founded on their experiences and capacities. It would be firmly rooted in immediate realities, not in abstract ideas or theories. It would be applied, immediate, and relevant, which means that it cannot be restricted to the classroom.[34]

Like Bickmore, Bush and Saltarelli conceive of education very broadly. They argue that education includes all kinds of learning activities including contents and pedagogies in the different subjects of math, sciences and humanities, delivered formally, non-formally and informally and targets all age groups. Such a broad conception is necessary because, as Bush and Saltarelli state, children are not 'blank slates'.[35] The context and environment in which children live transmit attitudes, knowledge, values and skills to them. But this is not a one-way street: while parents and society influence children, these youngsters can also transmit the values and attitudes they learn from schools to the wider society.[36] Therefore, it is necessary to expand the objectives of education and use it to target both children and adults in order to have maximum impact.

War-torn societies do not often have the luxury of functioning institutions such as schools and hospitals. Therefore, peacebuilding educators are forced to employ non-formal and informal programmes that are suitable for the context. In fact, Bickmore argues, peace could be taught and it could be learned formally, informally and non-formally.[37] Although peace education and peacebuilding education programmes would be more effective when integrated into the curriculum, non-formal and informal programmes have also proven effective in certain contexts. In fact, sometimes non-formal and informal programmes yield better results than do formal ones. It is preferable to have both so that they complement each other, but this is not always possible.

In 2003, although the use of peace education and peacebuilding education programmes in formal schools was minimal, there was one non-formal peacebuilding education programme that attracted the attention of most Somalis. Somalia's legendary poet and composer, Mohamed I. Warsame 'Hadrawi', during his famous peace caravan in 2003, visited most of the country from Kismayo to Bosaso and shared with the Somalis a message of peace. When Hadrawi announced his intention to travel to the chaotic south to share his message, most civil society organizations welcomed and supported it. INXA, an umbrella organization for civil society groups, provided the logistics that the trip required.[38] Hadrawi composed one long poem called 'Dabahuwan' (Covered from the bottom) and a short poem called 'Badbaado' (Rescuer). He also delivered speeches wherever he visited.

In the longer poem, 'Dabahuwan', Hadrawi employs an 'exculpatory approach'. According to Johan Galtung this approach is one of twelve used when reconciling groups that are in conflict. In this approach the peace worker starts from the assumption that nobody is guilty.[39] Hadrawi does not blame one Somali group or even one Somali regime. Rather, he eloquently and openly argues that whatever happened to Somalis was the result of the colonialist policies that partitioned and ruled Somalia for most of the nineteenth and twentieth centuries. The first part of this poem critiques Western colonial policies and values while the last part encourages Somalis to use their own traditional dispute resolution mechanisms to solve their own problems. The second poem, 'Badbaado', is mostly a prayer. Hadrawi prays for God to relieve Somalis from the formidable forces that perpetuate the conflict. Wherever he went, Hadrawi read these two poems for his audiences.

Although the substance of Hadrawi's ideas had been the values of Somali society, he delivered his message of peace mainly through poems. Mohammed Abu Nimer identifies 16 Islamic values: (1) the pursuit of justice; (2) social empowerment by doing good (*Ihsan*); (3) the universality of dignity and humanity; (4) equality; (5) the sacredness of human life; (6) a quest for peace (peacemaking); (7) knowledge and reason; (8) creativity and innovation; (9) forgiveness; (10) the importance of deeds and actions; (11) involvement through individual responsibility; (12) patience (*Sabar*); (13) collaborative actions and solidarity; (14) the concept of *Ummah* (universal

Muslim nation); (15) inclusivity and participatory processes; and (16) pluralism and diversity.[40] Detailed content analysis of Hadrawi's speeches and the two poems reveals that he emphasizes the values of doing good, pursuing justice, equality, peacemaking and patience. These values sound universal, but different cultures perceive them in different ways.

Close observation of Hadrawi's perspectives reveals that he has mixed baggage. First, the Islamic perspective is the dominant paradigm that informs Hadrawi's frame of reference. Both of his poems for this peace caravan heavily draw from the Islamic religion. His conception of the world is religious. He repeatedly refers to Allah (i.e., God as understood by the Muslim communities he is addressing). The values that he considers useful and relevant for life are largely drawn from the Islamic religion.

Moreover, Hadrawi explains the importance of the Somali culture and argues that such culture helped the Somali people survive in that part of the world for hundreds of years. In addition, Hadrawi considers education as any experience that helps individuals to survive or progress in the environment in which they live. He articulates this conception through most of his poems. This understanding leads Hadrawi to consider everywhere as a school – one is a student throughout his or her lifetime in every place. John Dewey has a similar understanding of education, although Hadrawi's conception is far broader.

A critical perspective is Hadrawi's second dominant theme. Hadrawi critiques Western culture. He links this culture to the colonial system that was based on insatiable demands for wealth (capitalism). Hadrawi convincingly argues that the Western colonialists who divided Somalia into five regions are responsible for most of the social ills that Somalia faces today. 'They destroyed the socio-cultural and economical systems that withstood life's formidable challenges for hundreds of years without providing an alternative system,' he argues.

Hadrawi's peace caravan was delivered in a way that addressed sensitive issues yet avoided causing problems. As in any other war-torn society, trust among Somali groups is very low. Different clans fought each other over resources and power. Hadrawi belongs to one of these clans. His team members were from different clans. For them to go to areas where they were not under the protection of their own clans and discuss these issues and yet take a position was not an easy task. Yet these poets completed their trip with no disruptions.

One factor that helped the mission to succeed is worth mentioning here. As Hadrawi said in his interview with Himilo Online, one of his major goals was to break the psychological barriers that keep people from intermingling with each other. When he was addressing this point it was as though he was explaining how to build positive inter-group relations. Hadrawi has not only called for people to live together in the cities, as was the case before 1990, he also openly called for the people to travel to different regions and open all channels of communications. His belief is that when people see and talk to each other, their perception of each other will change. While conceding the fact that there were fundamental problems that must be addressed, Hadrawi said, 'I want my people to understand, there exist devious plans to perpetuate the division among them by certain groups who want to secure their personal interests.'[41] Such is not difficult to prove, however, because by now most Somalis understand the forces that have prolonged the civil war.

Hadrawi's peace caravan was the first of its kind, and its effects are hard to quantify. What is clear is that this peace journey created a national debate about the reconciliation of Somalis at the time. While there is no data that measures the impact of the peace caravan, Hadrawi himself was highly satisfied with the outcome. He gave several interviews to different Somali and international media outlets such as Hiiraan Online, Himilo Online and the BBC Somali service. Several civil society groups have also publicly commented on the impact. In addition, when Hadrawi visited different cities and towns, the general public welcomed him in large numbers; militias decided not to disrupt his mission; and warlords did not undermine him even though they did not like his message. The Somali Diaspora organized a follow-up peace caravan in which Hadrawi visited several European countries including Great Britain. At the time it created euphoria among many Somalis who had never seen him but had heard his poems and songs. It is safe to say that Hadrawi's peace caravan has had a significant impact on different actors, albeit a short-lived one.

Like other non-formal programmes, Hadrawi's peace caravan had its shortcomings. Although the values he emphasized were important and home-grown, there were other relevant values that Hadrawi and his team did not address. The most important of these is the value of forgiveness. Indeed, most peace education and peacebuilding education programmes for war-torn societies address the value of forgiveness. Examples include the truth and reconciliation commissions in South Africa, Chile, Peru and Rwanda, which show the importance of this value in moving beyond conflict. In addition, Islam and the Somali culture have rich resources encouraging this value. Neglecting the idea of forgiving is a major shortcoming.

Detailed analysis of Hadrawi's peace caravan shows that there is a huge need for such peacebuilding education programmes, and for them to be delivered in a variety of ways. Clearly, the leaders of reconstruction in education neglected to utilize peacebuilding education programmes. Moreover, when developing such projects both the Somali culture and Islam can be employed because the values that these two sources present resonate with Somali people. Finally, a lesson that can be drawn from the success of Hadrawi's peace caravan is the importance of involving credible, respected figures. Religious scholars, intellectuals, poets, and other people of stature can all be involved in the efforts of building peace.

CHALLENGES OF USING EDUCATION FOR SOCIAL CHANGE: ANALYSIS AND IMPLICATIONS

Education can be a vehicle for long-term social transformation. Above, I examined three ways that education can be used: to provide opportunities, to instil positive peace, and to create citizenship values. However, in this section, I identify and analyse the major challenges that hinder the effective use of education for positive ends in Somalia. Two major challenges can be identified: the lack of resources and the lack of collaboration between those in the education sector.

As in other areas of peacebuilding, a lack of resources haunts the availability of education for Somali children. There is no functioning national ministry of education tasked with providing an education service to Somalis. According to officials from the UNDP, UNICEF and Save the Children, the three largest organizations that help Somalia in education, there is a lack of capacity for even Somaliland and Puntland education departments. In 2006 Somaliland allocated only 6 per cent of its $30 million budget to the social service sector and Puntland gave only 2 per cent of its $18 million budget.[42]

Obviously, such meagre resources cannot expand the access to education for all Somalis. In fact, this illustrates that the small number of students currently in education in Somalia have this access because of externally provided resources. The three education sector leaders UNICEF, UNESCO and Save the Children (Western IGOs and NGOs) and many Islamist NGOs fill the void in some cases and provide some assistance to Somali children. But such assistance, although appreciated, is far from sufficient for Somalia to meet UNESCO's Education for All and/or the Millennium Development Goals. If any substantial development is to be made in this area of expanding access to education for Somali children, a comprehensive nation-building project that helps build schools and train teachers would be needed.

In addition to lack of resources at the macro level, there is a shortage in professional educators, curriculum experts and education policy advisers in Somalia. One of FPENS' coordinators, Said Sheikh, explained to me why most Somali schools decided to use Arabic textbooks. He provided three reasons. First, Said argued that several Arab countries such as Saudi Arabia, United Arab Emirates and Yemen made their curriculum and textbooks available to the Somalis who were working in the education system. Second, Somali people and these Arab countries share a cultural and religious background, thus making the content provided to them largely compatible. Finally, most of the schools were earlier funded by Arab and Islamic based NGOs. If this argument is taken to its logical conclusion, the choices for the Somali educators have been limited. They have used whatever resources available to them and have delivered education services to as many students as they have been able. While this can be expected in a collapsed state context, one cannot reasonably expect a planned education system that would be used for social transformation.

The lack of resources is further complicated by the presence of two distinct groups within the education sector. Western organizations and the international community have negative perceptions about the Islamists who dominate the few educational institutions that exist in Somalia. Islamists also suspect ulterior motives in the Western agenda. This mutual suspicion is not helpful as it affects collaboration between the two groups. This is further fuelled by US policy toward Somalia, which supported the destruction of the Islamist regime in Mogadishu in 2006.

Moreover, since the Somali state collapsed in 1991, there has been no one group that has monopoly over violence. As Said Sheikh asserted, due to the recent conflict in southern Somalia, particularly in Mogadishu and Belet-weyne, many schools have been destroyed or abandoned and thousands of students have fled from their homes. As such, the small gains that were achieved during the past decade have been reversed in a few months. Recovering from this will take several years, at least.

In the midst of these challenges, however, an interesting opportunity has arisen. The presence of diasporic Somalis in Europe, North America and the Arab world is having a positive impact on education in Somalia. Since the 1970s, Somalis have emigrated overseas for work and education. Hundreds of thousands of them have gone to Europe and North America and have sent more than $1 billion back to Somalia. Moreover, since Somalis are organized along clan lines, building schools in small districts has proliferated. Abroad, in the mosques and in communities, fundraising events are often held for building schools and universities in Somalia. For example, with the help of many Somalis, one community built the Amoud University in 1997. Many more communities followed this example and built schools in Hargeysa, Buro, Las Anod, Bosaso, Galkayo, Belet-weyne, Mogadishu, Baidoa, Kismayo and other major cities.

While the presence of conscious and helpful Diaspora Somalis helps, the challenge that is associated with the lack of resources such as schools, books and teachers still remains. Diaspora assistance cannot replace the need for national educational institutions. Most important of all, the absence of so many educated Somalis from their home country is itself a negative factor, as it means that a large number of potential educators have gone. The Diaspora reflects a brain drain.

CONCLUSION

Education can play a key role in building durable peace and a functioning state in Somalia. At present, access to formal education is limited as only one in five children in Somalia is enrolled in school. Despite the limited access, both indigenous and colonial education systems are directly and indirectly present in the Somali context. An examination of the different stakeholders' perceptions of pertinent educational issues reveals two separate approaches. An analysis of UNESCO/UNICEF and FPENS textbooks in social studies and citizenship education respectively shows two distinct emphases. Somali students learn little conflict resolution and peacebuilding skills from schools. There are different identities present in Somalia and there are education systems that nourish some and not others. Somalia's national identity has been neglected for many years. The concepts of citizenship and citizenship education directly relate to identity and national identity in Somalia. As the interviews reveal and content analysis of the textbooks confirms, more work needs to be done in peace education. An examination of the extent to which peace education and peacebuilding education programmes are available within Somalia's education system reveals that few such projects can be found, although a few non-formal programmes have been occasionally used in the past.

8
Role for the International Community: Options and Implications

An American diplomat, in late 2001, visited an institute in Mogadishu called Mogadishu University. The diplomat asked a question to the rector of the University, Dr Ali Sheikh Ahmed: Do your students pray when they are on campus? Dr Ali was befuddled and didn't quite know how to react to the question. Dr Ali said, 'Those who want to pray do pray and those who do not want to pray that is their business.' What the American diplomat was trying to get is… if you had students praying when they are on campus this must be breeding some kind of lunatic terrorists. That is our world today and that is the method [by which] American politics works today.

Abdi Samatar[1]

This chapter discusses the international community and how its actions or inactions affect peacebuilding efforts in Somalia. It looks at the mismatch between the Western ideology that drives peacebuilding efforts and the indigenous values and institutions that are present in Somalia. Finally the chapter assesses three options that the United Nations often uses to address civil conflicts: trusteeship, transitional administration, and the support of home-grown solutions.

UNDERSTANDING THE INTERNATIONAL COMMUNITY AND ITS ROLE IN PEACEBUILDING

Policymakers and writers usually use the term 'international community' without defining it. In fact, according to the then editor of the *Financial Times*, Andrew Gowers, the term is not allowed to be used in the columns of that newspaper. Gowers argues that, 'The true international community – the one whose health and togetherness will determine the course of world events – is the group of states that created the rules and institutions in the first place. It is, essentially, the United States and Europe.'[2] Noam Chomsky comes to a similar conclusion arguing that while the common-sense definition of international community would have been the United Nations General Assembly, in practical terms it is much smaller. Chomsky contends that like other concepts such as 'terrorism', 'crime', and 'security', the 'doctrinal meaning' of the term *international community* differs from its 'technical meaning'. As such, Chomsky writes that the term 'is regularly used in a technical sense to describe the United States joined by some allies and clients'.[3] General Jama Mohamed Ghaleb agrees with Gowers and Chomsky by saying that, in the Somali context, the embassies of the Western governments in Nairobi constitute the international community. 'They mean those embassies in Nairobi when they say the international community wants this or that,' he said.[4] Gowers, Chomsky and Ghaleb are correct that the values and the institutions that are dominant in the current unipolar world are those of the West. Samuel P. Huntington has argued that the leading Western civilization, which has its roots in Christianity, is at odds with other civilizations.[5] Moreover, Francis Fukuyama argues that liberal democracy won the war between ideologies and it will remain the dominant ideology in the future.[6]

With respect to peacebuilding, in an ideal sense, it should be about creating a secure and peaceful environment for societies that have experienced wars. However, according to Roland Paris and Shalmali Guttal, international peacebuilders are interested in creating a particular type of peace.[7] In other words, the international community has predetermined the 'universal' way of organizing a nation-state. For these authors, all internationally-sponsored peacebuilding activities so far have been based on the assumption that a liberal democracy and market economy have to be the cornerstones of the state. Roland Paris argues that working with these assumptions makes peacebuilding an 'updated version' of civilizing missions from the colonial era: during the colonial era Europeans believed that they were obliged to 'civilize' colonized regions. Peacebuilders believe a liberal democracy and market economy are superior models, and therefore recovering societies have to use them for managing their conflicts.[8]

Paris contends that the current civilizing project is altruistic in that the West pays the bills while earlier colonialist missions benefited Europe. Taken to its logical conclusion, Paris's language suggests that 'peacebuilding is less mercenary'.[9] Guttal questions Paris's assertion that there are benign interventions; she thinks that so-called reconstruction programmes are beneficial for the UN and the international financial institutions (IFIs) because they give these institutions a new role.[10] Paris also identifies four mechanisms used by the West to impose liberal democracy and a market economy on war-torn societies: (1) shaping the content of peace accords, (2) providing expert advice, (3) imposing conditionalities, and (4) commissioning transitional administrations.[11] Guttal takes this argument further and contends that the main goal behind the 'reconstruction model' promotes 'neo-liberalism – unregulated, market economy, liberal democracy, free flow of private capital, privatizations'.[12] She argues that the actions of peacebuilders undermine the democratically elected governments of recovering societies because those who finance peacebuilding projects determine the direction of society.[13] For Guttal, states failed in the first place because colonialism drained the wealth of weak nations. In short, as Guttal suggests, modernizing should be distinguished from westernizing. Modernization should be a process that comes gradually within a society and indigenous values and institutions have to be in conformity with it. Otherwise, there will be a clash.

In Somalia, the 'international community', as defined by Gowers and Chomsky, has been driving peacemaking and peacebuilding efforts. Since the Somali state collapsed, the rest of the world followed the United States's lead in Somalia. When the US left Somalia in 1991 the United Nations and all of the other countries left as well. When the US launched Operation Restore Hope in 1992, many countries pledged their support by contributing troops or other types of funding. In other words, much-needed world attention to the Somali tragedy has followed US interests or disinterest since 1991.

After the US pulled out of Somalia, the United Nations, and to a lesser extent the European Union, were involved in helping with short-term humanitarian issues. Mostly, they operated from their Horn of Africa headquarters in Nairobi and had field offices in three different regions: Northwest (Somaliland), Northeast (Puntland), and South-Central. Individuals from the United Nations, the European Union, and many non-governmental organizations that have been interviewed for this book when I visited Nairobi in 2007 have conceded to this fact. When the United States became interested in Somalia after 9/11, some European countries became interested again, arguing that the European Union supports stable regions because it follows a peace-dividend.[14]

Like the EU, the UN is also involved in a number of areas in Somalia. In fact, many Somalis I met during my field research told me that the United Nations is the de-facto government of Somalia as it makes most of the decisions that a local and national government should have made. I asked the UN and European diplomats in

Nairobi whether Somalia was a de-facto undeclared United Nations trust – although the Trusteeship Council was dissolved in 2005. Some of the interviewees said they were there to help Somalia and they do not take over the role of the Somali state. However, one senior UN official said to me unapologetically that, 'a government ministry that has only a minister and deputy minister cannot be a counter-part to the UN agency that has field offices in every region and delivers services to the Somalis'.[15] Moreover, when he was explaining the resources and time that the agency spends on Somalia and the lack of a domestic partner, the country director of UNESCO said, 'We are the de-facto ministry of education for Somalia.'[16]

The agencies of the United Nations have produced a document that describes their activities for 2008 to 2009, 'United Nations Transition Plan for Somalia'. In it the UN identifies five areas of focus: governance, local governance, security, social services, and development. This document, although the UN argues that it has consulted with relevant stakeholders, became controversial as the Somali transitional government of the time protested it. I was in Nairobi when seven ministers came to talk to the United Nations about their understanding of the Transition Plan.[17] However, the UN insisted it had done nothing wrong. The idea that the UN, its backers, and the NGOs in Nairobi control what is happening in Somalia is not just limited to Somali intellectuals. In fact, Abdullahi Yusuf, former president of Somalia, said openly that his government did not control anything, and that NGOs in Nairobi and fundamentalists in Somalia run Somali society.[18]

Europe continues to support some programmes in Somalia, particularly in the northern more peaceful areas of the country. The EU also funded the Kenyan-hosted and IGAD-sponsored Somali peace process of 2002–04. One official told me that while the United States gave verbal support to the talks, it had taken actions that undermined the conference. For example, according to this official some US officials visited areas that were controlled by allied warlords not interested in peace – such an act was interpreted that Washington was not supportive of the Kenya-hosted peace process. In addition, a European diplomat argued that the United States considered Somalia another 'war on terror' front. When the Somali transitional government was established, according to this diplomat, the US was not interested and instead established good relations with Somali warlords in Mogadishu. After these warlords were defeated the US started to engage with the transitional government simply because it wanted to deal with alleged terrorists in Somalia.[19]

The United States's policy toward Somalia, as articulated by Bush administration officials, has been one of seeking a local partner to remove what it called 'terrorist threats' and to contain the Somalia problem within its borders. It appears, though, that this strategy has not addressed the major source of the problem which is the statelessness in the country. Moreover, one way or another, the actions and inactions of the US-led international community affect the perpetuation of the Somali conflict. As evidence from other failed or failing states suggests, the international community drives peacebuilding efforts. Literature pertaining to peacebuilding and reconstructing collapsed states offers a variety of useful responses to war-torn societies. These range from externally imposed solutions to the support of home-grown solutions.

SOMALIA UNDER A UN TRUSTEESHIP SYSTEM

Although no Somali political organization or major civil society group has formally called for placing Somalia under a UN trusteeship, the idea has been alive in the debates of some Somalis who are tired of the status quo.[20] Those who support this approach argue that Somalis have proven that they are not capable of self-governance. Thus, the argument goes, it is better to recognize this and ask the world to help through the establishment of a trusteeship-type form of governance. Other commentators on the Somali civil war disagree with this position, claiming that the southern part of Somalia, the part now facing difficulties, has effectively been under UN trusteeship for ten years and there is little to show for it.

William Bain argues that 'Trusteeship presupposes, by definition, a relationship of unequals; it is a practice that assumes that some people are incompetent in such a way that they do not understand their situation... Someone must choose for them.'[21] Bain has written in support of amending the UN Charter and giving a new mandate to the Trusteeship Council, which has been out of a job since the last trust country, Palau, became independent in 1994. Other African scholars, such as Ali A. Mazrui, have suggested that failed and failing states in Africa should be placed under an African trusteeship administration.[22]

Placing failed or failing states under UN trusteeship would require the General Assembly to amend the Charter.[23] Article 78 of the UN Charter reads: 'The trusteeship system shall not apply to territories which have become Members of the United Nations, relationship among which shall be based on respect for the principle of sovereign equality.'[24] Even if the UN wants to recommission the Trusteeship Council, it has to amend its Charter. This is not likely because such an amendment requires support from the UN member states. Paradoxically, a good number of the member states that would have to approve the amendment are (if Rotberg's state classifications are used) either weak or failed states themselves.[25] Thus, under normal circumstances, these countries would not support anything that can undermine their sovereignty.

Many Somalis would also find this option of either a UN or an African trusteeship system unacceptable. The very notion would trigger nationalistic feeling because of the historical experience in which Italy, a former colonial power, abused Somalis using the Trusteeship Council. Italy was given ten years to prepare Southern Somalia for independence from 1950 to 1960. Yet after the trusteeship period ended, Somalia did not inherit from Italy any effective state institutions. For this reason, the word *trusteeship* is a loaded term for Somalis. Regarding the African trusteeship proposal, Somalia's African neighbours, Kenya and Ethiopia, are themselves struggling in terms of capacity. Ethiopia's brutal occupation did not deliver a semblance of peace even though they occupied the country for more than two years.

The proposal to establish a UN trusteeship in Somalia is based on two assumptions. First, it assumes all other available and practical alternatives have been pursued and have failed. It assumes the many reconciliation conferences failed because of the Somalis. Thus, the implication is that Somalis either do not want peace or even if they want it they cannot make and maintain it. This assumption is not warranted. Arguably, Somalia lacks peace in large part because of both internal and external factors. Ethiopia's meddling and the international community's indifference to assisting with genuine peace initiatives combine with the warlords' disinterest in peace. This is not to say that Somalis and internal factors have not contributed to the problem. They have, and, in fact, warlords and business warlords significantly participated in the destruction of Somalia.

Second, Somalia is not only the south or Mogadishu. There are peaceful areas in the country that have had functioning, albeit weak, administrations for many years. 'Somaliland', for example, has been safe and recovering from civil war for the past 15 years. In fact, many people consider Hargeysa, the capital of Somaliland, to be safer than Nairobi. Although this region wants to secede, under international law, it still remains part of Somalia as it has not been recognized by any country. The north-eastern region of Puntland also has had relative peace and a functioning administration since 1998. Both regions achieved peace without the presence of foreign peacekeeping troops or a trusteeship administration – one important factor to keep in mind is that unlike other southern areas, Ethiopia supported these regions by not undermining them. Moreover, the Union of Islamic Courts established peace in most of chaotic southern Somalia in 2006. Yet, the American-supported Ethiopian invasion destroyed that peace.

In summary, the chances for putting Somalia under a UN trusteeship are slim as such a decision would require an international agreement on adjusting the UN Charter. Because of UN reform efforts in 2005, the Trusteeship Council is out of business. Even if it did exist, Somalia has been an 'independent' state for decades, and under peaceful conditions Somalis have the will and perhaps some capacity to run their own affairs. As such, whether it is sponsored by an international organization or by Africans, a trusteeship is not a feasible option.

UNITED NATIONS TRANSITIONAL ADMINISTRATION

Another way for the international community to respond to failed states is by commissioning a United Nations transitional administration. For instance, post-Cold War, the UN has intervened in several countries for different reasons using Chapter VII of the Charter – Somalia being the first, in 1992. The Security Council argued, with respect to Article 39, that a humanitarian disaster of the magnitude displayed in Somalia was a threat to international peace. In addition to Somalia, the Security Council has intervened in East Timor, Cambodia, Abkhazia, Bosnia, Kosovo, Sierra Leone, Liberia, Mozambique, Namibia and Haiti. For instance, in Haiti, according to David Thürer, the Security Council decided to intervene when a dictatorship replaced the democratic government. In Cambodia, the intervention was because of a genocide that warlords committed against civilians.[26]

Such interventions often avoid using the term *trusteeship*. However, in essence the assumptions behind and the functions of transitional administrations are almost the same as the trusteeship system. Commenting on the similarities, Edward Marks states, 'without consciously meaning to do so, the international community has revived the trusteeship system'.[27] Moreover, James Fearon and David Laitin call the system that the Security Council uses a 'neotrusteeship system'.[28]

Fearon and Laitin argue that there are four challenges with transitional administrations or the neotrusteeship system: recruitment, coordination, accountability, and exit strategies. First, the question is, according to these authors, who should pay for the mission? Fearon and Laitin suggest the nation receiving the mission and donor countries should foot the bill. They note that a good example is East Timor which, with its potential resources, will pay back Australia for some of the costs incurred.[29] With regard to who should coordinate, Fearon and Laitin argue that the Security Council should give the mandate to one nation, not to the UN. Again, Australia in East Timor, the United States in Haiti and Russia in Abkhazia illustrate their point. These authors also believe that to make sure that citizens of the reconstructing state are not abused, the UN should come up with a way to ensure accountability. Finally, Fearon and Laitin argue that the mission should be clear about a possible end date.

In addition, transitional administrations have not always been implemented in the same way. At times UN troops directly delivered and supervised interventions. Other times the UN gave member states the mandate while it supervised (e.g., East Timor by Australia). In some cases, the international community and donor agencies paid for some of these interventions (e.g., Somalia and Afghanistan) whereas, as stated above, in East Timor the future citizens of that small country will repay the costs that Australia is presently incurring.[30]

The Security Council's practices show that its five permanent members – China, France, Russian Federation, the United Kingdom, and the United States – have the most influence when mandating transitional administration missions.[31] The support of the US, in particular, was crucial for many of these interventions. This means that the international community has legal and moral power if it wants to intervene in the Somali conflict. But, as Milbrey Wallin McLaughlin suggests, we should keep two things in mind: the will and capacity of those who are expected to implement.[32] First, the will of the powerful nations is very important here. If the will is not there, even genocide won't compel them to act (e.g., Congo and Rwanda). Moreover, the Security Council approaches each situation in a way that reflects the five permanent powers' interests and preferences.

Indeed, after 9/11, global politics changed. The US started to pursue a more interventionist agenda. Since it is the sole superpower, Washington is determined to maintain its global hegemony. In addition, due to recent events, such as US support of warlords and Ethiopian invasion forces, and piracy, the American government has shown major security concerns regarding Somalia. Nevertheless, on 20 February 2007, the Security Council passed resolution 1744 which authorized the African Union to organize peace support forces for Somalia. The council passed another resolution (1814) which also says that the Somalia operation will become a United Nations operation in the future. However, as of late 2009 the nature and scope of the future UN involvement is not clear, albeit the government and the international community both call for a UN intervention force. A lot will depend on the political situation of Somalia. But, given the interventionist mood in Washington and the security concerns it has voiced, it is highly likely that this option will get the international support it needs. Like East Timor, if Somalia's potential resources are on the table there might be some powerful countries, maybe China, Italy, Indonesia, Turkey or Malaysia, that are interested in exploiting these resources in exchange for pacifying and developing Somalia.

The war-weary Somalis would welcome a transitional administration. After two decades of civil war most Somalis realize they need the assistance of the international community. The fact that there is a hostile neighbour perpetuating the conflict and which has even occupied their country, has now convinced many Somalis that they need the international community to lead and help implement peacemaking and peacebuilding efforts. Even most Islamists, who oppose international intervention on principal, may support this option.

Any way one looks at the situation, the transitional administration option seems politically viable at the international and local levels. Unlike the Ethiopian occupation, it is also appropriate because this option is temporary in nature. There is no need to justify whether the international community will leave the country or not. This is also within the parameters of the principles and goals that inform the 'threat to world peace thesis'.

As Pinar Bilgin and Adam David Morton argue, through its containment policy the Bush administration and the international community focused on the 'supposed symptoms of "state failure" (international terrorism) rather than the structural conditions that permit such "failure" to occur'.[33] When one looks at the principles and goals that the United States-led international community employs for the war on terror and the practices in place in Somalia now, one cannot help but conclude that there are serious flaws in this approach. If terrorism means using violence against innocent people for political reasons and the international community's goal is to discredit terrorism to the extent of slavery or piracy, then the focus should be on those who have perpetuated Somalia's conflict and statelessness: Ethiopia, warlords, and the international community's indifference. Rewarding Somali warlords and their foreign backers would put the international community in a morally untenable position. Although it appears to be learning from past mistakes, the United States's previous policies toward Somalia were counter-productive. For the Obama administration, much will depend on the recommendations of the inter-agency policy review team and how the administration implements those recommendations.

SUPPORTING HOME-GROWN SOLUTIONS

Interestingly, supporting home-grown solutions should have been the convenient, logical and common-sense approach for the international community. Yet, as Mohamed Sahnoon noted in his book, the international community missed many opportunities in which it could have affected the direction of the Somali conflict. Four major periods stand out. First, when the Somali state collapsed in 1991, the United States, the United Nations and many European countries left Somalia. This was a critical period because most Somalis at the time knew the importance of state institutions. Large numbers of bureaucrats, intellectuals and urban Somalis were still in the country. Most important of all, although warlords did not want peace, the presence, let alone sustained pressure, could have changed the situation.

Second, although it came late, the US-led intervention ended the famine and created a great opportunity to pacify the country. Unfortunately, the leaders of UNISOM made a number of mistakes. The courtesy that UNISOM provided to the warlords (such as Aideed and Ali Mahdi), giving the status of credible leaders, and policy prescriptions from the Addis Ababa conference contributed to the failure of the international community. Most importantly, the United States prematurely decided to quit when it lost 18 of its soldiers, despite public support for the mission.

Third, good opportunities presented themselves after the conclusion of Arta Peace Process in Djibouti in 2000 and Mbagathi

Peace Process in Kenya in 2004. The Arta peace process was Somali-owned and it deserved support at the time. Yet, because of the 11 September 2001 attacks, Ethiopia and its proxy warlords undermined this. Regarding the Mbagathi peace process, I consider it a good opportunity, though it was tainted and the warlords were given undue influence. Had the international community delivered timely and effective assistance, much could have been saved. Unfortunately, the United States supported Mogadishu warlords instead of the transitional government, thus missing another opportunity.

Finally, in 2006, a coalition of Islamists defeated the warlords, pacified most of southern Somalia and opened Mogadishu port and airport. The Union of Islamic Courts consisted of heterogeneous groups – some radical and some moderate. Although European diplomats considered this as the best opportunity for Somalia peace, again the United States disagreed. It supported – in fact for many Washington sponsored – the Ethiopian troops to destroy the Islamist groups. These policies had unintended consequences as they empowered the radicals who at the time could not even use their own name at the expense of moderates. After the occupation ended Al-Shabab came out stronger and more confident.

Fortunately, when one opportunity is missed another one knocks. With the conclusion of the Djibouti peace process in January 2009, another good opportunity presented itself. The Transitional Federal Government and the Alliance for the Re-liberation of Somalia agreed to what they called the government of national unity. This was a great milestone. Earlier, most Somali leaders neither had the will nor the capacity to address the insecurity problems – some even benefited from chaos. This seems to have changed as new, younger and more credible leaders have emerged – and so far, based on their actions and rhetoric, these leaders have shown they at least have the will and the commitment to face the challenges.

President Sheikh Sharif Sheikh Ahmed and Prime Minister Omar Abdulrashid Ali Sharmarke (son of a former president) come to Somali politics with a clean record. Participating in the negotiated settlement that eventually led to the withdrawel of Ethiopia and adopting Islamic Sharia as the basis of legislation were smart moves. Most important of all, the Djibouti conference effectively removed the Somalia file from IGAD and Ethiopian hands and placed it with the United Nations. These three achievements within such a short period tell us how different the new leadership are from the old-school politicians and notorious warlords. In fact, although still weak, the government enjoys broad public support among the Somali people (inside and outside the country). That said, many challenges lie ahead, including the rebuilding of Somali security forces, and the government will be evaluated on how it performs with respect to addressing those challenges.

In short, the United States and the international community claim that they understand this new government and its leadership as a rare opportunity and would seize it so they can help to end the statelessness in Somalia – the root cause of the insecurity. Secretary of State Hillary Clinton even described this as the best opportunity for Somalia. Let us hope that this happens.

9
Conclusion: A Way Forward

Xaraabada sokeeyiyo xigtada maanta kala guurtay.
Xal u raadi Soomaaliyeey xaasid ha u jabine.

The civil war and the relatives who have fled apart.
Oh Somalis, look for a solution to this problem
lest you do not lose [the war] to your enemies.[1]

Mohamed Ga'al Hayow, Xal u Raaddi

As the previous chapters elaborated, two important domestic and two external challenges haunt the Somali peace processes. Clan identity and the presence of strong Islamist movements are the main domestic challenges. While conceding the difficulty of dealing with clan identity, power-sharing for the short term and identity reconstruction, for the long term, could help address the challenges that are associated with clan identity. As we have seen, there are many opponents against the use of the clan system in order to address the problems of representation. Any sound policy prescription on representation has to deal with the perception of the people. Somalis, including Islamists, use clan identity for one reason or another when dealing with these complex political problems. As long as the prevailing societal conditions persist, the clan-based system may have to be accommodated in order to address representation problems at least for the short term. But the number of clans can change from 4.5 to six or seven or even more. Also, a system that empowers the individual can be introduced within the political system.

With respect to Islamic values and Islamic movements, most interviewees believe that inclusion of the Islamists in the peace process and accommodation of their values are necessary. How combining these things can play out will depend on the future peace processes. As in other Muslim countries, moderate Islamists and hardliners are both present within the Somali context. With the end of Ethiopian occupation, adoption of the Sharia system, and removal of the Somalia file from Ethiopia to the United Nations, the moderates and nationalists will be empowered as the causes and conditions that provide hardliners' ammunition have been removed from the equation. If the Ethiopian occupation returns, hardliners will easily win the hearts and minds of the people. Giving a popular cause to the hardliners would be another grave mistake.

US policy, which is based on its 'war on terror', and Ethiopian meddling have been identified as the two major external challenges to peacebuilding in Somalia. Since 9/11, the United States has considered Somalia the third front on its war on terror. Washington argues that three of the individuals who were involved in the bombing of the American embassies in Kenya and Tanzania were sheltered in Somalia.[2] As a result, the US added the Al-Ittihad and Al-Shabab Islamic movements to its terrorist list. The US also froze the assets of Al-Barakaat money transfer and telecommunication companies. Most important, Washington helped destroy the Union of Islamic Courts. Interestingly, Washington's actions coincided with Ethiopia's geopolitical agenda. Ethiopia is the regional power and it has long had hostile relations with Somalia. As a result, for Addis Ababa, this was a golden opportunity to eliminate an historic enemy. A change of US policy toward 'political Islam' is in the making. Washington accepted and is willing to work with a well-known Islamist-dominated government in Mogadishu, albeit they are moderates. Moreover, international pressure on Ethiopia helped end its occupation and Addis Ababa, it seems, has realized that it needs to change its strategies. That said, the United States's positive involvement is necessary for a restoration of the Somali state. With respect to Ethiopia, I believe that if it does not actively undermine and frustrate the efforts of state-building in Somalia, then Somalis can succeed in reestablising their state.

In short, as Susan Rice argues, the most appropriate response to collapsed states is to address the problem at its root causes. She notes, 'If the United States is to deal decisively with failed states and to succeed at post-conflict rehabilitation, it must engage in nation-building.'[3] Problems that are associated with statelessness pose significant threats in terms of health, refugee exits, piracy on the high seas, and humanitarian crises in Somalia. Many agree with Rice. The most appropriate way to address the problem at its root is a combination of encouraging and supporting home-grown initiatives – i.e. supporting the current transitional government – and commissioning a limited transitional administration that is linked to comprehensive peacebuilding – one that addresses security, economic development, political governance, and justice. Finally, those people interviewed for this book considered education as the long-term solution to Somali problems. Education opens unlimited opportunities for those who have access to it, and it can be used to change the negative behaviour that promotes violence.

FURTHER RESEARCH

As in other parts of the Muslim world, heterogeneous powerful and well-organized Islamist movements are present in Somalia. More research is urgently needed in this area as the presence of Islamists has raised Somalia's profile in the international arena. For instance, how do Somalia's Islamists want to deal with peaceful transition of power? What are the conditions that have necessitated most of Somalia's Islamists to take up arms? How do Islamists want to deal with clan identity?

More investigation is also needed regarding the inclusion of Islamists in political processes. This is significant for other parts of the world, such as Egypt, Afghanistan, Palestine and Sudan, where Islamists enjoy significant popular support. As such, how Islamists can be included and what implications their inclusion might have on the political process need to be investigated.

This book highlights the mismatch between proposed institutional mechanisms that are used for addressing the Somali conflict and the peculiarities of the Somali context. In particular, investigating how inclusive political parties can be created and developed in Somalia is urgent.

Further research is required in the area of designing a Somali national education curriculum that promotes peace. In addition, since 1991, free media has flourished in the country. Many cities have radio stations and small newspapers, and major media outlets such as the Voice of America and BBC Somali services are widely listened to. Unfortunately, there has been little analysis of this important area. Questions that need to be investigated include: How does Somali media impact peacebuilding? How do the stakeholders use media in order to propagate their viewpoints? Perhaps, comparing the VOA and BBC Somali services would help in the understanding of Somali issues. Finally, further study is required into reconciling secular-Islamist agendas with those of the external actors, such as the United States and Ethiopia.

RECOMMENDATIONS

1. While the UN provides assistance, Somalis must be given the opportunity to define their issues and discuss them. Striking a balance is necessary here.

2. Holding more peace conferences will not deliver peace. State-building, particularly creating a secure environment, should be the main goal of the international community. This will require participating countries to send more troops to Somalia in the short term while building Somalia's security forces would be the long-term response to building lasting peace. Success will hinge on the progress that is made in building an inclusive, professional and well-disciplined force.

3. With respect to the context-appropriate institutions, the parliamentary system and the federal model have to be revisited. There is a mismatch, as the prescribed institutions do not respond to local needs. As the experiences in Somaliland and Puntland suggest, a presidential system would be more appropriate. Somaliland has accommodated the clan system within a bicameral setting. Somalia can adopt what worked since both regions are Somali regions and their experiences count as Somali experiences. Regarding the electoral system, because of its simplicity and fairness, a proportional system which is largely based on a closed national list would be appropriate for the Somali context.

4. Although there are examples where Somalis made and implemented peace, some sort of international presence is necessary. This will help reduce Ethiopia's meddling and the impunity of Somali warlords. Moreover, since there is a trust deficit among Somalis, such a presence could be a confidence-building measure. Perhaps giving a long-term mandate to the AMISOM forces would be helpful.

5. Current American policy toward Somalia perpetuates the statelessness as its 'war on terror' strategy focuses on symptoms. Washington's actions have alienated a large segment of Somali society and have uncritically bundled together heterogeneous Islamist groups in Somalia. As such, there is a need for a reformed US policy toward Somalia. As the renewed commitment from Secretary of State Clinton suggests, it appears that Washington has learned from its past mistakes. But, a lot will depend on how the Obama administration approaches the Somali conflict after the inter-agency policy review team reports back.

6. The United States must realize that Somalia's Islamists are the best organized political group and most of them have a national agenda. These groups have to be included in the peace process.

7. The international community must understand that Ethiopia has its own agenda. Pressuring Ethiopia not only to withdraw from the Somali territories but to stop meddling in Somalia's internal affairs is necessary. Ethiopia is determined to prevent the emergence of a Somali state. The international community must do all it can to convince Ethiopia that a stable Somalia is in the best interests of the region and the world. For Somali governments, balancing the demands of domineering Ethiopia and the Somali people's defiant public reaction, will be a huge challenge. The Transitional government will need to reassure neighbouring countries, the donor countries and, most important of all, the Somali people – this will be the most difficult task for any government in Somalia.

8. Education is the long-term solution to the many problems that breed violence and poverty. Widening the access to education for all Somalis is needed. As such, as many resources as possible must be allocated to build schools and train teachers. In particular, there is a large need for professional teachers.

9. Besides access to education, education policy, curriculum, and pedagogy have to be used for the goal of building peace in Somalia.

Notes

PREFACE

1. See Alexander E. Wendt, 'The Agent-Structure Problem in International Relations Theory', *International Organization* 41, no. 3 (1987): 335–70; Emanuel Adler, 'Seizing the Middle Ground: Constructivism in World Politics', *European Journal of International Relations* 3, no. 3 (1987): 319–63.
2. Robert J.C. Young, *Post-colonialism: An Historical Introduction* (Oxford: Blackwell, 2001).
3. See Bill Ashcroft, Gareth Griffiths and Helen Tiffin, *Key Concepts in Post-Colonial Studies* (New York: Routledge, 1998); L. Gandhi, *Postcolonial Theory: A Critical Introduction* (New York: Columbia University Press, 1998).
4. Edward Said, *Orientalism* (London: Routledge and Kegan Paul, 1978).
5. This is taken from the film, 'Edward Said: The Last Interview', Charles Glass, interviewer, directed by Mike Dibb and produced by D.D. Guttenplan, Icarus Films, 2004.
6. See Said *Orientalism*; see also Said's *Culture and Imperialism* (London: Vintage Books, 1994).

CHAPTER 1

1. A Somali Youth League (SYL) poet, Ali Hussein was one of the pioneers of the nationalist movement. He composed this poem in the early 1960s when Somalia became independent. In it he observes that the Somali leaders' behaviour raises concern that Somalis might not be able to keep the independence and freedom that they had struggled for decades to attain.
2. J. Fearon and D.D. Laitin, 'Neotrusteeship and the Problem of Weak States', *International Security* 28, no. 4 (2004): 5–43.
3. On the importance of Africa as a source of energy, see Jeremy Keenan, *The Dark Sahara: America's War on Terror in Africa* (London: Pluto Press, 2009). Regarding Somalia, see Mark Fineman, 'The oil factor in Somalia', *Los Angeles Times*, 17 January 1993, Headline: Part A; page 1; column 1; Foreign Desk.
4. Robert Rotberg, 'The Failure and Collapse of Nation-States: Breakdown, Prevention and Repair', in Robert Rotberg (ed.), *When States Fail: Causes and Consequences* (Princeton, NJ: Princeton University Press), p. 9.
5. See ibid., p. 2.
6. See Jeffrey Herbst, 'Let Them Fail', in Rotberg (ed.), 'When States Fail'; and Pinar Bilgin and Adam David Morton, 'From "Rogue" to "Failed" States? The Fallacy of Short-termism', *Politics* 24, no. 3 (2004): 169–80. See also Susan E. Rice, *The New National Security Strategy: Focus on Failed States*, Policy Brief #116 (Washington, DC: Brookings Institution, 2003).
7. See Ken Menkhaus, 'Political Islam in Somalia', *Middle East Policy* 9, no. 1 (2002): 109–23. Also see Ken Menkhaus, 'Somalia: In the Crosshairs of the War on Terrorism', *Current History* 101, no. 655 (2002): 210–18; and Ken

Menkhaus, 'State Collapse in Somalia: Second Thoughts', *Review of African Political Economy* 30, no. 97 (2003): 405–22.

8. See Menkhaus, 'State Collapse in Somalia'; and Ted Dagne, 'Africa and the War on Terrorism: The Case of Somalia', *Mediterranean Quarterly* 13, no. 4 (2002): 62–73.

9. See Ken Menkhaus, *Somalia: State Collapse and the Threat of Terrorism* (New York: Oxford University Press, 2004), p. 71.

10. Ibid.

11. See Thomas Ricks's *Washington Post* report 'Allies step up Somalia watch: U.S. aims to keep Al Qaeda at bay', *Washington Post*, 4 January 2002, www. washingtonpost.com/ac2/wpdyn?pagename=article&contentId=A59310-2002Jan3&notFound=true.

12. Nurudin Farah, 'Somalia is no hideout for bin Laden', *New York Times*, 9 January 2002, p. 23, col. 2.

13. See Herbst, 'Let Them Fail'; Rotberg, 'The Failure and Collapse of Nation-States'.

14. The disease, which Somalis call 'Kaduudiyow', causes a wasting of the body and possible death within days.

15. 'Haamo Waaweyn oo kusoo Caariyey Xeebaha Gobolka Jubbada Hoose', *Somalitalk Online*, 16 April 2005, www.somalitalk.com/sun/14.html.

16. See Department of the Treasury, Office of Public Affairs, Statement by Treasury Secretary Paul O'Neill, 7 November 2001, para. 5, www.treas.gov/press/ releases/po770.htm.

17. Ibid., para. 6.

18. Ibid.

19. See International Maritime Bureau, *Piracy and Armed Robbery against Ships: Annual Report* (1 January–31 December, 2008).

20. Robert D. Kaplan, 'Center Stage for the Twenty-First Century', *Foreign Affairs* 82 (March–April 2009). See also Abukar Arman, 'Piracy, geopolitics, and private security', *The Huffington Post*, 24 April 2009.

21. See Peter Lennox, 'Contemporary Piracy off the Horn of Africa', Canadian Defence and Foreign Affairs Institute. Retrieved April 2008, from www.cdfai. org/PDF/Contemporary%20Piracy%20off%20the%20Horn%20of%20Africa. pdf.

22. Nick Amies, 'Shipping insurance sky-rockets as pirate attacks increase', Deutsche Welle. www.dw-world.de/dw/article/0,,4278642,00.html.

23. See Jeffrey Gettleman, 'For Somali pirates, worst enemy may be on shore', *New York Times*, 8 May 2009; Stephanie McCrummen, 'Somalia's godfathers: ransom-rich pirates', *Washington Post*, 20 April 2009. See also Sahal Abdulle and Rob Crilly, 'Somali fishermen opt for piracy's rich pickings', *Times Online*, 7 April 2009.

24. See FAO, 'Fishery and Aquaculture Country Profiles: Somalia'. Retrieved May 2008, from www.fao.org/fishery/countrysector/FI-CP_SO/en.

25. Personal communication.

26. See Roy Licklider, 'The Consequences of Negotiated Settlements in Civil Wars, 1945–1993', *American Political Science Review* 89, no. 3 (1995): 681–90.

27. D.P. Barash and C.P. Webel (eds), *Peace and Conflict Studies* (Thousand Oaks, CA: Sage Publications, 2002); J. Galtung, 'Cultural Violence', *Journal of Peace Research* 27, no. 3 (1990): 291–305; B. Reardon, *Comprehensive*

Peace Education: Educating for Global Responsibility (New York: Teachers College Press, 1988).

28. UN Secretariat, 'An Agenda for Peace: Preventive Diplomacy, Peacemaking and Peace-Keeping', *Report of the Secretary-General pursuant to the statement adopted by the Summit Meeting of the Security Council on 31 January 1992*, A/47/277 - S/24111, 17 June 1992, www.un.org/Docs/SG/agpeace.html (last accessed 23 January 2009), para. 2.

29. Barbara F. Walter, *Committing to Peace: The Successful Settlement of Civil Wars* (Princeton, NJ: Princeton University Press, 2003).

30. See George Downs and Stephen John Stedman (eds), *Evaluation Issues in Peace Implementation* (London: Lynne Rienner, 2002).

31. See Fen Osler Hampson, *Nurturing Peace: Why Peace Settlements Succeed or Fail* (Washington, DC: United States Institute of Peace Press, 1996).

32. Thomas F. Keating and Andrew W. Knight (eds), *Building Sustainable Peace* (Edmonton: University of Alberta Press, 2004), p. xxxiii.

33. See Alina Rocha Menocal and Kate Kilpatrick, 'Towards More Effective Peace Building: A Conversation with Roland Paris', *Development in Practice* 15 (2006): 767–77.

34. See Kathy Bickmore, 'Education for Conflict Resolution and Peacebuilding in Plural Societies: Approaches from Around the World', in Karen Mundy, Kathy Bickmore, Ruth Hayhoe, Meggan Madden and Kathy Madjidi (eds), *Comparative and International Education: Issues for Teachers* (Toronto: Canadian Scholars Press, 2008), pp. 259–72.

35. Michael G. Wessels, 'The Role of Peace Education in a Culture of Peace: A Social Psychological Analysis', http://eric.ed.gov/ERICWebPortal/contentdelivery/servlet/ERICServlet?accno=ED384549 (last accessed May 2007).

36. See Gavriel Salomon, 'The Nature of Peace Education: Not All Programs Are Created Equal', in Gavriel Salomon and Baruch Nevo (eds), *Peace Education: The Concept, Principles, and Practices Around the World* (Mahwah, NJ: Lawrence E. Associates, 2002).

37. Susan Fountain, 'Peace Education in UNICEF', Working Paper, Education Section, Programme Division, UNICEF New York, June 1999, www.unicef.org/girlseducation/files/PeaceEducation.pdfp.1 (last accessed 25 January 2009), p. 1.

CHAPTER 2

1. See Michael E. Brown, 'The Causes of Internal Conflict: An Overview', in Michael E. Brown (ed.), *Nationalism and Ethnic Conflict* (Cambridge, MA: MIT Press, 1997), pp. 3–25; Chaim Kauffman, 'Possible and Impossible Solutions to Ethnic Civil Wars', *International Security* 20 (1996): 136–75; Dan Smith, 'Trends and Causes of Armed Conflicts', in M.F. Norbert Ropers, Alexander Austin and Claus-Dieter Wild (eds), *The Berghof Handbook for Conflict Transformation* (Berlin: Berghof Research Centre for Constructive Conflict Management, 2000), www.berghof-handbook.net/uploads/download/smith_handbook.pdf (accessed August 2008).

2. Afyare Elmi and Abdullahi Barise, 'The Somali Conflict: Root Causes, Obstacles, and Peace-building Strategies', *African Security Review* 15, no. 1 (2006): 32–54.

3. The major clans are Dir, Darod, Isaq, Hawaye, and Digil and Mirifle. See I.M. Lewis, *Saints and Somalis: Popular Islam in a Clan-based Society* (Lawrenceville, NJ: Red Sea Press, 1998).

4. See I.M. Lewis, *Blood and Bone: The Call of Kinship in Somali Society* (Lawrenceville, NJ: Red Sea Press, 1994).

5. A.A. Castagnio, 'Political Party System in Somalia', 1964; Lewis, *Saints and Somalis*.

6. Although this is the widely held view, the leaders and supporters of this coup argue that the officers who wanted to overthrow the government belonged to all clans, but the regime played politics with this and punished only one clan.

7. Africa Watch, *Somalia: A Government at War with Its Own People* (London: Africa Watch, 1990), p. 10.

8. See Elmi and Barise, 'The Somali Conflict'.

9. A. Mansur, 'The Nature of the Somali Clan System', in A.J. Ahmed (ed.), *The Invention of Somalia* (Lawrenceville, NJ: Red Sea Press, 1995), pp. 117–33.

10. It would be simplistic to say that clan X fought clan Y over Z resources because militias organizing along clan lines used these clan names and committed atrocities against civilian members of all clans. Although most civilian members of clans did not play a notable part in the fighting, the war nevertheless affected them. In this book, I mean militias of respective clans fought, not all the members of a clan against all members of another clan. There are many examples where militias from two clans fought in one part of the country, but the same two clans coexisted peacefully in other areas.

11. Charles L. Geshekter, 'Anti-colonialism and Class Formation: The Eastern Horn of Africa before 1950'. Paper presented at Somali Studies Conference, Boston, 1992; Lee V. Cassanelli, *The Shaping of Somali Society: Reconstructing the History of a Pastoral People, 1600–1900* (Philadelphia: University of Pennsylvania Press, 1982).

12. Ahmed Ismail Qasim is one of Somalia's most well-known poets. He composed this poem during the 1960s.

13. See Elmi and Barise, 'The Somali Conflict'.

14. In the last few lines of this poem Hadrawi graphically explains the atrocities that the military regime committed in the northeast and central regions. In Somali, he writes, 'Hadimada Garoowiyo, hanaq go'a Nugaaleed, halka aad tummaatiday, waxa kaga habboonaa, dar kaloo i hawlee, huqdaad reebtay weynaa, hibashiyo ladh kululaa. Colka Bari harraatiyey, hubka Mudug ku talax tegey, Allaylehe hubsiiniyo, hakin buu u baahnaa'. In this poem, Hadrawi is talking about the troops that attacked the Bari and Mudug regions of Somalia and the atrocities they committed. For him, the Somali state cannot be excused for such a crime. He concludes that the implication for such a crime is huge.

15. See Africa Watch, *Somalia*.

16. See Otomar J. Bartos and Paul Wehr, *Using Conflict Theory* (Cambridge: Cambridge University Press, 2002).

17. Raage Ugaas, one of Somalia's classical poets, was quoted as saying, 'Qab qab dhaafay baa, laba qabiil qaran ku waayaane. Qaabiilba Haabiil markuu, qoonsaduu dilaye' (Two clans lose nationhood or brave man because of clan pride. Qabil, the first son of Adam killed Habil, his younger brother when he felt anguish.)

18. See Stephen John Stedman, Donald Rothchild and Elizabeth Cousens, *Ending Civil Wars: The Implementation of Peace Agreements* (Boulder: Lynne Rienner, 2002), pp. 43–70.
19. See Elmi and Barise, 'The Somali Conflict'.
20. Economic and Security Pact between Ethiopia and Kenya.
21. See the Aden Declaration for the details of the agreement between Sharif Hassan Sheikh Adan and Abdullahi Yusuf, www.hiiraan.com/news/2006/jan/eng/Aden_ Declaration.htm (last accessed February 2006).

CHAPTER 3

1. 'Damane' (Foolish) is part of the chain of poems called Guba (*Silsiladda Guba: Guba Poems*). Several clans were involved in tribal wars for about forty years. Mohomed Omar Dage was born the year that these wars began. When he grew up he participated in these wars and began writing poems. In this poem, he is trying to send a message to his rival poet, Ali Dhuh.
2. Henry Hale, 'Explaining Ethnicity', *Comparative Political Studies* 37, no. 4 (2004): 466.
3. See Amartya Sen, *Identity and Violence: The Illusion of Destiny* (New York: W.W. Norton, 2006).
4. See I.M. Lewis, *Pastoral Democracy: A Study of Pastoralism and Politics Among the Northern Somali of the Horn of Africa* (London: Oxford University Press, 1961); Said Sheikh Samatar, *Somalia: Nation in Turmoil* (London: Minority Rights Group Report, 1991).
5. Mohamud Khalif, 'The Limits of Clan Politics', unpublished paper, 2004.
6. See Afyare Elmi and Abdullahi Barise, 'The Somali Conflict: Root Causes, Obstacles, and Peace-building Strategies', *African Security Review* 15, no. 1 (2006): 33–54.
7. Lewis, *Pastoral Democracy*.
8. Personal communication, Hargeysa, August 2000.
9. See Abdi M. Kusow, 'The Somali Origin: Myth or Reality', in Ali Jimale Ahmed (ed.), *The Invention of Somalia* (Lawrenceville, NJ: Red Sea Press, 1995), pp. 81–106; Bernhard Helander, 'Rahanweyn Sociability: A Model for Other Somalis', in I.M. Lewis and R.J. Hayward (eds), *Voice and Power: The Culture of Language in North-East Africa. Essays in Honour of B.W. Andrzejewski*, African Language and Cultures, suppl. 3 (London: School of Oriental and African Studies, University of London, 1996), pp. 195–204.
10. See Lewis, *Pastoral Democracy*, p. 128.
11. Ibid., pp. 132, 134.
12. See Janet Carsten, 'The Substance of Kinship and the Heat of the Hearth: Feeding, Personhood, and Relatedness among Malays in Pulau Langkawi', *American Ethnologist* 22, no. 2 (1995): 223–41. See also Janet Carsten (ed.), *Cultures of Relatedness: New Approaches to the Study of Kinship* (Cambridge: Cambridge University Press, 2000).
13. See Helander, 'Rahanweyn Sociability'.
14. See Lewis, *Pastoral Democracy*.
15. I.M. Lewis, *Blood and Bone: The Call of Kinship in Somali Society* (Lawrenceville, NJ: Red Sea Press, 1994), p. 22.
16. See A.H. Roble (ed.), *Silsiladda Guba: Guba Poems* (Sweden: Scansom Publishers, 1999). These poems present the harsh realities that existed in early

twentieth-century Somalia. As the poets narrate, these Somali clans have been fighting for decades.

17. A.S.B. Ahmed, *Xeerkii Soomaalidii Hore* (Somalia's traditional legal system) (Muqdisho: Somali National Printing Agency, 1977), p. 3.

18. Ibid., pp. 7–8.

19. Ibid., p. 22.

20. Lewis, *Pastoral Democracy*, p. 1.

21. The ayas say: 'O mankind! We created you from a single [pair] of a male and a female, and made you into nations and tribes, that ye may know each other not that ye may despise [each other]. Verily the most honoured of you in the sight of Allah is [he who is] the most righteous of you. And Allah has full knowledge and is well acquainted [with all things]' (Surah 49:11–13).

22. Lewis, *Pastoral Democracy*, p. 2.

23. Bobe Yusuf Duale, commenting on a presentation at the Somali Studies conference in Djibouti in December 2007.

24. See John Burton, *Conflict: Basic Human Needs* (New York: St Martin's Press); Johan Galtung, 'Cultural Violence', *Journal of Peace Research* 27, no. 3 (1990): 291–305.

25. Interview with Omar Iman, Asmara, 2008.

26. Interview with Abdirahman, Asmara, 2008.

27. Lewis, *Pastoral Democracy*, p. 3.

28. In the last ten years there have been a number of fundraising events held for different causes. Members of different clans collecting money to build schools and universities is a recent and increasing phenomenon. There is a thriving university in Borama which members of that community built – albeit with the help of other Somalis. There have also been publicized events in which Diaspora communities from the Hiran, Bay and Sool regions conducted fundraising events.

29. Samatar, *Somalia: Nation in Turmoil*, p. 13.

30. Interview with Islamist, Asmara, February 2008.

31. See, for example, Lewis, *Blood and Bone*; Samatar, *Somalia: Nation in Turmoil*; Abdalla Omar Mansur, 'The Nature of the Somali Clan System', in Ali Jimale Ahmed (ed.), *The Invention of Somalia* (Lawrenceville, NJ: Red Sea Press), pp. 117–33.

32. For example Ahmed I. Samatar (ed.), *The Somali Challenge: From Catastrophe to Renewal* (Boulder, CO: Lynne Rienner, 1994); Ahmed I. Samatar, 'Leadership and Ethnicity in the Making of African State-models: Botswana versus Somalia', *Third World Quarterly* 18, no. 4 (1997): 687–707; Elmi and Barise, 'The Somali Conflict'.

33. See Deborah P. Britzman, *Lost Subjects, Contested Objects: Toward a Psychoanalytic Inquiry of Learning* (Albany: State University of New York Press, 1998).

34. Ibid, p. 97.

35. Elmi and Barise, 'The Somali Conflict', p. 36.

36. Britzman, *Lost Subjects, Contested Objects*.

37. See Dan Smith, 'Trends and Causes of Armed Conflicts', in M.F. Norbert Ropers, Alexander Austin and Claus-Dieter Wild (eds), *The Berghof Handbook for Conflict Transformation* (Berlin: Berghof Research Centre for Constructive Conflict Management, 2000), www.berghof-handbook.net/uploads/download/smith_handbook.pdf (accessed August 2008).

38. For more on this see Burton, *Conflict: Basic Human Needs*; Galtung, 'Cultural Violence'.

39. See Johan Galtung, 'Three Approaches to Peace: Peacekeeping, Peacemaking, and Peacebuilding', in Johan Galtung (ed.), *Peace, War and Defense: Essays in Peace Research*, vol. 2 (Copenhagen: Christian Ejlers, 1975), pp. 297–8.

40. Boutros Boutros-Ghali, 'An Agenda for Peace: Preventive Diplomacy, Peacemaking and Peace-keeping, United Nations, 31 January 1992, para. 4, www.un.org/Docs/SG/agpeace.html (accessed August 2008).

41. Taisier M. Ali and Robert O. Matthews, 'Conclusion: The Long and Difficult Road to Peace', in Taisier and Matthews (eds), *Durable Peace: Challenges for Peacebuilding in Africa* (Toronto: University of Toronto Press, 2004), pp. 393–426.

42. I have heard this story from a number of people who narrate it differently. Even Abdi Kusow (2004) narrates it in different form. But, the fact that Rajis complained about the criteria of inclusion and exclusion of the peace process remains the same.

43. See Robert Rotberg, *When States Fail: Causes and Consequences* (Princeton, NJ: Princeton University Press, 1996).

44. Interview with Islamist, Asmara, 2008. The Hadith is in Bukhari.

45. See Lewis, *Pastoral Democracy*.

46. Interview with Islamist, Asmara, 2008.

47. Interview with civil society member, Djibouti, 2008.

48. Interview with Islamist, Djibouti, 2007.

49. Interview with Islamist, Dubai, 2007.

50. Interview with Gaandi, Djibouti, 2007.

51. Chaim Kaufmann, 'Possible and Impossible Solutions to Ethnic Civil Wars', *International Security* 20 (1996): 136–75.

52. Interview with Islamist, Dubai, 2008.

53. Interview with businessman, Dubai, 2008.

54. Interview with Islamist, Asmara, 2008.

55. Traditionally, clan chiefs, such as Sultan, Ugaas, Malaaq or Garaad, are the heads of clans. They make the decisions for clans. However, the current system empowers warlords.

56. Interview with Islamist, Asmara, 2008.

57. Interview with Islamist, Asmara, 2008.

58. Arend Lijphart, *Democracy in Plural Societies: Comparative Explanation* (New Haven, CT: Yale University Press, 1977).

59. George Downs and Stephen John Stedman, 'Evaluation Issues in Peace Implementation', in Donald Rothchild, Stephen John Stedman and Elizabeth M. Cousens (eds), *Ending Civil Wars: The Implementation of Peace Agreements* (Boulder, CO: Lynne Rienner, 2002), pp. 43–70, at p. 55.

60. See D.L. Horowitz, 'Constitutional Design: Proposals Versus Processes', in Andrew Reynolds (ed.), *The Architecture of Democracy: Constitutional Design, Conflict Management and Democracy* (Oxford: Oxford University Press, 2002), pp. 15–36. Lijphart, *Democracy in Plural Societies*.

61. Timothy D. Sisk, *Power-Sharing and International Mediation in Ethnic Conflicts* (Washington, DC: US Institute of Peace Press, 1996), p. 38.

62. Interview with Islamist, Asmara, 2008.

63. Interview with Islamist, Dubai, 2008.

64. See Lewis, *Pastoral Democracy*; Samatar, *Somalia: Nation in Turmoil*.

CHAPTER 4

1. Sheikh Mohamed Moallim Hassan is considered the founder of Somalia's Islamic movements. There are many lectures that he recorded on cassettes. This quote is taken from a lecture recorded in early 1992.
2. International Crisis Group, 'Somalia's Islamists', African Report No. 100, 12 December 2005, http://merln.ndu.edu/archive/icg/terrorismsomalia.pdf, p. 1.
3. See I.M. Lewis, *Pastoral Democracy: A Study of Pastoralism and Politics among the Northern Somali of the Horn of Africa* (London: Oxford University Press, 1961); see also Enrico Cerulli, 'New Notes on Islam', in Enrico Cerulli (ed.), *Somalia, scritti vari editi ed inediti*, vol. 3, trans. Biancani (Roma: Ministero degli Affari Esteri, 1964).
4. See Ali Abdirahman Hersi, *The Arab Factor in Somali History: The Origins and the Development of the Arab Enterprise and Cultural Influences in the Somali Peninsula* (Los Angeles: University of California Press, 1977); Mohammed Haji Mukhtar, 'Islam in Somali History: Fact and Fiction', in Ali Jimale Ahmed (ed.), *The Invention of Somalia* (Lawrenceville, NJ: Red Sea Press, 1995), pp. 1–29.
5. Mukhtar, 'Islam in Somali History', pp. 8–9.
6. Abu-Bakar Sidiq is the first Khalifa or Amir of the Muslims. He is also the first man who believed in the message of Islam.
7. Mukhtar, 'Islam in Somali History', p. 5.
8. See Hersi, *The Arab Factor in Somali History*; Mukhtar, 'Islam in Somali History'.
9. Ash'ari is a branch of Islamic faith which first articulated by Imam Abul-Hassan Al-Ash'ari.
10. Imam Shafi'i is the founder of the Shafi'i Fiqi Mad-hab. The other three founders are Imam Abu Hanifa, Imam Malik and Imam Ahmed Bin Hanbal.
11. Lewis and Cerulli translate the Arabic word *tariqa* as brotherhoods. I use the same term for this research.
12. See I.M. Lewis, *Saints and Somalis: Popular Islam in a Clan-based Society* (Lawrenceville and Asmara: Red Sea Press, 1998), p. 12.
13. See ibid.
14. Sheikh Mohamed Guled lived in the early twentieth century in the Gosha area. He should not be confused with another modern Somali scholar of the same name, who was a prominent Sufi politician during the military regime era (1969–91).
15. See ibid.; Cerulli, 'New Notes on Islam'.
16. The Darwish movement was an anti-colonial movement that fought against Great Britain for more than twenty years in Somaliland.
17. See Said Sheikh Samatar, *Oral Poetry and Somali Nationalism: The Case of Sayyid Mahammad Abdille Hassan* (Cambridge: Cambridge University Press, 1982); Abdi Sheik-Abdi, *Divine Madness: Mohammed Abdulle Hassan (1856–1920)* (London: Zed Books, 1993); Lewis, *Pastoral Democracy*.
18. Hersi, *The Arab Factor in Somali History*, p. 109.
19. Abdi Al-Qader, *The Conquest of Abyssinia: 16th Century*, trans. Paul Lester Stenhouse, with annotations by Richard Pankhurst (Hollywood, CA: Tsehai Publishers, 2003).
20. Samatar, *Oral Poetry and Somali Nationalism*; Sheikh-Abdi, *Divine Madness*; Lewis, *Pastoral Democracy*.
21. Samatar, *Oral Poetry and Somali Nationalism*; Sheik-Abdi, *Divine Madness*.

22. This series of poems edited by Abullahi Hassan Roble, *Silisilladii Guba: Guba Poems* (Sweden: Scansom Publishers, 1999) marks a forty-year war between Darod sub-clans of Ogaden and Dhulbahante against Isaaq sub-clans of Habar Yonis and Habar Je'lo. Many classical poets participated in this series including Ali Dhux, Salaan Arrabey and Qaman Bulxan.

23. See Bobby S. Sayyid, *A Fundamental Fear: Eurocentrism and the Emergency of Islamism* (London: Zed Books, 1997).

24. David Harrington Watt, 'The Meaning and End of Fundamentalism', *Religious Studies Review* 33, no. 4 (1997): 271.

25. Sayyid, *A Fundamental Fear*.

26. See J.L Esposito, *The Islamic Threat: Myth or Reality* (New York: Oxford University Press, 1993); Fawaz A. Gerges, *America and Political Islam: Clash of Cultures or Clash of Interests?* (Cambridge: Cambridge University Press, 1999); Graham Fuller, *A Sense of Siege: The Geopolitics of Islam and the West* (Boulder, CO: Westview Press, 1995); Graham Fuller, *The Future of Political Islam* (New York: Palgrave Macmillan, 2004); Edward Said, *Covering Islam: How the Media and the Experts Determine How We See the Rest of the World* (New York: Routledge, 1981).

27. Stephen Schwartz, 'What is "Islamofascism"?' *TCS Daily*, 16 August 2008, www.tcsdaily.com/article.aspx?id=081606C (accessed August 2008).

28. David Horowitz announced that he would raise the awareness of the American people and he called his campaign the 'Islamo-Fascim' week (22–26 October), 2007.

29. The White House, 'President Bush discusses terror plot upon arrival in Wisconsin', 10 August 2006, www.whitehouse.gov/news/releases/2006/08/20060810-3. html (accessed August 2008), para. 1.

30. Fuller, *The Future of Political Islam*, p. xi.

31. Guilain Denoeux, 'The Forgotten Swamp: Navigating Political Islam', *Middle East Policy* 9, no. 2 (2002): 52, see also 61.

32. See Mohammed Ayoob, 'The Future of Political Islam: The Importance of External Variables', *International Affairs* 81, no. 5 (2005): 951–61.

33. See Sheikh Yusuf Al-Qaradawi, *State in Islam* (Cairo: AL Falah Foundation for translation, publication and distribution, 2004), p. 121.

34. See ibid., pp. 121–42.

35. See Esposito, *Islamic Threat*.

36. Written by Shakib Arsalan, the book was re-published in 1975 (Beirut: Maktaba-Alhey'ah).

37. Ikhwan orientation stems from Imam Hassan Al-Banna's approach and the Muslim Brotherhood movement he established.

38. The term *Salafi* is derived from *Salaf-Salih*, meaning the Muslim scholars who lived in the first three centuries of Islam. Those who call themselves Salafis claim that they want to follow the path of the Salaf-Salih.

39. See Denoeux, 'The Forgotten Swamp'.

40. Abdelwhab El-Affendi, *Turabi's Revolution: Islam and Power in Sudan* (London: Grey Seal, 1991).

41. See Esposito, *Islamic Threat*; Fuller, *The Future of Political Islam*; Gerges, *America and Political Islam*.

42. See Ayoob, 'The Future of Political Islam'.

43. Mohammed Ayoob, 'Challenging Hegemony: Political Islam and the North–South Divide', *International Studies Review* 9 (2007): 635.

44. Interview with Islamist, Mogadishu, 2006.
45. In a conference held in Bosaso in 2008, Dr. Ahmed Abdirahman, a scholar who is identified with this school of thought, recently argued that Sheikh Ali Majeerteen was the first pioneer of the Salafi school in Somalia.
46. See Stig Jarle Hansen and Atle Mesøy, 'The Muslim Brotherhood in the Wider Horn of Africa'. The paper is available online at www.scribd.com/doc/24601810/Jarle-Hansen-Atle-Mes%C3%B8y-The-Muslim-Brotherhood-in-the-Wider-Horn-of-Africa. See also Abdurahman M. Abdullahi (Baadiyow), 'The Islah Movement: Islamic Moderation in Somalia'. This paper was presented at the Second Nordic Horn of Africa Conference held on 31 October to 1 November 2008, Oslo University, Norway. Retrieved June 2009, from www.scribd.com/doc/14642683/The-Islah-Movement-Islamic-Moderation-in-Somalia.
47. For seven of these years the Sheikh was in a prison near Baidoa called Labatan Jirow.
48. This merger took place because these movements wanted to organize their efforts in order to resist the Ethiopian occupation of Somalia. The Islamist website www.beerdhiga.org reported the merger.
49. See the websites of the two wings: www.al-islah.org and www.islahonline.org.
50. Personal communication with several Islamists in Asmara, Djibouti, Mogadishu and Dubai, December 2007 to March 2008.
51. See Ken Menkhaus, *Somalia: State Collapse and the Threat of Terrorism* (New York: Oxford University Press, 2004).
52. Ibid.; A. Le Sage, 'Prospects for Al-Ittihad and Islamist Radicals in Somalia', *Review of African Political Economy* 27, no. 89 (2001): 472–7; R. Marchal, *Somalia: A New Front Against Terrorism*, Social Science and Research Council: Horn of Africa, 2007. Retrieved from http://hornofafrica.ssrc.org/marchal/.
53. See the circular issued by 70 Somali scholars in 2007, at Goobjoog Online. Retrieved April 2007, from www.goobjoog.net/news/125/ARTICLE/5164/2007-04-15.html.
54. I visited Mogadishu in 2006 when Islamists controlled southern Somalia. There was euphoria in the streets of the city. It was obvious that these movements enjoyed popular support.
55. Interview with Jama Ghaleb, Djibouti, December 2007.
56. Interview with Islamist, Dubai, August 2006.
57. Abdinur N. Hashi, *Leadership Vacuum: Weapons and Clan Politics in Somalia* (Mogadishu: Horn of Africa Printing Press, 1996), p. 105.
58. Interview with Islamist, Asmara, 2008.
59. Interview with Islamist, Asmara, 2008.
60. Hashi, *Leadership Vacuum*, p. 103.
61. Personal communication, July 2007.
62. The change seems to be slow and indirect. In Djibouti in June 2008, the Security Council met with the leadership of the Alliance for the Re-liberation of Somalia which is dominated by the Islamists.
63. See US Department of State, Jendayi E. Frazer, Assistant Secretary of African Affairs, *Statement Before the Senate Committee on Foreign Relations Subcommittee on African Affairs*, 'Somalia: US Government Policy and Challenges', 11 July 2006, www.state.gov/p/af/rls/rm/2006/68870.htm.
64. Ethiopia invaded Somalia several times and destroyed Islamist movements and the US supported this military move.
65. Interview with Islamist, Djibouti, 2008.

66. Interview with Islamist, Asmara, 2008.
67. See Abdisalam M. Issa-Salwe, *Cold War Fallout: Boundary Politics and Conflict in the Horn of Africa* (London: HAAN Publishing, 2000).
68. See Roland Paris, 'Peacebuilding and the Limits to Liberal Internationalism', *International Security* 22, no. 2 (1997): 54–89; Alina Rocha Menocal and Kate Kilpatrick, 'Towards More Effective Peace Building: A Conversation with Roland Paris', *Development in Practice* 15 (2006): 767–77.
69. Interview with Islamist, Asmara, 2008.
70. Interview with Islamist, Djibouti, 2008.
71. Interview with businesswoman, Dubai, 2008.
72. Interview with businessman, Dubai, 2007.
73. Interview with Jama Ghaleb, Djibouti, 2007.
74. Interview with Islamist, Asmara, 2008.
75. Interview with businesswoman, Dubai, 2008.
76. Ayoob, 'Challenging Hegemony', 641.
77. Ibid., 642.
78. See Gerges, *America and Political Islam*.
79. Condoleezza Rice, 'Rethinking the National Interest: American Realism for a New World', *Foreign Affairs* 87, no. 4 (2008): 2–27, www.foreignaffairs. org/20080701faessay87401-p50/condoleezza-rice/rethinking-the-national-interest.html (accessed August 2008).

CHAPTER 5

1. The then US Assistant Secretary of State for African Affairs, Jendayi Frazer, gave an interview to the Associated Press a few days after the US-assisted Ethiopian occupation occurred. See 'America's top diplomat to Africa says U.S. must lead from behind in Somalia', *International Herald Tribune*, 7 January 2007, www.iht.com/articles/ap/2007/01/07/africa/AF-GEN-Somalia-US.php (accessed August 2008).
2. Terrence Lyons and Ahmed I. Samatar, *Somalia State Collapse, Multilateral Intervention and Strategies for Political Reconstruction* (Washington, DC: Brookings Institution, 1990), p. 26.
3. Most news agencies reported the event. See, for example, Agence France-Presse, 4 October 1993.
4. 'Combined Joint Task Force-Horn of Africa', Global Security.org, 2002, www. globalsecurity.org/military/agency/dod/cjtf-hoa.htm, para. 9.
5. William Pope, 'Remarks to the Conference on the Middle East Terrorist Connection in Latin America and the Caribbean', Center for International Policy's Columbia Program, 3 March 2004, available at America.gov, www. america.gov/st/washfile-english/2004/March/20040312160347FRllehct iMo.7013208.html See also www.ciponline.org/colombia/040303pope.htm.
6. Executive Order 13224, *Code of Federal Regulations*, title 3, 23 September 2001, www.state.gov/s/ct/rls/fs/2002/16181.htm.
7. Thomas Ricks, 'Allies step up Somalia watch: U.S. aims to keep Al Qaeda at bay', *Washington Post*, 4 January 2002, www.washingtonpost.com/ac2/wpdy n?pagename=article&contentId=A59310-2002Jan3&notFound=true.
8. Ken Menkhaus has written extensively about these issues. See 'Political Islam in Somalia', *Middle East Policy* 9, no. 1 (2002): 109–23. See; see also his 'Somalia: In the Crosshairs of the War on Terrorism', *Current History* 101,

no. 655 (2002): 210–18; 'State Collapse in Somalia: Second Thoughts', *Review of African Political Economy* 30, no. 97 (2003): 405–22; and *Somalia: State Collapse and the Threat of Terrorism* (New York: Oxford University Press, 2004).

9. There are several versions of Snyder's speech. I had received an e-mail from the UCLA African Studies Center which contained Snyder's speech of 14 November 2003. There is also a revised and edited version by Leslie Evans, 'Acting Assistant Secretary of State for African Affairs Surveys the Continent', UCLA International Institute, 3 December 2003, www.international.ucla.edu/article.asp?parentid=5373.

10. Chris Tomlinson, 'U.S. general calls Somalia terror haven', Associated Press, 15 May 2005, Xanga, New Yorker in DC, 'More on Somalia', www.xanga.com/home.aspx?user=NYkrinDC&nextdate=5%2F18%2F2005+23%3A59%3A59.999.

11. See US Department of State, Jendayi E. Frazer, Assistant Secretary of African Affairs, *Statement Before the Senate Committee on Foreign Relations Subcommittee on African Affairs*, 'Somalia: U.S. Government Policy and Challenges', 11 July 2006. The statement is online at www.state.gov/p/af/rls/rm/2006/68870.htm.

12. See Menkhaus, *Somalia: State Collapse and the Threat of Terrorism*.

13. White House, National Security Council, *National Security Strategy of the United States of America* (Washington, DC: GPO, 2003), pp. 1, 5. See the full report at www.whitehouse.gov/nsc/nss/2002/index.html.

14. Ibid., pp. 23–4.

15. Jeffrey Record, 'Bounding the Global War on Terrorism', Global Security.org, December 2003, www.globalsecurity.org/military/library/report/2003/record_bounding.pdf.

16. The White House, National Security Council, *National Strategy for Combating Terrorism* (Washington, DC: GPO, 2003), www.whitehouse.gov/nsc/nsct/2006/nsct2006.pdf.

17. See the S/CRS website for more information: www.state.gov/s/crs/.

18. See Andrew Natsios' announcement of the creation of this office: United States Embassy Stockholm, *U.S. Threatened by 'Failed States', USAID's Natsios Says Official Outlines U.S. Development Strategy for Helping Failed States*, Thursday 17 February 2005, www.au.af.mil/au/awc/awcgate/usaid/natsios021705.htm.

19. See Kansteiner's testimony in the US Senate, Senate Committee on Foreign Relations, Subcommittee on African Affairs, *Somalia: U.S. Policy Options: Hearing before the Subcommittee on African Affairs of the Committee on Foreign Relations*, 107th Congress 2nd sess., 6 February 2002, http://purl.access.gpo.gov/GPO/LPS19719.

20. See ibid., p. 7.

21. US Department of State, Secretary Condoleezza Rice, *Remarks at the American University in Cairo*, 20 June 2005, www.state.gov/secretary/rm/2005/48328.htm. See para. 8.

22. See Andre Le Sage, 'Prospects for Al-Ittihad and Islamist Radicals in Somalia', *Review of African Political Economy* 27, no. 89 (2001): 472–7. See also Menkhaus, 'Political Islam in Somalia'. Al-Ittihad used to publish a magazine called *Al-Bushraa*. In particular, see 'Wareysi lala yeeshay hoggaamiyaha Al-Itixaad' (An interview with the leader of Al-Ittihad), *Al-Bushraa* (July–August 1991).

23. See 'Wareysi lala yeeshay hoggaamiyaha Al-Itixaad'.
24. See Le Sage, 'Prospects for Al-Ittihad and Islamist Radicals in Somalia'; and Menkhaus 'Political Islam in Somalia'.
25. See Le Sage, 'Prospects for Al-Ittihad and Islamist Radicals in Somalia'; Menkhaus, 'Somalia: In the Crosshairs of the War on Terrorism'; and Menkhaus, *Somalia: State Collapse and the Threat of Terrorism.*
26. See Menkhaus, *Somalia: State Collapse and the Threat of Terrorism.*
27. See Menkhaus, 'Political Islam in Somalia'.
28. Ibid., 112.
29. See T.S. Dagne, 'Africa and the War on Terrorism: The Case of Somalia', *Mediterranean Quarterly* 13, no. 4 (2002): 16.
30. See Menkhaus, *Somalia: State Collapse and the Threat of Terrorism*, p. 65.
31. Ibid.
32. John L. Hirsch and Robert B. Oakley, *Somalia and Operation Restore Hope: Reflections on Peacemaking and Peacekeeping* (Washington, DC: United States Institute of Peace, 1995), p. 84.
33. This perception seems to be changing slowly. There are reports now that when Secretary of State Hillary Clinton visited Kenya in August 2009, Al-Shabab attempted to attack some Western targets in Nairobi. As most Somali media outlets reported, one of the spokesmen of Al-Shabab, Hassan Yacquub, also threatened Kenya in June 2009. Threats against Yemen have also been released by this group.
34. See Mohamed Ibrahim, 'Somali Rebels Pledge to Send Fighters to Aid Yemen Jihad', *New York Times*, 1 January 2010, available at www.nytimes.com/2010/01/02/world/africa/02somalia.html. See also Abdiaziz Hassan and Linda Muriuki, 'Somali Hardline Rebels Threaten Kenya Attack', Reuters, 21 January 2010, available at http://af.reuters.com/article/worldNews/idAFTRE60K49X20100121.
35. The National Commission on Terrorist Attacks Upon the United States (9-11 Commission) released its report on 22 July 2004; available online at http://govinfo.library.unt.edu/911/report/index.htm.
36. Several news agencies reported when Suleiman Abdalla Hamed was arrested. See for example, Associated Press, 6 November 2003.
37. See Evans, 'Acting Assistant Secretary of State for African Affairs Surveys the Continent'.
38. International Crisis Group, *Counter-Terrorism in Somalia: Losing Hearts and Minds?*, Crisis Group Africa Report No. 95, 11 July 2005, 'Executive Summary', www.crisisgroup.org/home/index.cfm?id=3555&l=2.
39. See Snyder, in Evans, 'Acting Assistant Secretary of State for African Affairs Surveys the Continent'.
40. Ibid., para. 109.
41. See 'America's top diplomat to Africa says U.S. must lead from behind in Somalia', www.iht.com/articles/ap/2007/01/07/africa/AF-GEN-Somalia-US.php. See also Stephanie McCrummen, 'U.S. diplomat meets with Somali leaders', *Washington Post*, Sunday 7 January 2007.
42. See International Crisis Group, *Counter-Terrorism in Somalia*.
43. Shabelle Radio is the most popular radio station in Mogadishu. It reported, in detail, the events that unfolded in 2006. The station has one of the most visited Somali websites.
44. The Department of State issued a press release regarding the creation of the Anti-Terrorism Warlords Alliance. The statement said that Washington was

working with a number of actors in order to contain terrorism in that part of the world.

45. Adulkadir Osman of Goobjoog Online interviewed Sheikh Sharif Sheikh Ahmed, chairman of the Union of Islamic Courts. See www.goobjoog.net.

46. See 'Somalia, revisited', *New York Times*, 7 June 2006, editorial page; 'Afghanistan in Africa', *Los Angeles Times*, 28 July 2006; 'Somalia simmers', *Washington Post*, 18 October 2006.

47. See Karen DeYoung, 'U.S. to hold international meeting on Somalia', *Washington Post*, 10 June 2006, sec. A, p. 12, www.washingtonpost.com/wp-dyn/content/article/2006/06/09/AR2006060901713.html.

48. See the BBC World Service report, 'Ethiopia says Somalia "a threat"', http://news.bbc.co.uk/2/hi/africa/5124068.stm.

49. Jeffrey Gettleman, 'U.S. strikes inside Somalia, bombing suspected militant hide-out', *New York Times*, 3 June 2007, www.nytimes.com/2007/06/03/world/africa/03somalia.html?scp=27&sq=JEFFREY%20GETTLEM.

50. See Michael Gordon and Mark Mazzetti, 'U.S. used base in Ethiopia to hunt Al Qaeda', *New York Times*, 23 February 2007. See also, 'US accused of using Ethiopia to launch air strikes on Somalia', *Guardian*, 24 February 2007.

51. See Jeffrey Gettleman and Eric Schmitt's *New York Times* article, 'U.S. kills top Qaeda militant in southern Somalia', www.nytimes.com/2009/09/15/world/africa/15raid.html.

52. Interview with Islamist, Asmara, February 2008.

53. The *New York Times* published this quote on 17 September 2001. See also Todd S. Purdum, 'After the attacks: the White House; Bush warns of a wrathful, shadowy and inventive war', *New York Times*, 15 September 2001, http://query.nytimes.com/gst/fullpage.html?res=9506E6DA173BF934A2575AC0A9679C8B63.

54. Interview with businessmen, Djibouti, December 2007.

55. Interview with Islamist, Asmara, February 2008.

56. Interview with Islamist, Doha, February 2008.

57. Mark Fineman, 'The oil factor in Somalia: four American petroleum giants had agreements with the African nation before its civil war began. They could reap big rewards if peace is restored', *Los Angeles Times*, Foreign Desk, Home Edition, Monday 18 January 1993, pt. A, p. 1, col. 1.

58. Telephone interview with Amina Said, May 2008.

59. Robert Weil, 'Somalia in Perspective: When the Saints Go Marching In', *Monthly Review* (March 1993), http://findarticles.com/p/articles/mi_m1132/is_n10_v44/ai_13607480.

60. Mohamed Said Samatar, interview, *Himilo Somali Magazine* 1 (1994): 28.

61. Jeffrey Gettleman, 'Clinton offers assurances to Somalis', *New York Times*, 6 August 2009.

62. Roland Marchal, 'Somalia: A New Front Against Terrorism', Horn of Africa: Social Science and Research Council, 2007, http://hornofafrica.ssrc.org/marchal/.

CHAPTER 6

1. Kenya's former president, Daniel Arap Moi, spoke at the National Defense University in Washington, DC, in September 2003. Also see the coverage of the African Digest at www.indo-african-society.org/pdf/africandigest.pdf.

2. See Ken Menkhaus, *Somalia: State Collapse and the Threat of Terrorism* (New York: Oxford University Press, 2004).

3. See Michael Brown (ed.), *The Causes of Internal Conflict: An Overview* (Cambridge, MA: MIT Press, 1996).

4. See Sihab ad-Din Ahmed bin Abd al-Qader, *The Conquest of Abyssinia*, which he wrote c. 1559. In 2003 Abd al-Qader's work was translated into English by Paul Stenhouse. *The Conquest of Abyssinia* provides a detailed account of Muslim–Christian wars in the sixteenth century.

5. Charles L. Geshekter, 'Anti-colonialism and Class Formation: The Eastern Horn of Africa before 1950', *International Journal of Historical African Studies* 18, no.1 (1985): 1–32.

6. John H. Spencer, *Ethiopia at Bay: A Personal Account of the Haile Sellassie Years* (Algonac, MI: Reference Publications, 1984), p. 141.

7. Ibid.

8. Ibid., p. 181.

9. See Abdi Sheik-Abdi, *Divine Madness: Mohammed Abdulle Hassan (1856–1920)* (London: Zed Books, 1993); Said Sheikh Samatar, *Oral Poetry and Somali Nationalism: The Case of Sayyid Mahammad Abdille Hassan* (Cambridge: Cambridge University Press, 1982).

10. See Spencer, *Ethiopia at Bay*. Airplanes dropped leaflets to Somalis in southern Somalia calling on them to join Ethiopia.

11. See Gebru Tareke, 'The Ethiopia–Somalia War of 1977 Revisited', *International Journal of African Historical Studies* 33, no. 3 (2000): 635–67.

12. See ibid.; see also Ruth Lapidoth-Eschelbacher, *International Straits of the World: Red Sea and the Gulf of Aden* (The Hague: Martinus Nijhoff, 1982).

13. See Terrence P. Lyons and Ahmed Ismail Samatar, *Somalia: State Collapse, Multilateral Intervention, and Strategies for Political Reconciliation* (Washington, DC: The Brookings Institute, 1994); I.M. Lewis, *Modern History of the Somali: Nation and State in the Horn of Africa* (London: Longman Group Limited, 1980).

14. Interview with Shamis, Dubai, 2008.

15. Abdelwhab El-Affendi, 'The Impasse in the Igad Peace Process for Sudan: The Limits of Regional Peacemaking?' *African Affairs* 100, no. 401 (2001): 581–99.

16. From Dr Abdi Aden's speech at the 2002 University of Toronto conference, which I attended.

17. See Bertrand Rosenthal, 'Ethiopia Shows Its Hand in Somalia Crisis', Agence France Presse, 23 March 2001, www.reliefweb.int/rw/rwb.nsf/AllDocsByUNID/d545bf44072de9f7c1256a18004c3c7a.

18. UN Security Council, 'Stressing Respect for Somalia's Sovereignty, Independence, Unity, Security Council Reaffirms Commitment to Comprehensive Settlement', 31 October 2001, SC/7190, www.un.org/News/Press/docs/2001/sc7190.doc.htm (last accessed 14 January 2009).

19. See A.I. Samatar and A. Samatar, 'Somali Reconciliation: Editorial Note', *Bildhaan: International Journal of Somali Studies* 3 (2003): 1–14; International Crisis Group, 'Somalia: Continuation of War by Other Means?' Crisis Group Africa Report No. 88, 21 December 2004, www.crisisgroup.org/home/index.cfm?l=1&id=3194.

20. James C. Mckinley, Jr., 'Ethiopian Army Attacks 3 Towns in Border Region of Somalia', *New York Times*, 10 August 1996, http://query.nytimes.com/gst/

fullpage.html?res=9501E5DE103EF933A2575BC0A960958260 (last accessed 14 January 2009).

21. See ibid.; see also Ken Menkhaus, *Somalia: State Collapse and the Threat of Terrorism* (New York: Oxford University Press, 2004).

22. Patrick Gilkes 'The Somali Connection', BBC Online Network, Battle in the Horn Special Report, 23 July 1999 http://news.bbc.co.uk/1/hi/special_report/1999/07/99/battle_in_the_horn/399898.stm (last accessed 14 January 2009).

23. BBC, 'Ethiopia Says Somalia "a Threat"', 28 June 2006, http://news.bbc.co.uk/2/hi/africa/5124068.stm (last accessed 14 January 2009).

24. See reports of these events at Shabelle Radio, Hiiraan Online, Qadisiya Online, and HornAfrik Online.

25. Afyare Elmi and A. Barise, 'The Somali Conflict: Root Causes, Obstacles, and Peace-building Strategies', *African Security Review* 15, no. 1 (2006): 42.

26. See Brown, *The Causes of Internal Conflict*. See also his chapters 'The Causes and Regional Dimensions of Internal Conflicts' (pp. 571–602) and 'Internal Conflict and International Action' (pp. 603–628) in M.E. Brown (ed.), *The International Dimension of Internal Conflicts* (Cambridge, MA: MIT Press, 1996).

27. Adam Mynott, 'Somali Crisis "Worse than Darfur"', 16 June 2008, BBC News, http://news.bbc.co.uk/2/hi/africa/7457974.stm (last accessed 14 January 2009).

28. The Federal Democratic Republic of Ethiopia Foreign Affairs and National Security Policy and Strategy, 'Ethiopia's Policy Towards Somalia', www.mfa.gov.et/Foreign_Policy_And_Relation/Relations_With_Horn_Africa_Somalia.php.

29. See Catherine Hoskyns, *Case Studies in African Diplomacy* (Dar es Salaam, Nairobi and Addis Ababa: Oxford University Press, 1969); John Drysdale, *The Somali Dispute* (New York: Fredrick A. Praeger, 1964).

30. See Hoskyns, *Case Studies in African Diplomacy*.

31. See ibid.; see also Spencer, *Ethiopia at Bay*.

32. See AFP article in 2007.

33. Farah Wa'ays Dhule was a member of Somalia's Revolutionary Council, which consisted of 25 senior military officers.

34. See Abdisalam M. Issa-Salwe, *The Collapse of the Somali State* (London: HAAN Publishing, 1996).

35. Interview with Dr Ali Khalif Galaidh, Dubai, January 2008.

36. See Samatar and Samatar, 'Somali Reconciliation: Editorial Note'; Elmi and Barise, 'The Somali Conflict'.

37. Interview with Islamist, Asmara, February 2008.

38. See Article 16 of the Charter of the Organization of African Unity.

39. In *Case Studies in African Diplomacy*, Catherine Hoskyns collects several important documents including the speech of President Aden Abdulle Osman. See pp. 32–3.

40. Hoskyns, *Case Studies in African Diplomacy*; Drysdale, *The Somali Dispute*.

41. Hoskyns, *Case Studies in African Diplomacy*.

42. Spencer, *Ethiopia at Bay*, p. 320.

43. See Thomas Kwasi Tieku, 'Explaining the Clash and Accommodation of Interests of Major Actors in the Creation of the African Union', *African Affairs* 103 (2004): 249–67.

44. See Corinne A.A. Packer and Donald Rukare, 'The New African Union and Its Constitutive Act', *American Journal of International Law* 96, no. 2 (2008): 365–79.
45. Ibid.
46. See El-Affendi, 'The Impasse in the Igad Peace Process for Sudan'.
47. Ibid.
48. I discussed this issue with several members of the Somali Parliament, former TNG officials, and a number of intellectuals who confirmed this to me.
49. See El-Affendi, 'The Impasse in the Igad Peace Process for Sudan'.
50. Ibid., 583.
51. Elmi and Barise, 'The Somali Conflict'. See also my article 'Meddling mars the Somali peace process', *The Toronto Star*, Editorial Page, 16 October 2003.
52. Peter Wallensteen and Margareta Sollenberg, 'Armed Conflict, 1989–2000', *Journal of Peace Research* 38, no. 5 (September 2001): 629–44.
53. Stephen John Stedman, 'Spoiler Problems in Peace Processes', *International Security* 22, no. 2 (1997): 51.
54. See Matt Bryden, 'New Hope for Somalia? The Building Block Approach', *Review of African Political Economy* 26, no. 79 (1999): 134–40.
55. The CIA World Factbook book suggests otherwise. See https://www.cia.gov/library/publications/the-world-factbook/geos/et.html.
56. Interview with Omar, Asmara, 2008.
57. *Ethiopian Herald*, 'The Jihad Siad Barre is waging', *Ethiopian Herald*, 28 July 1977.
58. Spencer, *Ethiopia at Bay*.
59. Mohamud Khalif has written several academic articles on the subject. I noted this from a personal communication I had with him during his visit to Edmonton on 30 July 2008.
60. Spencer, *Ethiopia at Bay*.
61. BBC, 'Clerics Killed in Somali Mosque', http://news.bbc.co.uk/2/hi/africa/7358198.stm.
62. See, for instance, Amnesty International, 'Somalia/Ethiopia: Deliberate Killing of Civilians Is a War Crime', 25 April 2008, www.amnesty.org/en/for-media/press-releases/somaliaethiopia-deliberate-killing-civilians-war-crime-20080425 (last accessed 18 January 2009).
63. *A Resolution Supporting Humanitarian Assistance, Protection of Civilians, Accountability for Abuses in Somalia, and Urging Concrete Progress in Line with the Transitional Federal Charter of Somalia toward the Establishment of a Viable Government of National Unity*, S.RES.541, 110 Cong., 2d sess. (29 April 2008), http://thomas.loc.gov/cgi-bin/bdquery/z?d110:sr541 (last accessed 18 January 2009).
64. See Louis Charbonneau, 'UN Council Meets Somalia Government, Opposition', *Reuters*, 2 June 2008, www.reuters.com/article/homepageCrisis/idUSL01118790._CH_.2400.
65. UN Monitoring Group, www.un.org/sc/committees/751/mongroup.shtml (last accessed 18 January 2009), p. 22.

CHAPTER 7

1. Hadrawi composed 'Gudgude' (Heavy Rain) in 1990, right before the Somali state collapsed. These two lines deal with the importance of education and how

those who do not have sufficient education would not learn from the events they themselves witnessed.

2. Mohamed I. Warsame (Hadrawi), 'Islam is the Solution to the Somali Problems', *Himilo Somali Newspaper* 1 (1995): 1–8.

3. B.W. Andrzejewski and I.M. Lewis, *Somali Poetry: An Introduction* (Oxford: Clarendon Press, 1964).

4. Ali Abdirahman Hersi, *Arab Factor in Somali History: The Origins and the Development of the Arab Enterprise and Cultural Influences in the Somali Peninsula* (Los Angeles: University of California Press, 1977).

5. See ibid.

6. Ali A. Abdi, 'Education in Somalia: History, Destruction, and Calls for Reconstruction', *Comparative Education* 34, no. 3 (1998): 327–40.

7. See ibid.

8. The major schools in Mogadishu are the following: General Daauud, Mohamud Ahmed Ali, Bartamaha, Sheikh Hassan Barsane l, Rage Ugaas, Polytechnic, Wadajir Sare, Banadir, 15 May School, Muse Galal, Hawlwadaag Sare, Osman Gedi Rage, Xisaabaatka iyo Cabiraadda Dhulka, Macallin Jaamac, Sakhaawaddiin, Jamaal Cabdi Naasir, Culuunta Badda, Baarbe, Kaasa bobollaare, Xamar sare.

9. See Clayton Thyne, 'ABC's, 123's and the Golden Rule: The Pacifying Effect of Education on Civil Conflict, 1980–1999', *International Studies Quarterly* 50, no. 4 (2006): 733–54; W.C. Parker, 'Toward Enlightened Political Engagement', in W.B. Stanley (ed.), *Critical Issues in Social Studies Research for the 21st Century* (Chicago: Information Age Publishing, 2001), pp. 97–118.

10. See Thyne, 'ABC's, 123's and the Golden Rule'.

11. See Ken Bickmore, 'Education for Conflict Resolution and Peacebuilding in Plural Societies: Approaches from Around the World', unpublished paper, 2006; Thyne, 'ABC's, 123's and the Golden Rule'; Kenneth D. Bush and Diana Saltarelli, *The Two Faces of Education: Towards a Peacebuilding Education for Children* (Florence: Innocenti Research Centre, UNICEF, 2000).

12. Terrance R. Carson and David C. Smith, *Educating for a Peaceful Future* (Toronto: Kagan & Woo, 1998).

13. See Paul Collier, 'Economic Causes of Civil Conflict and Their Implications for Policy', April 2006, http://users.ox.ac.uk/~econpco/research/pdfs/EconomicCausesofCivilConflict-ImplicationsforPolicy.pdf (last accessed 19 January 2009); Ibrahim Elbadawi and Nicholas Sambanis, 'Why Are There So Many Civil Wars in Africa? Understanding and Preventing Violent Conflict', *Journal of African Economies* 9 (2000): 244–69; Parker, 'Toward Enlightened Political Engagement'.

14. See Afyare Elmi and A. Barise, 'The Somali Conflict: Root Causes, Obstacles, and Peace-building Strategies', *African Security Review* 15, no. 1 (2006): 33–54.

15. Abdi, 'Education in Somalia'; L. Cassanelli and F. Abdilkadir, 'Education in Transition', *Bildhaan International Journal of Somali Studies* 7 (2007): 91–125.

16. See Abdi, 'Education in Somalia'.

17. A Somali educator told this story to me in Mogadishu in July 2006.

18. UNICEF, *Survey of Primary Education in Somalia 2005/2006: Technical Report* (Nairobi: UNICEF Office, 2006).

19. See UNDP, *Millennium Development Goals Report* (Nairobi: Springette House, 2007), www.so.undp.org/index.php/Viewcategory.html?dir=DESC&limit=5&limitstart=5&order=name (last accessed August 2008).

20. Ibid.
21. Interview with Mohamed Abdulkadir, Nairobi, July 2007.
22. Interview with Mohamed Abdulkadir, Nairobi, July 2007.
23. Interview with Paul Gomis, UNESCO Country Director for Somalia, Nairobi, July 2007.
24. Andrea Kathryn Talentino, 'Two Faces of Nation Building: Developing Function and Identity', *Cambridge Review of International Affairs* 17, no. 3 (2004): 559.
25. Ibid., 564.
26. I.M. Lewis, *Pastoral Democracy: A Study of Pastoralism and Politics among the Northern Somali of the Horn of Africa* (London: Oxford University Press, 1961).
27. In an interview by Ali Iman Sharmarke, Nairobi, 2003.
28. W.C. Parker, 'Toward Enlightened Political Engagement'.
29. See Ali Jimale Ahmed, *Daybreak Is Near: Literature, Clans and the Nation-state in Somalia* (Lawrenceville, NJ: Red Sea Press, 1996); Abdi M. Kusow, 'The Somali Origin: Myth or Reality?' in Ali Jimale Ahmed (ed.), *The Invention of Somalia* (Lawrenceville, NJ: Red Sea Press, 1995), pp. 81–106.
30. Interview with Paul Gomis, Nairobi, July 2007.
31. Interview with Toby Kay, Nairobi, July 2007.
32. Interview with Mohamed Abdulkadir, Nairobi, July 2007.
33. Interview with Paul Gomis, Nairobi, July 2007.
34. Bush and Saltarelli, *The Two Faces of Education*, p. 23.
35. Ibid.
36. Ibid.
37. See Ken Bickmore, 'Conflicts Global and Local: An Elementary Approach', *Social Education* 66, no. 4 (2000): 235–8.
38. See Elmi and Barise, 'The Somali Conflict'.
39. See Johan Galtung (ed.), *After Violence, Reconstruction, Reconciliation, and Resolution: Coping with Visible and Invisible Effects of War and Violence* (New York: Lexington Books, 2001).
40. Mohammed Abu Nimer, *Nonviolence and Peacebuilding in Islam: Theory and Practice* (Gainesville: University Press of Florida, 2003), pp. 42–84.
41. 'Wareysi: Hadrawi' (Interview with Hadrawi), *Himilo Newspaper,* October 2003.
42. Save the Children, 'What We Do in Somalia/Somaliland', 2007, www.savethechildren.org.uk/en/947.htm (last accessed June 2008).

CHAPTER 8

1. Professor Abdi Samatar narrated this story. He was speaking at Lund University, Sweden, in 2007. A video is available at http://video.google.ca/videoplay?docid=-4408652489162053739&q=samatar&ei=j3x QSLlmkIqqA5j1-MEM&hl=en (accessed July 2008).
2. Andrew Gowers, 'The Power of Two', *Foreign Policy* 132 (2002): 32–3.
3. Noam Chomsky, 'The Crimes of "Intcom"', *Foreign Policy* 132 (2002): 34.
4. Interview with General Jama Mohamed Ghaleb, Ali Sabih Hotel, Djibouti, December 2007.
5. Samuel P. Huntington, 'The Clash of Civilizations?' *Foreign Affairs* 72, no. 3 (1993): 22–49.

6. See Francis Fukuyama, *The End of History and the Last Man* (New York: Free Press, 1990).
7. See Roland Paris, 'Peacebuilding and the Limits to Liberal Internationalism', *International Security* 22, no. 2 (1997): 54–89; Roland Paris, 'International Peacebuilidng and the "Mission Civilisatrice"', *Review of International Studies* 28 (2002): 637–56; Shalmali Guttal, 'The Politics of Post-war/Post-conflict Reconstruction', *Development* 48, no. 3 (2005): 73–81.
8. Paris, 'International Peacebuilding and the "Mission Civilisatrice"', 638–9.
9. Ibid.
10. Guttal, 'The Politics of Post-war/Post-conflict Reconstruction'.
11. Paris, 'International Peacebuilding and the "Mission Civilisatrice"'.
12. Guttal, 'The Politics of Post-war/Post-conflict Reconstruction', 73.
13. Ibid., 74.
14. Interview with EU official, Nairobi, June 2007.
15. Interview with the Deputy of the Special Representative of the Secretary General of the United Nations, Nairobi, July 2007.
16. Interview with the Country Director of UNESCO, Nairobi, June 2007.
17. Interview with an official who was close to the talks, Nairobi, June 2007.
18. Abdullahi Yusuf gave a speech in Baidoa. He was talking to senior employees of his government and he urged them to come up with a way that the government can re-gain control of the situation.
19. Interview with European diplomat, Nairobi, June 2007.
20. For instance, intellectuals from the Somali Diaspora had a debate on this issue. All were members of the Israaca Organization, and some even met with Dr Ali Mazrui who is a proponent of inter-African trusteeship.
21. William Bain, 'Trusteeship: A Response to Failed States?' Paper presented at the Conference on Failed States and Global Governance, Purdue University, Florence, Italy, 10–14 April 2001. A draft of this paper is available online at www.comm.ucsb.edu/research/mstohl/failed_states/2001/papers/bain.pdf (last accessed 19 January 2009); see p. 3.
22. See Ali Mazrui, 'Blood of Experience: The Failed State and Political Collapse in Africa', *World Policy Journal* 12, no. 1 (1995): 28–34; Ali Mazrui, *Islam between Globalization and Counter-terrorism* (Trenton, NJ: Africa World Press, 2006).
23. See Bain, 'Trusteeship: A Response to Failed States?'; William Bain, 'The Idea of Trusteeship in International Society', *The Round Table* 368 (2003): 67–76; Harry A. Inman and Walter Gary Sharp, Sr., 'Revising the U.N. Trusteeship System: Will It Work?' *American Diplomacy* 4, no. 4 (1999), www.unc.edu/depts/diplomat/AD_Issues/amdipl_13/inman_somalia.html (last accessed 20 January 2009); David Thürer, 'The "Failed State" and International Law', *International Review of the Red Cross* 836 (1999): 731–61.
24. United Nations Charter, Article 78, www.un.org/aboutun/charter/.
25. See Bain, 'The Idea of Trusteeship'.
26. See Thürer, 'The "Failed State" and International Law'.
27. Edward Marks, 'Transitional Governance: A Return to the Trusteeship System', *American Diplomacy* 9, no. 1 (1999), www.unc.edu/depts/diplomat/AD_Issues/amdipl_10/marks2.html (last accessed 20 January 2009), para. 15.
28. See James D. Fearon and David D. Laitin, 'Neotrusteeship and the Problem of Weak States', *International Security* 28, no. 4 (2004): 5–43.
29. Ibid.

30. See Fearon and Laitin, 'Neotrusteeship and the Problem of Weak States'; Marks, 'Transitional Governance'; and Thürer, 'The "Failed State" and International Law'.
31. William Bain, 'Trusteeship: A Response to Failed States?'.
32. See Milbrey Wallin McLaughlin, 'Learning from Experience: Lessons from Policy Implementation', *Educational Evaluation and Policy Analysis* 9, no. 2 (1987): 171–8.
33. See Pinar Bilgin and Adam David Morton, 'From Rogue to Failed States? The Fallacy of Short-termism', *Politics* 24, no. 3 (2004): 169–80.

CHAPTER 9

1 This is one of seven peace poems that Mohamed Ga'al Hayow composed in the 1990s. I transcribed this from a cassette. The recording can be accessed at www.newbanadir.com/GacalXaayow-22.rm (last accessed 25 January 2009).
2 Al-Jazeera interviewed Al-Qaeda's leader in Afghanistan, Abul-Yazed, and asked him about the link between Al-Shabab and Al-Qaeda. Abul-Yazid revealed that one of the three individuals was a member of Al-Qaeda and he was killed in Somalia in 2007. Moreover, the United States killed Saleh Nebhan, the second man, in an operation in southern Somalia. Washington argues that the third individual, Fuzul Rahman, is still in Somalia.
3 Susan E. Rice, *The New National Security Strategy: Focus on Failed States*, Policy Brief # 116 (Washington, DC: Brookings Institution, 2003), p. 6.

Selected Bibliography

Abd al-Qader, S.A. (2003). *The conquest of Abyssinia: 16th Century* (trans. Paul Lester Stenhouse, with annotations by Richard Pankhurst). Hollywood, CA: Tsehai Publishers.

Abdi, A.A. (1998). Education in Somalia: History, destruction, and calls for reconstruction. *Comparative Education*, 34(3): 327–40.

Abdi, A.A. (2003). Reconstructing the collapsed Somali state, and the promise (and possible pitfalls) of federation. *Horn of Africa*, 21: 20–9.

Abdi, A. and Elmi, A. (2008). Nationalism, nation-building and education in Somalia. Paper presented at the Canadian Association of African Studies conference, held at the University of Alberta, Edmonton, Canada, 3 May.

Abdulle, S. and Crilly, R. (2009, 7 April). Somali fishermen opt for piracy's rich pickings. *Times Online*.

Abu-Nimer, M. (ed.) (2000). *Reconciliation, justice and coexistence: Theory and practice*. New York: Lexington Books.

Abu-Nimer, M. (2003). *Nonviolence and peace building in Islam: Theory and practice*. Gainesville: University Press of Florida.

Abu Sulayman, A. H. (1993). *Towards Islamic theory of international relations: New directions for methodology and thought*. Herndon, VA: International Institute of Islamic Thought.

Adar, K.G. (2001). Somalia: The reconstruction of a collapsed State. *Conflict Trends*, 2.

Adler, E. (1997). Seizing the middle ground: Constructivism in world politics. *European Journal of International Relations*, 3(3): 319–63.

Adorno, T.W. (1950). *The authoritarian personality*. New York: Harper.

Africa Watch. (1990). *Somalia: A government at war with its own people*. London: Africa Watch.

Ahmed, A.J. (1995). Dervishization of the Somali state. In A.J. Ahmed (ed.), *The invention of Somalia*. Lawrenceville, NJ: Red Sea Press.

Ahmed, A.J. (1996). *Daybreak is near: Literature, clans and the nation-state in Somalia*. Lawrenceville, NJ: Red Sea Press.

Ahmed, A.S.B. (1977). *Xeerkii Soomaalidii hore* (Somalia's traditional legal system). Muqdisho: Somali National Printing Agency.

Alexander, J.L. (1987). Twenty lectures: Sociological theory since World War II. New York: Columbia University Press.

Ali, A.Y. (1930). *The meaning of the Holy Qur'an*. Beltsville, MD: Amana Publications.

Ali, T.M. and Matthews, R.O. (2004). Conclusion: The long and difficult road to peace. In T.M. Ali and R.O. Matthews (eds), *Durable peace: Challenges for peacebuilding in Africa* (pp. 393–426). Toronto: University of Toronto Press.

Al-Qaradawi, S.Y. (2004). *State in Islam*. Cairo: AL Falah Foundation for translation, publication and distribution.

Amies, N. (2009, 27 May). Shipping insurance sky-rockets as pirate attacks increase. *Deutsche Welle*. www.dw-world.de/dw/article/0,,4278642,00.html.

Amnesty International. (2008). *Somalia/Ethiopia: Deliberate killing of civilians is a war crime*. Retrieved 12 August 2008, from www.amnesty.org/en/for-media/press-releases/somaliaethiopia-deliberate-killing-civilians-war-crime-20080425.

Andeweg, R.B. (2000). Consociational Democracy. *Annual Reviews of Political Science*, 3: 509–36.

Andrzejewski, B.W. and Lewis, I.M. (1964). *Somali poetry: An introduction*. Oxford: Clarendon Press.

Arman, A. (2009, 24 April). Piracy, geopolitics, and private security. *The Huffington Post*.

Arsalan, S. (1975). *Limadha ta'akhkhara al-Muslimun wa-limadha taqaddama ghayruhum?* (Why have Muslims regressed while others progressed?). Beirut: Maktaba-Alhey'ah.

Ashcroft, B., Griffiths, G. and Tiffin, H. (1998). *Key concepts in post-colonial studies*. New York: Routledge.

The Associated Press. (2005). Americans seek warlords' help in hunt for terrorists in Somalia. CNN published this report and I retrieved May 2007 from www.cnn.com/2003/WORLD /africa/11/06/somalia.terrorism.ap/index.html.

The Associated Press. (2007, 7 January). America's top diplomat to Africa says U.S. must lead from behind in Somalia. (AP Interview). *International Herald Tribune*. Retrieved August 2008, from www.iht.com/articles/ap/2007/01/07/africa/AF-GEN-Somalia-US.php.

Ayoob, M. (2005). The future of political Islam: The importance of external variables. *International Affairs*, 81(5): 951–61.

Ayoob, M. (2007). Challenging hegemony: Political Islam and the North–South divide. *International Studies Review*, 9: 629–43.

Bain, W. (2001). Trusteeship: A response to failed states? Paper presented at the Conference on Failed States and Global Governance, organized by Purdue University, Florence, Italy, 10–14 April. A draft of this paper is available at www.comm.ucsb.edu/research/mstohl/failed_states/2001/papers/bain.pdf.

Bain, W. (2003). The idea of trusteeship in international society. *The Round Table*, 368: 67–76.

Baldwin, D.A. (2006). The concept of security. *Review of international studies*, 23: 5–26.

Bandura, A. (1971). *Social learning theory*. New York: General Learning Press.

Barash, D.P. (ed.) (2000). *Approaches to Peace*. New York: Oxford University Press.

Barash, D.P. and Webel, C.P. (eds) (2002). *Peace and conflict studies*. Thousand Oaks, CA: Sage Publications.

Barise, A.A. and Elmi, Afyare A. (2004, 20 September). Somalia is the hen in a fox-brokered peace. *Globe and Mail*, opinion/editorial section.

Bar-Tal, D. (ed.) (2002). *The elusive nature of peace education*. Mahwah, NJ: Lawrence E. Associates.

Bartos, O.J. and Wehr, P. (2002). *Using conflict theory*. Cambridge: Cambridge University Press.

BBC World Service. (2006). *Ethiopia says Somalia 'a threat'* (2006). Retrieved 12 August 2008, from http://news.bbc.co.uk/2/hi/africa/5124068.stm.

BBC World Service. (2008). *Clerics killed in Somali mosque*. Retrieved 8 August 2008, from http://news.bbc.co.uk/2/hi/africa/7358198.stm.

Bemath, A.S. (ed.) (1992). *The Sayid and the Salihiya Tariqa: Reformist anti-colonial hero in Somalia*. Trenton, NJ: Red Sea Press.

Berdal, M. and Malone, D.M. (eds) (2000). *Greed and grievance: Economic agendas in civil wars*. Boulder: Lynne Rienner.

Bergesen, A.J. (2008). *The Sayyid Qutb reader: Selected writings on politics, religion, and society*. New York: Routledge.

Bhabha, H. (1994). *The location of culture*. London: Routledge.

Bickmore, K. (2002). Conflicts global and local: An elementary approach. *Social Education*, 66(4): 235–8.

Bickmore, K. (2002). Peer mediation training and program implementation in elementary schools: Research results. *Conflict Resolution Quarterly*, 20(2): 137–60.

Bickmore, K. (2003). Kinds of conflict. Class handout given to students in summer 2003 at OISE/University of Toronto.

Bickmore, K. (2006). Education for conflict resolution and peacebuilding in plural societies: Approaches from around the world. Unpublished paper.

Boulding, E. (1999). Peace culture. *Encyclopedia of Violence, Peace and Conflict*, vol. 2, pp. 653–67.

Boulding, E. (2000). *Cultures of peace: The hidden side of history*. Syracuse: Syracuse University Press.

Boutros-Ghali, B. (1992, 31 January). An agenda for peace: Preventive diplomacy, peacemaking and peace-keeping. Retrieved 12 August 2008, from www.un.org/Docs/SG/agpeace.html.

Boutros-Ghali, B. (1995, 3 January). Supplement to An agenda for peace: Position paper of the Secretary-General on the occasion of the fiftieth anniversary of the United Nations. Retrieved 12 August 2008, from www.un.org/Docs/SG/agsupp.html.

Brinkerhoff, D.W. (2005). Rebuilding governance in failed states and post-conflict societies: Core concepts and cross-cutting themes. *Public Administration and Development*, 25 (3): 3–14.

Britzman, D. (1998). *Lost subjects, contested objects: Toward a psychoanalytic inquiry of learning*. Albany: State University of New York Press.

Britzman, D. (2003). *Practice makes practice: A critical study of learning to teach*, Revised edition. Albany: State University of New York Press.

Brown, M.E. (1996). The causes and regional dimensions of internal conflicts. In M. Brown (ed.), *The international dimension of internal conflicts* (pp. 571–602). Cambridge, MA: MIT Press.

Brown, M.E. (1996). Internal conflict and international action. In M. Brown (ed.), *The international dimension of internal conflicts* (pp. 603–28). Cambridge, MA: MIT Press.

Brown, M.E. (ed.) (1997). *The causes of internal conflict: An overview*. Cambridge, MA: MIT Press.

Bryden, M. (1999). New hope for Somalia? The building block approach. *Review of African Political Economy*, 26 (79): 134–40.

Burrell, G. and Morgan, G. (1979). Sociological paradigms and organizational analysis. London: Heinemann Educational.

Burton, J. (1990). *Conflict: Basic human needs*. New York: St Martin's Press.

Bush, K.D. and Saltarelli, D. (2000). *The two faces of education: Towards a peacebuilding education for children*. Florence: Innocenti Research Centre, UNICEF.

Callaghy, T.M., Kassimir, R. and Latham, R. (eds) (2001). *Intervention and transnationalism in Africa: Global–local networks of power*. Cambridge: Cambridge University Press.

Carsten, J. (1995). The substance of kinship and the heat of the hearth: Feeding, personhood, and relatedness among Malays in Pulau Langkawi. *American Ethnologist*, 22(2): 223–41.

Carsten, J. (ed.) (2000). *Cultures of relatedness: New approaches to the study of kinship*. Cambridge: Cambridge University Press.

Cassanelli, L. and Abdilkadir, F. (2007). Education in transition. *Bildhaan International Journal of Somali Studies*, 7: 91–125.

Cassanelli, L.V. (1982). *The shaping of Somali society: Reconstructing the history of a pastoral people, 1600–1900*. Philadelphia: University of Pennsylvania Press.

Castagno, A.A. (1975). The development of political parties in the Somali republic. In J. Coleman and C. Rosberg (eds), *Political parties and national integration in tropical Africa*. Berkeley: University of California Press.

Cerulli, E. (1964). New notes on Islam. In E. Cerulli (ed.), Biancani (trans.), *Somalia, scritti vari editi ed inediti* (vol. 3). Roma: Ministero degli Affari Esteri.

Charbonneau, L. (2008, 2 June). UN Council meets Somalia government, opposition. *Reuters*. Retrieved 12 August 2008, from www.reuters.com/article/homepageCrisis/idUSL01118790._CH_.2400.

Chomsky, N. (2002). The crimes of 'Intcom'. *Foreign Policy*, 132: 34–5.

Circular issued by 70 well-known scholars. (2007). Goobjoog Online. Retrieved April 2007, from www.goobjoog.net/news/125/ARTICLE/5164/2007-04-15.html.

Collier, P. (1999). Doing well out of war. Paper presented at the Conference on Economic Agendas in Civil Wars.

Collier, P. (2001). Economic causes of civil conflict and their implications for policy. Retrieved 12 August 2008, from http://users.ox.ac.uk/~econpco/research/pdfs/EconomicCausesofCivilConflict-ImplicationsforPolicy.pdf.

Collier, P. and Hoeffler, A. (1999). *Justice-seeking and loot-seeking in civil war*. Oxford: World Bank.

Collins, K. (2004). The logic of clan politics: Evidence from the central Asian trajectories. *World Politics*, 56: 224–61.

Commission on Human Security. (2004). *Final Report of the Commission on Human Security*. Retrieved July 2004, from: www.humansecurity-chs.org/finalreport/index.html.

Connell, D. (2002). War clouds over Somalia. *Middle East Report Online*. Retrieved 1 August 2008, from www.merip.org/mero/mero032202.html.

Cornwell, R. (2004). *Fourteenth time lucky?* (Occasional Paper 87, April 2004) Retrieved 1 August 2008, from Institute for Security Studies website: www.iss.co.za/pubs/papers/87/Paper87.htm.

Crocker, C.A. and Hampson, F. (1996). Making peace settlement work. *Foreign Policy*, 104: 54–71.

Dage. M. (n.d.). *'Damane'* (Foolish). Retrieved August 2008, from http//www.doollo.com.

Dagne, T.S. (2002). Africa and the war on terrorism: The case of Somalia. *Mediterranean Quarterly*, 13 (4): 62–73.

Colardyn, D. and Bjornavold, J. (2004). Validation of formal, non-formal and informal learning: Policy and practices in EU member states. *European Journal of Education*, 39(1): 69–89.

Darby, J.P. (2003). *Introduction*. In J.P. Darby (ed.), *Contemporary peace making: Conflict, violence and peace processes*. Hawaii: University of Hawaii Press.

Davies, L. (2005). Schools and war: Urgent agendas for comparative and international education. *Compare*, 35(4): 357–71.

Dawns, G. and Stedman, S.J. (eds) (2002). Evaluation issues in peace implementation. In D. Rothchild, S.J. Stedman and E.M. Cousens (eds), *Ending civil wars: The implementation of peace agreements* (pp. 43–70). Boulder: Lynne Rienner.

De Soto, A. and Del Castillo, G. (1994). Obstacles to peace-building. *Foreign Policy*, 94: 69–81.

DeYoung, K. (2006, 10 June). U.S. to hold international meeting on Somalia. *Washington Post*, PA12. Retrieved June 2008, from http://www. washingtonpost. com/wpdyn/content/article/2006/06/09/AR2006060901713.html.

Dempsey, G.T. (2002, 21 March). Old folly in a new disguise: Nation building to combat terrorism. *Policy Analysis*, 429.

Denoeux, G. (2003). The forgotten swamp: Navigating political Islam. *Middle East Policy*, 9: 56–81.

Deutsch, M. (1993). Educating for a peaceful world. *American Psychologist*, 48: 510–17.

Deutsch, M. and Coleman, P.T. (2000). *The handbook of conflict resolution: Theory and practice*. San Francisco: Jossey-Bass.

Dougherty, J.E. and Pfaltzgraff, R.L. (2001). *Contending theories of international relations: A comprehensive survey*. New York: Longman.

Drysdale, J. (1964). *The Somali dispute*. New York: Fredrick A. Praeger.

Duhs, T. (2004). The war on terrorism in the Horn of Africa. *Marine Corps Gazette*, 88(4): 54–60.

Ekeh, P. (2004). Individual's basic security needs and the limits of democratization in Africa. In B. Berman, E. Dickson and W. Kymlicka (eds), *Ethnicity and democracy in Africa*. Oxford: James Currey Press.

El-Affendi, A. (1991). *Turabi's revolution: Islam and power in Sudan*. London: Grey Seal.

El-Affendi, A. (2001). The impasse in the Igad peace process for Sudan: The limits of regional peacemaking? *African Affairs*, 100(401): 581–99.

Elbadawi, I.N.S. (2000). Why are there so many civil wars in Africa? Understanding and preventing violent conflict. *Journal of African Economies*, 9: 244–69.

Elbadawi, I.N.S. (2002). How much war will we see? Explaining the prevalence of civil war. *Journal of Conflict Resolution*, 46: 307–34.

Elmi, Afyare Abdi. (2005). Does the Cultivating Peace program contribute to the promotion of a culture of peace? Unpublished MA thesis. Ontario Institute for Studies in Education, University of Toronto, Department of Theory and Policy Studies in Education.

Elmi, A. and Barise, A. (2006). The Somali conflict: Root causes, obstacles, and peace-building strategies. *African Security Review*, 15(1): 33–54.

England, A. (2001, 21 December). *Top U.S. military officials link Somalia to bin Laden's Al-Qaeda*. Associated Press.

Englander, E.K. (2003). *Understanding violence*. Mahwah, NJ: Lawrence Erlbaum Associates.

Esposito, J.L. (1993). *The Islamic threat: Myth or reality*. New York: Oxford University Press.

Esposito, J.L., Fasching, D.J. and Lewis, T. (eds) (2008). *Religion and globalization: World religions in historical perspective*. New York: Oxford University Press.

Ethiopian Herald. (1977, 28 July). The jihad Siad Barre is waging.

Etzione, A. (2006). A neo-communitarian approach to international relations: Rights and the good. *Human Rights Review*, 7(4): 69–80.

Evans, L. (2003). Acting Assistant Secretary of State for African Affairs surveys the continent. Retrieved 12 August 2008, from www.international.ucla.edu/article.asp?parentid=5373.

Executive Order No. 13224 (2001, 23 September). Retrieved 23 August 2007, from the US Department of State website: www.state.gov/s/ct/rls/fs/2002/16181.htm.

Failks, K. (2000). *Citizenship*. London: Routledge.

Falk, R. (2005). The communitarian approach to international relations and the future of world order. *American Behavioral Scientist*, 48(12): 1577–90.

Farah, N. (2002, 9 January). Somalia is no hideout for bin Laden. *New York Times*, p. 23, col. 22.

Fearon, J. and Laitin, D.D. (2004). Neotrusteeship and the problem of weak states. *International Security* 28(4): 5–43.

Fearon, J.D. (1999). What is identity (As we now use the word)? Retrieved 12 August 2008, from www.stanford.edu/~jfearon/papers/iden1v2.pdf.

Feldeman, N. (2008). *The fall and rise of the Islamic state*. Princeton, NJ: Princeton University Press.

Fineman, M. (1993, 17 January). The oil factor in Somalia:. Four American petroleum giants had agreements with the African nation before its civil war began. They could reap big rewards if peace is restored. *Los Angeles Times*, headline: part A; p. 1; col. 1; Foreign desk (18 January 1993, Monday, home edition).

Finkelstein, L.S. (1995). What is global governance? *Global Governance*, 1: 367–72.

Finnel, B. (1998). What is security? Why the debate matters. *National Security Studies Quarterly*, 4(4): 1–18.

Fisk, L. (ed.) (2000). *Shaping visionaries: Nurturing peace through education*. Peterborough, Ontario: Broadview Press.

Food and Agriculture Organization of the United Nations (FAO). *Fishery and aquaculture country profiles: Somalia*. Retrieved May 2008, from www.fao.org/fishery/countrysector/FI-CP_SO/en.

Fountain, S. (1999). Peace education in UNICEF. Retrieved 12 August 2008, from www.unicef.org/girlseducation/files/PeaceEducation.pdf.

Frazer, J. (2006). The Assistant Secretary for African Affairs' testimony before the Senate Foreign Relations Subcommittee on African Affairs, Somalia: U.S. Government policy and challenges. *Senate Foreign Relations Subcommittee on African Affairs*.

Frazer, J. (2007, 6 February). Somalia: Interagency team working toward restoring effective governance. *Testimony before the Senate Foreign Relations Subcommittee Hearing on Somalia*. Retrieved 12 August 2008, from www.hiiraan.com/news2/2007/feb/somalia_interagency_team_working_toward_restoring_effective_governance.aspx.

Fukuyama, F. (1990). *The end of history and the last man*. New York: Free Press.

Fuller, G. (2004). *The future of political Islam*. New York: Palgrave Macmillan.

The Fund for Peace and Foreign Policy. (2008). The failed states index 2008. *Foreign Policy*, July/August 2008. Retrieved July 2008, from www.foreignpolicy.com/story/cms.php?story_id=4350

Gage, R.L. (ed.) (1995). *Choose peace: A dialogue between Johan Galtung and Daisaku Ikeda*. London: Pluto Press.

Galtung, J. (ed.) (1975). *Three approaches to peace: Peacekeeping, peacemaking and peace-building* (vol. 2). Copenhagen: Christian Ejlers.

Galtung, J. (1990). Cultural violence. *Journal of Peace Research*, 27(3): 291–305.

Galtung, J. (ed.) (1995). *Cultural peace: Some characteristics*. Paris: UNESCO Publishing.

Galtung, J. (1996). *Peace by peaceful means: Peace and conflict, development and civilization*. London: Sage Publications.

Galtung, J. (ed.) (2001). *After violence, reconstruction, reconciliation, and resolution: Coping with visible and invisible effects of war and violence*. New York: Lexington Books.

Galtung, J. (2004). Peace education: Typology. Retrieved 12 August 2008, from www.dadalos.org/frieden_int/grundkurs_2/typologie.htm.

Gandhi, L. (1998). *Postcolonial theory: A critical introduction*. New York: Columbia University Press.

Gerges, F.A. (1999). *America and political Islam: Clash of cultures or clash of interests?* Cambridge: Cambridge University Press.

Gerges, F.A. (2007). *Understanding the many faces of Islamism and Jihadism. Neiman Reports*. Retrieved 12 August 2008, from www.nieman.harvard.edu/reports/07-2NRsummer/p07-0702-gerges.html.

Gerges, F.A. (2008). Gauging terror. *Yale Global Online*. Retrieved 12 August 2008, from http://yaleglobal.yale.edu/display.article?id=7996.

Geshekter, C. (1985). Anti-colonialism and class formation: The eastern Horn of Africa before 1950. *International Journal of Historical African Studies*, 18(1): 1–32.

Geshekter, C.L. (1992). Anti-colonialism and class formation: The Eastern Horn of Africa before 1950. Paper presented at the Somali Studies Conference in Boston 1992.

Gettleman, J. (2007, 3 June). U.S. strikes inside Somalia, bombing suspected militant hide-out. *New York Times* (electronic version). Retrieved June 2007, from www.nytimes.com/2007/06/03/world/africa/03somalia.html?scp=27&sq=JEFFREY%20GETTLEMAN%20and%20Somalia%20and%20Bush%20Administration&st=cse.

Gettleman, J. (2009, 8 May). For Somali pirates, worst enemy may be on shore. *New York Times*.

Gettleman, J. (2009, 6 August). Clinton offers assurances to Somalis. *New York Times*.

Gettleman, J. and Schmit, E. (2009, 14 September). U.S. kills top Qaeda militant in Southern Somalia. *New York Times*. Retrieved from www.nytimes.com/2009/09/15/world/africa/15raid.html.

Ghalib, J.M. (1995). *The cost of dictatorship: The Somali experience*. New York: Lilian Barbar Press.

Ghalib, J.M. (2002). Ethiopian distortions vis-à-vis the Somali reconciliation. Retrieved from www.somalisite.com/ethiopia.htm.

Gilkes, P. (1999, 23 July). Battle in the Horn: The Somali connection. BBC Online Network. Retrieved 10 September 2008, from http://news.bbc.co.uk/1/hi/special_report/1999/07/99/battle_in_the_horn/399898.stm.

Glesne, C. and Peshkin, A. (eds) (1992). *Meeting qualitative inquiry*. White Plains, NY: Longman.

Gordon, M. and Mazzetti, M. (2007, 23 February). U.S. used base in Ethiopia to hunt Al Qaeda. *New York Times* (electronic version). Retrieved 10 September 2008, from www.nytimes.com/2007/02/23/world/africa/23somalia.html.

Gowers, A. (2002). The power of two. *Foreign Policy*, 132: 32–3.

Green, M. (2002, 14 January). U.S. war on terror causes anxiety in the Horn of Africa. *East African Standard*. Retrieved 10 September 2008, from http://news. newamericamedia.org/news/view_article.html?article_id=217.

Gurr, T.R. (1994). *Ethnic conflict in world politics*. Boulder: Westview Press.

Gurr, T.R. and Ruttenberg, C. (1967). *The conditions of civil violence: First test of causal model*. Princeton, NJ: Princeton University Press.

Guttal, S. (2005). The politics of post-war/post-conflict reconstruction. *Development*, 48(3): 73–81.

Hale, H. (2004). Explaining ethnicity. *Comparative Political Studies*, 37(4): 458–84.

Hampson, F.O. (1996). *Nurturing peace: Why peace settlements succeed or fail*. Washington, DC: United States Institute of Peace Press.

Harris, H.V. (1997). Causes of violence. Retrieved January 2004, from http:// www-mcnair.berkeley.edu:16080/97Journal/.

Harris, I. (ed.) (2003). *Conceptual underpinning of peace education*. Mahwah, NJ: Lawrence E. Associates.

Hashi, A.N. (1996). *Leadership vacuum: Weapons and clan politics in Somalia*. Mogadishu: Horn of Africa Printing Press.

Hassan, S.M. (1976). *Diiwaankii gabayadii Sayid Maxamed Cabdulle Xasan* (Collections of the poems of Sayid Mohamed Abdulle Hassan) (S.J.C. Ciise, ed.). Mogadishu: Somali National Printing Agency.

Hayow, M.G. (n.d.). *'Xal u raadi'* (Look for a solution). Retrieved August 2008, from www.newbanadir.com/suugaan.html.

Helander, B.D.C. (1996). Rahanweyn sociability: A model for other Somalis. *African Languages and Cultures*. In I.M. Lewis and R.J. Hayward (eds), *Voice and power: The culture of language in North-East Africa. Essays in honour of B.W. Andrzejewski* (*African Language and Cultures*, Suppl. 3): 195–204.

Helsing, J.W. (2006). Education, sustainable peace and reconciliation. Paper presented at the International Studies Association Annual Meeting. San Diego, CA, 24 March 2006.

Herbst, J. (2004). Let them fail: State failure in theory and practice. In R. Rotberg (ed.), *When states fail: Causes and consequences*. Princeton, NJ: Princeton University Press.

Hersi, A.A. (1977). *The Arab factor in Somali history: The origins and the development of the Arab enterprise and cultural influences in the Somali Peninsula*. Los Angeles: University of California Press.

Hewitt De Alcantara, C.H. (1998). Uses and abuses of the concept of governance. *International Social Science Journal*, 50(155): 105–13.

Hirsch, J.L.O. and Oakley, R.B. (1995). *Somalia and Operation Restore Hope: Lessons learned*. Washington United States Peace Institute.

Hogg, M. and Grieve, P. (1999). Social identity theory and the crises of confidence in social psychology: A commentary, and some research on uncertainty reduction. *Asian Journal of Social Psychology*, 2: 79–93.

Holsti, K. (1996). *The state, war and the state of war*. Cambridge: Cambridge University Press.

Horowitz, D.L. (1985). *Ethnic groups in conflict*. Berkeley: University of California Press.

Horowitz, D.L. (1999). Constitutional design: Proposals versus processes. Paper presented at the Kellogg Institute conference on Constitutional Design 2000: International Design, Conflict Management, and Democracy in the Late Twentieth Century.

Hoskyns, C. (ed.) (1969). *Case studies in African diplomacy.* Dar es Salaam, Nairobi and Addis Ababa: Oxford University Press.

Howard, D., Schweitzer, C. and Stieren, C. (2001). Nonviolent peaceforce feasibility study. Retrieved 10 September 2008, from www.nonviolentpeaceforce.org/en/feasibilitystudy.

Huntington, S.P. (1993). The clash of civilizations? *Foreign Affairs*, 72(3): 22–49.

IGAD (2001). Resolution: Press Release. Retrieved from www.un.org/News/Press/docs/2001/sc7190.doc.htm.

IGAD (2002, 11 January). Resolution of the 9th IGAD Summit of the Heads of State and Government on Somalia. Retrieved 12 August 2008, from Egypt State Information Service website: www.sis.gov.eg/En/Pub/africanperspective/8thissue Winter2001/110408000000000006.htm.

Ignatieff, M. (2005). The rights revolution. In K. Fierlbeck (ed.), *The development of Canadian political thought in Canada: An anthology* (pp. 311–21). Peterborough: Broadview Press.

Inman, H. and Sharp, W.G. (1999). Revising the U.N. trusteeship system: Will it work? *American Diplomacy*, 4(4). Retrieved May 2007, from www.unc.edu/depts/diplomat/AD_Issues/amdipl_13/inman_somalia.html.

International Commission on Intervention and State Sovereignty. (2001). *The responsibility to protect.* Retrieved 12 August 2008, from www.iciss.ca/report-en.asp.

International Crisis Group (2004, 21 December). Somalia: Continuation of war by other means?: Crisis Group Africa Report No. 88. Nairobi: ICG. Retrieved 10 September 2008, from www.crisisgroup.org/home/index.cfm?l=1&id=3194.

International Crisis Group (2005, 11 July). *Counter-terrorism in Somalia: Losing hearts and minds?* Crisis Group Africa Report No. 95. Nairobi: ICG. Retrieved 10 September 2008, from www.crisisgroup.org/home/index.cfm?id=3555&l=2.

Issa-Salwe, A.M. (1996). *The collapse of the Somali state.* London: HAAN Publishing.

Issa-Salwe, A.M. (2000). *Cold War fallout: Boundary politics and conflict in the Horn of Africa.* London: HAAN Publishing.

Jensen, H. (2002, 8 January). U.S. won't evade fallout by waging 'proxy wars'. Retrieved 12 August 2008, from www.usagold.com/gildedopinion/jensen/index.html.

Johnson, D. and Johnson, R. (2005). Essential components of peace education. *Theory into practice*, 44(4): 280–92.

Jones, B.G. (2006). Introduction: International relations, Eurocentrism and imperialism. In B.G. Jones (ed.), *Decolonizing international relations* (pp. 1–22). New York: Rowman and Littlefield.

Joshee, R. (2004). Is peace the answer? Paper presented at the annual meeting of the American Educational Research Association.

Kansteiner, W.H. (2002). Somalia: U.S. policy options. *Testimony to United States Congress. Senate Committee on Foreign Relations. Subcommittee on African Affairs.* Washington, DC. Retrieved 12 August 2008, from Office of the Press Secretary website: www.state.gov/p/af/rls/rm/7872.htm.

Kauffman, C. (1996). Possible and impossible solutions to ethnic civil wars. *International Security*, 20: 136–75.

Keating, T. and Knight, W.A. (eds) (2004). *Building sustainable peace*. Edmonton, Alberta: University of Alberta Press.

Keen, D. (2000). Incentives and disincentives for violence. In D. Malone and M. Berdal (eds), *Greed and grievance: Economic agendas in civil wars* (pp. 19–42). Boulder: Lynne Rienner.

Keenan, J. (2009). *The dark Sahara: America's war on terror in Africa*. London: Pluto Press.

Khalif, M. (2004). The limits of clan politics. Unpublished paper: The author shared the paper with me in 2004.

Kriesberg, L. (1998). *Constructive conflicts: From escalation to resolution*. Oxford: Rowman and Littlefield Publishers.

Kuhn, T.S. (1970). *The structure of scientific revolutions*. Chicago: University of Chicago Press.

Kusow, A. (1995). The Somali origin: Myth or reality. In A.J. Ahmed (ed.), *The invention of Somalia* (pp. 81–106). Lawrenceville, NJ: Red Sea Press.

Kymlicka, W. (1994). Return of the citizen: A survey of recent work on citizenship theory. *Ethics Journal*, 104: 352–81.

Kymlicka, W. (1995). *Multicultural citizenship*. Oxford: Clarendon Press.

Kymlicka, W. (2002). *Contemporary political philosophy: An introduction*. Oxford: Oxford University Press.

Kymlicka, W. (2004). Nation-building and minority rights: Comparing African and West. *Journal of Ethnic and Migration Studies*, 26(2): 183–212.

Lake, D. and Rothchild, D. (2002). Political decentralization and civil war settlement. Retrieved from http://weber.ucsd.edu/~dlake/Working%20Papers/LakeRothchilh.pdf.

Lapidoth-Eschelbacher, R. (1982). *International straits of the world: Red Sea and the Gulf of Aden*. The Hague: Martinus Nijhoff.

Le Sage, A. (2001). Prospects for Al-Ittihad and Islamist radicals in Somalia. *Review of African Political Economy*, 27 (89): 472–7.

Lederach, J.P. (1991). *Beyond prescription: New lenses for conflict resolution training across cultures*. Waterloo, Ontario: Inter-Racial and Cross-Cultural Conflict Resolution Project.

Lederach, J.P. (1997). *Building peace: Sustainable reconciliation in divided societies*. Washington, DC: United States Institute of Peace Press.

Lennox, P. (2008). *Contemporary piracy off the Horn of Africa*. Canadian Defence and Foreign Affairs Institute. Retrieved April 2008, from www.cdfai.org/PDF/Contemporary%20Piracy%20off%20the%20Horn%20of%20Africa.pdf.

Lewis, I.M. (1961). *Pastoral democracy: A study of pastoralism and politics among the northern Somali of the Horn of Africa*. London: Oxford University Press.

Lewis, I.M. (1980). *Modern history of Somalia: Nation and state in the Horn of Africa*. London: Longman Group Limited.

Lewis, I.M. (1994). *Blood and bone: The call of kinship in Somali society*. Lawrenceville and Asmara: Red Sea Press.

Lewis, I.M. (1998). *Saints and Somalis: Popular Islam in a clan-based society*. Lawrenceville and Asmara: Red Sea Press.

Lewis, I.M. (2004). Visible and invisible differences: The Somali paradox. *Africa*, 74(4): 489–513.

Licklider, R. (1995). The consequences of negotiated settlements in civil wars, 1945–1993. *American Political Science Review*, 89(3): 681–90.

Lijphart, A. (1977). *Democracy in plural societies: Comparative explanation.* New Haven, CT: Yale University Press.

Lijphart, A. (1994). *Prospects for power-sharing in the New South Africa.* London: James Currey.

Lyons, T. and Samatar, A. (1994). *Somalia: State collapse, multilateral intervention, and strategies for political reconciliation.* Washington, DC: The Brookings Institute.

Mamdani, M. (2001). *When victims become killers: colonialism, nativism, and the genocide in Rwanda.* Princeton, NJ: Princeton University Press.

Mamdani, M. (2004). Good *Muslim, bad Muslim: America, the Cold War, and the roots of terror.* New York: Three Leaves Press.

Mamdani, M. (2009). Saviors and survivors: Darfur, politics, and the War on Terror. New York: Pantheon Books.

Mansur, A. (1995). Contrary to a nation: The cancer of the Somali state. In A.J. Ahmed (ed.), *The invention of Somalia* (pp. 107–16). Lawrenceville, NJ: Red Sea Press.

Mansur, A. (1995). The nature of the Somali clan system. In A.J. Ahmed (ed.), *The Invention of Somalia* (pp. 117–33). Lawrenceville, NJ: Red Sea Press.

Marchal, R. (1995). Let's talk about governance in Somalia: A few provocative remarks on governance in Somalia. Retrieved from http://meltingpot.fortunecity.com/lebanon/254/marchal.htm.

Marchal, R. (2007). *Somalia: A new front against terrorism.* Social Science and Research Council: Horn of Africa. Retrieved from http://hornofafrica.ssrc.org/marchal/.

Markakis, J. (1998). *Resource conflict in the Horn of Africa.* London: Sage Publishing.

Marks, E. (1999). Transitional governance: A return to the trusteeship system. *American Diplomacy*, 9(1). Retrieved 12 August 2008, from www.unc.edu/depts/diplomat/AD_Issues/amdipl_10/marks2.html.

Marshall, T.H. (1965). *Class, citizenship, and social development; essays. With an introduction by Seymour Martin Lipset.* Garden City, NY: Anchor Books.

Marshall, T.H. (1981). *The right to welfare.* London: Heinemann Educational Books.

Martin, B.G. (1992). Shaykh Zayla'i and the nineteenth century Somali Qadirya. In S.S. Samatar (ed.), *In the shadow of conquest: Islam in colonial Northeast Africa* (pp. 11–32). Trenton, NJ: Red Sea Press.

Martin, J.L. (2001). The authoritarian personality, 50 years later: What lessons are there for political psychology? *Political Psychology*, 22(1): 1–26.

Mazrui, A. (1995). Blood of experience: The failed state and political collapse in Africa. *World Policy Journal*, 12(1): 28–34.

Mazrui, A. (2006). *Islam: Between globalization and counterterrorism.* Trenton, NJ: Africa World Press.

McConnell, K. (2005, 17 February). U.S. threatened by 'failed states', USAID's Natsios says. Retrieved 12 August 2008, from www.au.af.mil/au/awc/awcgate/usaid/natsios021705.htm.

McCrummen, S. (2009, 20 April). Somalia's godfathers: Ransom-rich pirates. *Washington Post*.

Mckinley, J.C.J. (1996, 10 August). Ethiopian Army attacks 3 towns in border region of Somalia. *New York Times*. Retrieved July 2008, from http://query.nytimes.com/gst/fullpage.html?res=9501E5DE103EF933A2575BC0A960958260.

McLaughlin, M.W. (1987). Learning from experience: Lessons from policy implementation. *Educational Evaluation and Policy Analysis*, 9(2): 171–8.

Menkhaus, K. (2002). Political Islam in Somalia. *Middle East Policy*, 9(1): 109–23.

Menkhaus, K. (2002). Somalia: In the crosshairs of the war on terrorism. *Current History*, 101(655): 210–18.

Menkhaus, K. (2002). *Somalia: Next up in the war on terrorism?* CSIS Africa Notes. Retrieved May 2007, from www.csis.org/component/option,com_csis_pubs/task,view/id,2139/type,3/.

Menkhaus, K. (2003). State collapse in Somalia: Second thoughts. *Review of African Political Economy*, 30(97): 405–22.

Menkhaus, K. (2004). *Somalia: State collapse and the threat of terrorism.* New York: Oxford University Press.

Menocal, A.R. and Kilpatrick, K. (2006). Towards more effective peace building: A conversation with Roland Paris. *Development in Practice*, 15: 767–77.

Merriam, S. (1998). *Qualitative research and case study in education.* San Francisco: Jossey-Bass Publishers.

Mills, G. (2004). Africa's new strategic significance. *Washington Quarterly*, 27(4): 157–69.

Morton, A.D. (2004). From rogue to failed states? The fallacy of short-termism. *Politics*, 24(3): 169–80.

Mukhtar, M.H. (1995). Islam in Somali history: Fact and fiction. In A.J. Ahmed (ed.), *The invention of Somalia* (pp. 1–29). Lawrenceville, NJ: Red Sea Press.

Mukhtar, M.H. (1996). The plight of agro-pastoral society in Somalia. *Review of African Political Economy*, 23(70): 543–53.

Mullin, B. and Hogg, M. (1999). Motivations for group membership: The role of subjective importance and uncertainty. *Basic and Applied Psychology*, 21(2): 91–102.

Muro-Ruiz, D. (2002). State of the art: The logic of violence. *Politics*, 22(2): 109–17.

Musah, A.F. (2000). A country under siege: State decay and corporate military intervention in Sierra Leone. In A.F. Musah and J.K. Fayeme (eds), *Mercenaries: An African security dilemma* (pp. 76–116). London: Pluto Press.

Mwanasali, M. (2000). The view from below. In M.R. Berdal and D.M. Malone (eds), *Greed and grievance: Economic agendas in civil wars* (pp. 137–53). Boulder: Lynne Rienner.

Mynott, A. (2008). Somali crisis 'worse than Darfur'. Retrieved from http://news.bbc.co.uk/2/hi/africa/7457974.stm.

Narayan, U. and Harding, S. (eds) (2000). *Decentering the center: Philosophy for a multicultural, postcolonial, and feminist world.* Bloomington: Indiana University Press.

Nash, R. (1992). *Worldviews in conflict: Choosing Christianity in a world of ideas.* Grand Rapids, MI: Zondervan.

National Commission on Terrorist Attacks Upon the United States. (2004). Al-Barakaat case study: The Somali community and al-Barakaat. Chapter 5 in *Terrorist Financing Staff Monograph*. Retrieved 12 August 2008, from http://govinfo.library.unt.edu/911/staff_statements/911_TerrFin_Ch5.pdf.

Naylor, R.T. (2006). *Satanic purses: Money, myth and misinformation.* Montreal: McGill-Queens University Press.

Nevo, B. and Brem, I. (2002). Peace education programs and the evaluation of their effectiveness. In G. Solomon and B. Nevo (eds), *Peace education: The concept, principles, and practices around the world* (pp. 271–83). Mahwa, NJ: Lawrence Erlbaum Associates.

North, D. (1990). *Institutions, institutional change and economic performance.* Cambridge: Cambridge University Press.

Ogata, S. (2002). Guilty parties. *Foreign Policy*, 132: 39–40.

O'Neill, P. (2001). Statement by Treasury Secretary Paul O'Neill. Retrieved 12 August 2008, from US Department of Treasury website: www.treas.gov/press/releases/po770.htm.

Onyango, D. (2002, April, 29). No links with Osama: UN moves to save Al Barakaat. *The East African Standard.* Retrieved from www.nationaudio.com/News/EastAfrican/06052002/Regional/Regional2.html.

Packer, C.A.A. and Rukare, D. (2008). The new African Union and its constitutive Act. *American Journal of International Law*, 96(2): 365–79.

Paris, R. (1997). Peacebuilding and the limits to liberal internationalism. *International Security*, 22(2): 54–89.

Paris, R. (2002). International peacebuilding and the 'mission civilisatrice'. *Review of International Studies*, 28: 637–56.

Paris, R. (2004). *At war's end: Building peace after civil conflict.* Cambridge: Cambridge University Press.

Paris, R. (2006). Towards more effective peace building: A conversation with Roland Paris. *Development in Practice*, 15: 767–77.

Parker, W.C. (2001). Toward enlightened political engagement. In W.B. Stanley (ed.), *Critical issues in social studies research for the 21st century.* Chicago: Information Age Publishing.

Parker, W.C. (ed.) (2001). *Toward enlightened political engagement.* Greenwich, Chicago: Information Age Publishing.

Pasha, M.K. (2006). Liberalism, Islam, and the international relation. In B.G. Jones (ed.), *Decolonizing international relations* (pp. 65–88). New York: Rowman and Littlefield.

Pogge, T. (1997). Group rights and ethnicity. In I. Shapiro and W. Kymlicka (eds), *Ethnicity and group rights.* New York: New York University Press.

Purdum, T. (2001, 15 September). After the attacks: The White House; Bush warns of a wrathful, shadowy and inventive war. *New York Times* (electronic version). Retrieved 12 August 2008, from http://query.nytimes.com/gst/fullpage.html?res=9506E6DA173BF934A2575AC0A9679C8B63.

Qudb, S. (1970). *Social justice in Islam.* New York: Octagon Books.

Qudb, S. (1974). *Islam: The religion of the future.* Delhi: Markazi Maktaba Islami.

Qudb, S. (1974). *The religion of Islam.* Delhi: Markazi Maktaba Islami.

Qudb, S. (1990). *Milestones* (Revised translation with forward by Ahmed Zaki Hammad). Indianapolis: American Trust Publications.

Qutb, S. (1999). *In the Shade of the Qur'an.* (M.A. Salahi and A.A. Shamis, eds) (vols. 1–10). Leicester: Islamic Foundation.

Rabi, O. (1989). North remains part of the nation. Unpublished paper.

Reardon, B. (1988). *Comprehensive peace education: Educating for global responsibility.* New York: Teachers College Press.

Reardon, B. (ed.) (1988). *Education for positive peace.* New York: Teachers College Press.

Reardon, B. (1994). *Tolerance: The threshold of peace.* Paris: UNESCO.

Record, J. (2003). Bounding the global war on terrorism. Retrieved from www.globalsecurity.org/military/library/report/2003/record_bounding.pdf.

Reno, W. (1998). *Warlord politics and African states.* Boulder: Lynne Rienner.

Reynolds, A. (1999). Majoritarian or power-sharing government. Paper presented at the International Conference on Constitutional Design 2000.

Rhodes, R.A.W. (1996). The new governance: Governing without government. *Political Studies*, 44(3): 652–67.

Rice, C. (2005, 20 June). Remarks at the American University in Cairo. Retrieved from www.state.gov/secretary/rm/2005/48328.htm.

Rice, C. (2008). Rethinking the national interest: American realism for a new world. *Foreign Affairs* (electronic version). Retrieved 12 August 2008, from http://www.foreignaffairs.org/20080701faessay87401-p50/condoleezza-rice/rethinking-the-national-interest.html.

Rice, S. (2003, 20 February). *The new national security strategy: Focus on failed states* (Policy Brief #116). Washington, DC: Brookings Institution.

Richards, H. (2000). On the concept of peacemaking. Retrieved 10 September 2008, from http://howardrichards.org/ontheconcept.html.

Richardson, G.H. and Blades, D.W. (2006). Introduction: Troubling the canon of citizenship education. In G.H. Richardson and D.W. Blades (eds), *Troubling the canon of citizenship education*. New York: Peter Lang.

Ricks, T. (2002, 4 January). Allies step up Somalia watch: U.S. aims to keep Al Qaeda at bay. *The Washington Post*. Retrieved 12 August 2008, from www.washingtonpost.com/ac2/wpdyn?pagename=article&contentId=A59310-2002Jan3&notFound=true.

Riker, W.H. (1964). *Federalism: Origin and operation significance*. Boston and Toronto: Little, Brown and Company.

Roble, A.H. (ed.) (1999). *Silisilladii Guba: Guba Poems*. Sweden: Scansom Publishers.

Roche, D. (2003). *The human rights to peace*. Toronto: Novalis.

Rosenau, J.N. (1995). Governance in the twenty-first century. *Global Governance*, 1: 3–13.

Rosenberg, M.J. (2002, 26 January). Somali warlords see opportunity in war on terrorism. Associated Press.

Rosenthal, B. (2001). Ethiopia shows its hand in Somalia crisis. Agence France-Presse.

Ross, M. (1993). The two faces of conflict. In M. Ross (ed.), *The management of conflict* (pp. 1–16). New Haven, CT: Yale University Press.

Ross, M.H. (2000). Creating the conditions for peacemaking: Theories of practice in ethnic conflict resolution. *Ethnic and Racial Studies*, 23(6): 1002–34.

Rotberg, R.I. (2004). The failure and collapse of nation-states: Breakdown, prevention, and repair. In R. Rotberg (ed.), *When states fail: Causes and consequences* (pp. 1–51). Princeton, NJ: Princeton University Press.

Rothe, J.P. (1993). *Qualitative research: A practical guide*. Toronto: RCI/PDE Publications.

Ruggie, J.G. (1993). *Multilateralism matters: The theory and praxis of an institutional form*. New York: Columbia University Press.

Ryan, S. (2001). *Nationalism and ethnic conflict* (2nd edition). New York: St Martin's Press.

Safi, L.M. (1991). The Islamic state: A conceptual framework. *American Journal of Islamic Social Science*, 8(2): 221–34.

Sahnoun, M. (1994). *Somalia: The missed opportunities*. Washington, DC: United States Institute of Peace Press.

Said, E. (1978). *Orientalism*. London: Routledge and Kegan Paul.

Said, E. (1981). *Covering Islam: How the media and the experts determine how we see the rest of the world*. New York: Routledge.

Said, E. (1994). *Culture and imperialism*. London: Vintage Books.

Said, E. (2004). Edward Said: Last interview (directed by Mike Dibb and produced by D.D. Guttenplan). Interviewer is Charles Glass.

Said, E. (2004). The clash of ignorance. In K.A. Mingst and J.L. Snyder (eds), *Essential readings in world politics* (pp. 170–3). New York: W.W. Norton.

Samatar, A. (1992). Destruction of state and society in Somalia: Beyond the tribal convention. *Journal of Modern African Studies*, 30(4): 625–41.

Samatar, A. (ed.) (1994). *The Somali challenge: From catastrophe to renewal*. Boulder: Lynne Rienner.

Samatar, A. (1997). Leadership and ethnicity in the making of African state-models: Botswana versus Somalia. *Third World Quarterly*, 18(4): 687–707.

Samatar, A.I. (2007). The porcupine dilemma: Governance and transition in Somalia. *Bildhaan International Journal of Somali Studies*, 7. Retrieved 12 August 2008, from Macalester College Department of International Studies website: www.macalester.edu/internationalstudies/Samatar-Porcupine.pdf.

Samatar, A.I. and Samatar, A. (2003). Somali reconciliation: Editorial note. *Bildhaan: International Journal of Somali Studies*, 3: 1–14.

Samatar, M.S. (1994). Interview. *Himilo Somali Magazine*, 1 (Himilo Group), p. 28.

Samatar, S.S. (1982). *Oral poetry and Somali nationalism: The case of Sayyid Mahammad Abdille Hassan*. Cambridge: Cambridge University Press.

Samatar, S.S. (1991). *Somalia: Nation in turmoil*. London: Minority Rights Group Report.

Samatar, S.S. (1992). Introduction. In S.S. Samatar (ed.), *In the shadow of conquest: Islam in colonial Northeast Africa* (pp. 3–10). Trenton, NJ: Red Sea Press.

Samatar, S.S. (1992). Sheikh Uweys Muhammad of Baraawe, 1847–1909: Mystic and reformer in East Africa. In S.S. Samatar (ed.), *In the shadow of conquest: Islam in colonial Northeast Africa* (pp. 48–74). Trenton, NJ: Red Sea Press.

Sambanis, N. (2000). Partition as a solution to ethnic war: An empirical critique of the theoretical literature. *World Politics*, 52: 437–83.

Save the Children. (2007). What we do in Somalia/Somaliland. Retrieved June 2008, from www.savethechildren.org.uk/en/947.htm.

Sayyid, B.S. (1997). *A fundamental fear: Eurocentrism and the emergency of Islamism*. London: Zed Books.

Schirch, L. (2001). Ritual reconciliation: Transforming identity /reframing conflict. In M. Abu-Nimer (ed.), *Reconciliation, justice, and coexistence: Theory and practice* (pp. 145–61). Lanham, MD: Lexington Books.

Schram, T.H. (2003). *Conceptualizing qualitative inquiry: Mindwork for fieldwork in education and social sciences*. Upper Saddle River, NJ: Merrill Prentice Hall.

Schwartz, S. (2006). What is 'Islamofascism'? Retrieved 12 August 2008, from www.tcsdaily.com/article.aspx?id=081606C.

Scott, G.M. (1990). A resynthesis of the primordial and circumstantial approaches to ethnic group solidarity. *Ethnic and Racial Studies*, 13(2): 147–17.

Sen, A. (2006). *Identity and violence: The illusion of destiny*. New York: W.W. Norton.

Shapiro, I. and Kymlicka, W. (1997). Introduction. In I. Shapiro and W. Kymlicka (eds), *Ethnicity and group rights*. New York: New York University Press.

Sheik-Abdi, A. (1993). *Divine madness: Mohammed Abdulle Hassan (1856–1920)*. London: Zed Books.

Shils, E. (1957). Primordial, personal, sacred and civil ties: Some particular observations on the relationships of sociological research and theory. *British Journal of Sociology*, 8(2): 130–45.

Sisk, T. (1996). *Power-sharing and international mediation in ethnic conflicts.* Washington, DC: US Institute of Peace Press.

Smith, D. (2000). Trends and causes of armed conflicts. In M.F. Norbert Ropers, Alexander Austin and Claus-Dieter Wild (eds), *The Berghof Handbook for Conflict Transformation.* Berlin: Berghof Research Center for Constructive Conflict Management. Retrieved 12 August 2008, from www.berghof-handbook. net/uploads/download/smith_handbook.pdf

Smith, D.C. and Carson, T.R. (1998). *Educating for a peaceful future.* Toronto: Kagan and Woo.

Smith, L.T. (1999). *Decolonizing methodologies: Research and indigenous peoples.* Dunedin, New Zealand: Otago University Press.

Smith, S. 1997. Epistemology, postmodernism and international relations theory: A reply to Osterud. *Journal of Peace Research*, 34(3): 330–6.

Snyder, C. (2003). Acting Assistant Secretary of State for African Affairs surveys the continent. Leslie Evans transcripted and published this speech. Retrieved 12 August 2008, from www.international.ucla.edu/article.asp?parentid=5373.

Solomon, G. (2002). The nature of peace education: Not all programs are created equal. In G.S.B. Nevo (ed.), *Peace education: The concept, principles, and practice around the world.* Mahwah, NJ: Lawrence E. Associates.

Somalitalk-Online. (2005). Haamo Waaweyn oo kusoo Caariyey Xeebaha Gobolka Jubbada Hoose (Big tanks were spotted around the Somali coastline). Retrieved 12 August 2008, from www.somalitalk.com/sun/14.html.

Spears, I.S. (2000). Understanding inclusive peace agreements in Africa: The problem of power-sharing. *Third World Quarterly*, 21(1): 105–18.

Spencer, J.H. (1984). *Ethiopia at bay.* Algonac, MI: Reference Publications.

Spivak, G.C. (1994). Can the subaltern speak? In P.W.L. Chrisman (ed.), *Colonial discourse and postcolonial theory: A reader* (pp. 66–111). New York: Columbia University Press.

Stedman, S.J. (1997). Spoiler problems in peace processes. *International Security*, 22(2): 5–53.

Stephan, W. (1999). Contact theory. In W. Stephan (ed.), *Reducing prejudice and stereotyping in schools.* New York: Teachers College Press.

Stevenson, J. (2002, 3 January). Somalia redux? *Wall Street Journal*, p. A6.

Stohl, R. and Stohl, M. (2001, 21 October). Fatally flawed? U.S. policy toward failed states. *The Defense Monitor*, 30(8): 1–7. Retrieved 12 August 2008, from www. cdi.org/dm/2001/issue8/dm8-2001.pdf.

Stoker, G. (1998). Governance as theory: Five propositions. *International Social Science Journal*, 50(155): 17–28.

Swank, G. (2008, 15 April). Islamo-fascism awareness week. Retrieved 12 August 2008, from www.theconservativevoice.com/article/31716.html.

Takeyh, R. (2003). Islamism in Algeria: A struggle between hope and agony. *Middle East Policy*, 10(2): 62–75.

Talentino, A.K. (2004). Two faces of nation building: Developing function and identity. *Cambridge Review of International Affairs*, 17(3): 557–75.

Tal-Or, N., Boninger, D. and Gleicher, F. (2003). Understanding the conditions and processes necessary to reduce prejudice. In G. Solomon and B. Nevo (eds), *Peace education: The concept, principles, and practice around the world* (pp. 89–107). Mahwah, NJ: Lawrence E. Associates.

Tareke, G. (2000). The Ethiopia–Somalia war of 1977 revisited. *International Journal of African Historical Studies*, 33(3): 635–67.

Tawil, S. (2004). Education and identity-based conflict: Assessing curriculum policy for social and civic construction. Retrieved 3 May 2008, from www.ibe.unesco. org/conflict/educ_ind_01.pdf.

Tesch, R. (1990). *Qualitative Research*. New York: Falmer Press.

Thurer, D. (1999). The 'failed state' and international law. *International Review of the Red Cross*, 836: 731–61.

Thyne, C. (2006). ABC's, 123's and the golden rule: The pacifying effect of education on civil conflict, 1980–1999. *International Studies Quarterly*, 50(4): 733–54.

Tieku, T.K. (2004). Explaining the clash and accommodation of interests of major actors in the creation of the African Union. *African Affairs*, 103: 249–67.

Toh, S.W. (1997). Education for peace: Towards a millennium of well-being. Paper for the Working Document of the International Conference on Culture of Peace and Governance, Maputo, Mozambique, 1–4 September. Retrieved 12 August 2008, from www.peace.ca/educationforpeace.htm.

Tomlinson, C. (2005). U.S. General calls Somalia terror haven. Retrieved May 2006, from www.xanga.com/home.aspx?user=NYkrinDC&nextdate=5%2F18%2F20 05+23%3A59%3A59.999.

Touval, S. (1963). *Somali nationalism: International politics and the drive for unity in the Horn of Africa*. Cambridge, MA: Harvard University Press.

Turyare, M.A. (1997). *Study on the conflict between the two main factions in Mogadishu*. Mogadishu: Saacid Centre for Peace Studies.

UN. (1945). United Nations Charter, Article 78. Retrieved May 2007, from www. un.org/aboutun/charter/.

UN. (1999). *Resolution adopted by the GA: Declaration and programme of action on a culture of peace. 53/243*. New York: United Nations.

UN. (2006). Situation on Somalia: Security Council Resolution 1724. Retrieved March 2008, from www.un.org.

UN. (2006). Situation on Somalia: Resolution 1725. Retrieved March 2008, from www.un.org.

UN. (2007). Situation on Somalia: Security Council Resolution 1744. Retrieved March 2008, from www.un.org.

UN. (2008). *Report of the Monitoring Group on Somalia pursuant to Security Council resolution 1766*. Retrieved 10 September 2008, from www.un.org/sc/ committees/751/mongroup.

UNDP. (1999). *Governance foundations for post-conflict situations: UNDP's experience*. UNDP Management Development and Governance Division, Bureau for Development Policy. Retrieved 12 August 2008, from http://mirror.undp.org/ magnet/Docs/crisis/AcknowledgementsandExecSummary.doc.html.

UNDP. (2007). *Millennium Development Goals Report*. Nairobi: Springette House. Retrieved 12 August 2008, from www.so.undp.org/index.php/Viewcategory.htm l?dir=DESC&limit=5&limitstart=5&order=name.

UNESCO. (1998). *A consolidated report submitted to the Secretary General of the United Nations to the fifty-third session of the General Assembly, Towards Culture of Peace*. New York: United Nations.

UNICEF. (2006). *Survey of primary education in Somalia 2005/2006: Technical report*. Nairobi: UNICEF Office.

UN Monitoring Group. (2002). Report of the team of experts submitted in accordance with resolution 1407 (2002). Retrieved July 2008, from www.un.org/sc/committees/751/mongroup.shtml.

UN Monitoring Group. (2003). Report of the panel of experts on Somalia submitted in accordance with resolution 1474 (2003). Retrieved July 2008, from www.un.org/sc/committees/751/mongroup.shtml.

UN Monitoring Group. (2004). Report of the Monitoring Group on Somalia submitted in accordance with resolution 1519 (2003). Retrieved July 2008, from www.un.org/sc/committees/751/mongroup.shtml.

UN Monitoring Group. (2005). Report of the Monitoring Group on Somalia submitted in accordance with resolution 1587 (2005). Retrieved July 2008, from www.un.org/sc/committees/751/mongroup.shtml.

UN Monitoring Group. (2006). Report of the Monitoring Group on Somalia submitted in accordance with resolution 1587 (2005). Retrieved July 2008, from www.un.org/sc/committees/751/mongroup.shtml.

UN Monitoring Group. (2007). Report of the Monitoring Group on Somalia submitted in accordance with resolution 1724 (2006). Retrieved July 2008, from www.un.org/sc/committees/751/mongroup.shtml.

UN Monitoring Group. (2008). Report of the Monitoring Group on Somalia pursuant to Security Council resolution 1811 (2008). Retrieved January 2009, from http://daccess-dds-ny.un.org/doc/UNDOC/GEN/N08/604/73/PDF/N0860473.pdf?OpenElement.

United States Institute of Peace. (2008). *Terrorism in the Horn of Africa* (Special Report No. 113). Retrieved 12 August 2008, from www.usip.org/pubs/specialreports/sr113.pdf.

US Naval Forces Central Command. (2002). Combined Joint Task Force-Horn of Africa. Retrieved July 2008, from www.globalsecurity.org/military/agency/dod/cjtf-hoa.htm.

US Senate. (2008). A resolution supporting humanitarian assistance, protection of civilians, accountability for abuses in Somalia, and urging concrete progress in line with the Transitional Federal Charter of Somalia toward the establishment of a viable government of national unity. Retrieved May 2008, from http://thomas.loc.gov/cgi-bin/query/D?c110:1:./temp /~c110K29D5A.

Van den Berghe, P.L. (1981). *The ethnic phenomenon.* New York: Elsevier.

Van Gunsteren, H.R. (1998). *A theory of citizenship: Organizing plurality in contemporary democracies.* Boulder, CO: Westview Press.

Wallenstein, P. and Sollenberg, M. (2000). Armed conflict 1989–1999. *Journal of Peace Research*, 37(5): 635–49.

Wallenstein, P. and Sollenberg, M. (2001) Armed Conflict, 1989–2000, *Journal of Peace Research*, 38(5) 629–44.

Walter, B.F. (2003). *Committing to peace: The successful settlement of civil wars.* Princeton, NJ: Princeton University Press.

Warde, I. (2007). *The price of fear: The truth behind the financial war on terror.* Berkeley: University of California Press.

Warsame, M.I. (1980). Hoombaro (Female monkey). Retrieved May 2007, from www.aftahan.com.

Warsame, M. (1982). Dibadyaal (Excluded). Retrieved August 2008, from www.aftahan.com.

Warsame, M. (1984). Sirta nolosha (Secrets of life). Retrieved August 2008, from www.aftahan.org.

Warsame, M.I. (1991). Gudgude (Heavy rain). Retrieved August 2008, from www. aftahan.com.

Warsame, M.I. (1995). Islam is the solution to the Somali problems. *Himilo Somali Newspaper*, 1: 1–8.

Warsame, M.I. (1995) Dabahuwan (Covered from the bottom). Retrieved August 2008, from www.aftahan.com.

Warsame, M.I. (2003). Wareysi: Hadrawi (Interview with Hadrawi). *Himilo Newspaper*, October 2003.

Watt, D.H. (2007). The meaning and end of fundamentalism. (Review essay.) *Religious Studies Review*, 33(4): 269–73.

Watts, R.L. (1999). *Comparing Federal Systems*. Montreal: McGill-Queens University Press.

Wax, E. and DeYoung, K. (2006, 17 May). U.S. secretly backing warlords in Somalia. *Washington Post*, PA01. Retrieved June 2008, from http://www. washingtonpost. com/wpdyn/content/article/2006/05/16/AR2006051601625_pf.html.

Weber, M. (1978). *Economy and society: An outline of interpretive sociology*. (Guanther Roth and Claus Wittich, eds). Berkeley: University of California Press.

Weil, R. (1993). Somalia in perspective: When the saints go marching in. *Monthly Review* (March 1993). Retrieved April 2008, from http://findarticles.com/p/articles/mi_m1132/is_n10_v44/ai_13607480.

Wendt, A. (1987). The agent-structure problem in international relations theory. *International Organization*, 41(3): 335–70.

Wendt, A. (1999). *Social theory of international politics*. Cambridge, UK; New York: Cambridge University Press.

Wessels, M. (1994). The role of peace education in a culture of peace: A social psychological analysis. Retrieved May 2007, from http://eric.ed.gov/ERICWebPortal/contentdelivery/servlet/ERICServlet?accno=ED384549.

The White House. (2002). *The National Security Strategy of the United States of America*. Retrieved 12 August 2008, from www.whitehouse.gov/nsc/nss.html.

The White House. (2003). *National Strategy for Combating Terrorism*. Retrieved 12 August 2008, from www.whitehouse.gov/nsc/nsct/2006/nsct2006.pdf.

The White House. (2006, 10 August). President Bush discusses terror plot upon arrival in Wisconsin. Retrieved 12 August 2008, from www.whitehouse.gov/news/releases/2006/08/20060810-3.html.

Willmot, P. (1957). Kinship and social legislation. *British Journal of Sociology*, 9(2): 126–42.

Woods, P. (1986). *Inside schools: Ethnography in educational research*. New York: Routledge and Kegan Paul.

World Bank. (2000). *Reforming public institutions and strengthening governance: A World Bank strategy*. Washington, DC: The International Bank for Reconstruction and Development/World Bank. Retrieved 12 August 2008, from http://www1. worldbank.org/publicsector/strategysummary.pdf.

World Bank. (2005). *Reshaping the future: Education and post-conflict reconstruction*. Washington, DC: World Bank. Retrieved February 2007, from http://www1. worldbank.org/education/pdf/Reshaping_the_Future.pdf.

Yanis, A. (2002). State collapse and its implications. *Development and Change*, 33(5): 817–35.

Young, R.J.C. (1995). *Colonial desire: Hybridity in theory, culture and race*. London: Routledge.

Index

Compiled by Sue Carlton

185